NEWSLETTER SOURCEBOOK

Mark Beach

NORTH
LIGHT
BOOKS

Cincinnati, Ohio

Acknowledgments

This book would have been impossible to create without the generous cooperation of hundreds of newsletter editors and designers. Almost 400 busy professionals responded to my request for their newsletters. Most sent several issues; many sent more than one publication.

Although I could include less than one-fourth of the publications submitted, each contributor added to the richness and variety found in the following pages. I deeply appreciate their efforts.

KiKi Canniff and Kathleen Ryan helped me keep track of and evaluate the newsletters that constituted the raw material that developed into this book. Paul Huckfeldt's keen eye for graphic detail saw many outstanding features that I had overlooked.

Newsletter Sourcebook.
Copyright © 1993 by Mark Beach. Printed and bound in Mexico. All rights reserved. No part of this book may be reproduced in any form or by any electronic or mechanical means including information storage and retrieval systems without permission in writing from the publisher, except by a reviewer, who may quote brief passages in a review. Published by North Light Books, an imprint of F&W Publications, Inc., 1507 Dana Avenue, Cincinnati, Ohio, 45207. 800-289-0963. First edition.
Printed and bound in Mexico.

97 96 95 94 93   5 4 3 2 1

Library of Congress Cataloging in Publication Data

Beach, Mark
    Newsletter sourcebook/by Mark Beach.
    p. cm.
    Includes index.
    ISBN 0-89134-469-1
    1. Newsletters—Publishing. I. Title.
PN4784.N5B42 1993
070.5'72—dc20   92-30665
                                CIP
Edited by Diana Martin
Designed by Brian Roeth

About the Author

Mark Beach holds B.S. and Ph.D. degrees from the University of Wisconsin in Madison. He taught at Cornell University and the University of Rochester, where he was also associate dean of the College of Arts and Science. During his academic career, he held research grants from the Smithsonian Institution, Ford Foundation and National Academy of the Arts, and wrote the book *Making It in College*.

In 1977, Mark moved to Oregon and established a publishing company with his wife Kathleen Ryan. Mark's books about graphic design and production are used throughout North America for corporate training and as college texts. Some titles include *Editing Your Newsletter*, *Getting It Printed*, *Papers for Printing* and *Graphically Speaking*.

Table of Contents

Chapter 4　56
Illustrations

Chapter 5　74
Color

Chapter 6　102
Photographs

Introduction

To describe the highly effective design of her newsletter, one editor explained that, "The bold nameplate makes readers notice, the layout of page one pulls them in, and the consistent format holds their attention."

Newsletter designers and editors who want to meet these same high standards will find help in this book. It features examples of well-done newsletter front and interior pages and selected design elements. With each newsletter you will find text that discusses the publication's well-designed aspects, plus brief publisher, designer and production notes. Newsletter publishers include trade associations, schools, businesses, government agencies and for-profit organizations from the U.S. and Canada.

Most newsletter designs are created in two stages. First, the editor selects a design for the nameplate, format and type specifications. In some cases, a professional graphic designer develops the design. In others, the design comes from the editor's own ideas or from a template in page layout software.

The second stage of design is laying out each issue. In large organiza-tions, the professional designer who developed the overall concept often plans each issue. In smaller organiza-tions, the editor, who is also responsible for writing and often for distributing, does layout.

Before developing a design, you must determine the purpose of the newsletter. In this guide, you'll see publications from the three main newsletter categories, which are:

• promotional newsletters for marketing or public relations to sell products, services or ideas. Audiences for promotional newsletters, such as previous customers, may already be affiliated with the publisher or, as with a target market, may not know the publisher and receive the newsletter at no cost.

• informational newsletters for employees or members that are about people, places and ideas. Informational newsletter audiences are already affiliated with the publisher and receive the newsletter as part of membership in the organization.

• subscription newsletters that try to make readers richer, smarter or healthier. Audiences for subscription newsletters pay to receive the specialized information.

Each of these categories has specific goals that will help guide your design decisions.

I hope you enjoy this book and find it useful. If you think of ways to improve it, or if you would like your newsletter considered for another edition, please write to me in care of North Light Books.

Mark Beach

Standard terms for the design elements of a newsletter are listed at right. To ensure clear communication about the newsletters reproduced in this book, these terms are used consistently throughout.

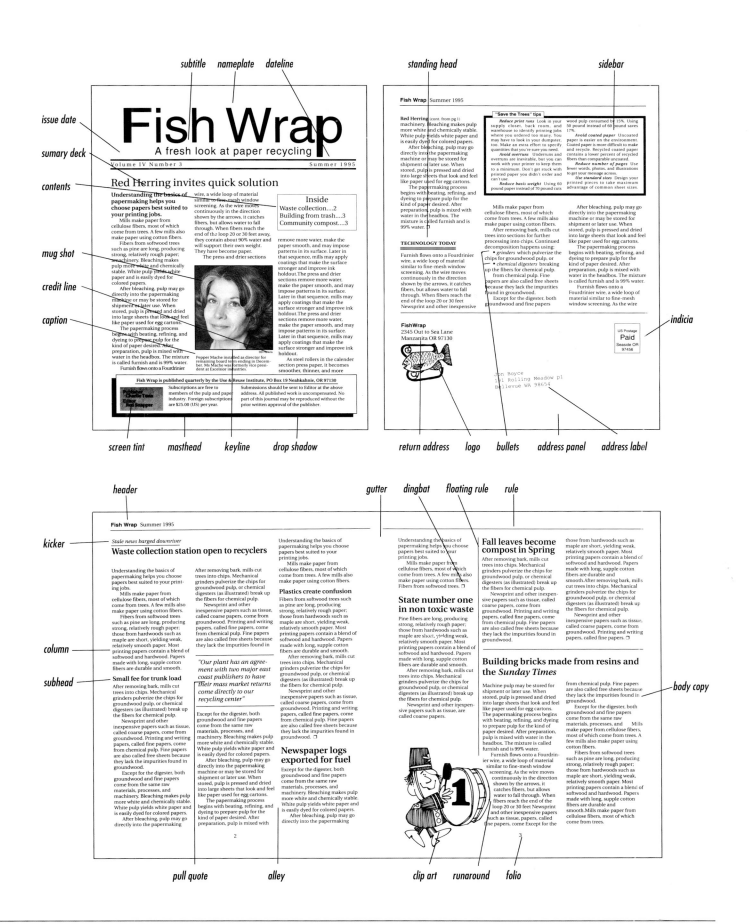

Chapter 1

Tricks and Tips to Control and Cut Newsletter Costs

Because most newsletter staffers have minimal training in print production and typically work on tight, busy schedules, newsletters often cost more to produce than they should. However, there are dozens of ways to cut costs and save yourself money and time. To cut your own newsletter's production expenses, start by considering your fixed vs. your variable costs.

Fixed costs, such as writing, design, photography and prepress, stay the same no matter how many copies you print. Fixed costs also include overhead, such as salaries and office space, which can increase the total of your other fixed costs by as much as 50 percent.

Variable costs, which include paper, press time and postage, change depending upon how many copies you print.

If you produce fewer than 1,000 copies per issue, fixed costs for each copy of your newsletter are relatively high and, therefore, represent your greatest potential savings. If you produce more than 2,000 copies per issue, your fixed costs per unit are relatively low. You'll find your greatest potential savings in variable costs.

For most newsletters, postage represents the largest variable cost. Many newsletters cost twice as much per copy to mail as to print. For that reason, cutting the cost of postage is the quickest way for most newsletters to save money. See page 5 for eight tips on cutting your mailing costs. On the next several pages you'll find more cost cutting tips.

Fifteen Tips for Money-Smart Management

1. *Set clear goals.* Define what you want your readers to know so you don't waste time and money dealing with subjects that aren't important.

2. *Study your readers.* Use reader reply cards, focus groups and informal conversations to learn about your audience and its needs.

3. *Define tasks.* Save time and money by determining who is responsible for what. Salaries represent the largest fixed cost.

4. *Set a schedule.* Tell everyone, from the president to the printer, when work is due. Make the schedule realistic, put it in writing and stick to it.

5. *Don't make people rush.* People in a hurry often make mistakes.

6. *Enforce deadlines.* Late work makes people rush and costs everyone money.

7. *Survey expenses.* Write down the cost of all services and supplies. Identify the value of staff time, in-house services and donations. Learn the true, full costs of production.

8. *Set a budget.* Use expense figures to forecast outlays of time and money.

9. *Shop for services.* Prices for services such as photography, illustrations, design and printing can vary as much as 100 percent among different suppliers.

10. *Consider dividing tasks.* Don't assume printers must also take care of outputting type or that design and illustration must go together. Using specialists or new combinations of services might save money.

11. *Work from your budget, not from supplier's fees.* Stay in control by letting vendors know how much you have to spend.

12. *Listen to the pros.* Good professionals know about sources of supplies, new technologies and creative approaches.

13. *Consider long-term contracts.* Take advantage of savings from long-range planning and quantity buying by building specifications for services and supplies around a period of a year or more.

14. *Pay bills on time.* Don't encourage vendors to quote high prices because they anticipate collection problems. Ask for discounts on bills paid promptly.

15. *Stay educated.* Take workshops; read books and periodicals; join organizations for communicators in your field; examine course offerings of community colleges and similar agencies serving nonprofit organizations; and go to trade shows to see the latest in supplies, equipment and techniques.

Four Easy Editorial Cost Savers

1. *Edit!* Cut issues from volumes, stories from issues, paragraphs from stories, sentences from paragraphs, and words from sentences. Every cut saves money on paper, printing and postage.

2. *Do your own writing.* Create efficient ways to gather information, then write all the copy yourself. Maximum control over content leads to control of deadlines and length.

3. *Copyfit as you write.* Know how many characters fill one line; how many words fill a column inch; and how many lines fill an issue.

4. *Avoid last minute scrambling.* Build a file of ideas, quotations and drawings to use when that final story falls through.

Six Creative Design Tips

1. *Stick to your format.* Resist changing elements, such as the number or width of columns, placement of regular features and typefaces.

2. *Avoid bleeds.* Pictures or art designed to run off the page require extra paper and cost more to print.

3. *Avoid tight register.* Fine rules around photos, duotones and color separations require extra care in printing.

4. *Scallop columns.* Hang all columns from a top horizontal line and leave the bottom of the text scalloped (uneven). Scalloped columns let you concentrate on content because you're not worrying about precision copyfitting.

5. *Use screen tints.* Use a different

screen percentage of a single color to create a tint that gives the effect of a second ink color. Overlapping screens of two different colors can create a third or fourth color.

6. *Design for self-mailing.* Save the cost of envelopes by building in an address panel on the back page.

Ten Practical Photography Tips

1. *Do your own photography.* Learn to feel as comfortable with a camera as you do with a computer keyboard.

2. *Select black-and-white photos from contact sheets.* Do your own photo editing. Order full-frame prints, then specify cropping to the printer. Keep maximum control of images as well as words.

3. *Select color photos from transparencies.* Make photocopies to show cropping and positioning on mock-ups.

4. *Scale photos yourself.* Learn to use a proportion wheel to determine percentages of reduction or enlargement. Ask your printer the best way to show percent changes for each image.

5. *Find inexpensive photo sources.* Using stock photo services can cost less than hiring a freelancer to create a special image. You could also give the assignment to a photo class or club, or use free photos from historical societies and other public collections, as well as from corporate public relations files.

6. *Think gang.* For a lot of images, you can save money by having the printer "gang shoot" them. Choose photos with similar uniform contrast. Reproduce the images at the same percentage of enlargement or reduction, then have them shot as halftones all at once.

7. *Use PMTs.* Service bureaus and printers make photomechanical transfers that allow you to paste halftones directly on your pasteup so they are shot for printing along with type and art.

8. *Start with a full range of tones in photos, from white whites to black blacks.* The printing process and paper surfaces will not improve poorly exposed or printed photos.

9. *Use students.* Let creative young people who are hungry for real-world experience show what they can do. Pay their expenses and a small fee and give them plenty of lead time

10. *Explore digital photography.* Save money on film and processing by using a camera that reads images directly into computer memory.

Forty-Two Proven Production Tips

1. *Double space manuscripts sent to typesetting.* Mark corrections clearly with standard proofreader marks. Help typesetters be efficient.

2. *Proofread all corrections.* Make sure mistakes are corrected and that there are no new mistakes.

3. *Point out TEs and PEs.* Clearly write TE (typesetter error) or PE (printer error) on proofs when a mistake is not your fault.

4. *Capture your keyboarding.* Regardless of how you set final type, transmit the manuscript by disk or modem so no one has to repeat your keystrokes.

5. *Don't set too much type.* Edit and copyfit carefully with the manuscript, not galley or production proofs.

6. *Verify that your printout matches your electronic files.* Don't confuse a service bureau or printer by providing electronic files that don't precisely match your laser proofs.

7. *Know what you're buying.* Some output services charge by the hour, others by the page. To compare costs, give several shops the same job specifications and ask what they would charge.

8. *Avoid elaborate desktop publishing.* Unless you're producing several different publications or one important publication, word processing software does fine for most newsletters.

9. *Avoid new software.* Upgrade the software you have instead of starting over with something new.

10. *Stick with standard typefaces.* Newsletters don't need special fonts.

11. *Proof your copy on-screen.* Pull up all hidden instructions and catch unwanted spaces and tabs and incorrect paragraph leading before making a printout.

12. *Use page layout software for design, not for writing.* It's more efficient to import final text from a word processing program.

13. *Don't tinker.* Resist the urge to make "little" design changes once you have chosen a format and type style.

14. *Proofread a second time after making changes to the electronic page.* A change at the top of the newsletter may create a disappearing act for type at the bottom of the page.

15. *Preprint color.* Don't pay to print two colors in each issue. Instead, preprint one color on an initial large print run, such as for your nameplate and other fixed elements. Then use the preprinted sheets to print your second color in future issues.

16. *Shop for a printer.* Don't assume that your regular printer, or the print shop down the street, is best suited to your newsletter.

17. *Use standard language.* Learn the correct terms for graphic design and reproduction. Poor communication is the number one source of mistakes.

18. *Use house sheets.* Specify that paper your printer buys in large quantity for many customers be used. Special-ordered paper costs much more.

19. *Stick with standard format sizes.* Certain newsletter formats, such as 8½-by-11 inches, make best use of common paper sizes. Nonstandard sizes, such as 9-by-12 inches, often put too much wasted paper into printers' dumpsters.

20. *Specify standard colors.* Avoid

special colors or color matches. Ask your printer which colors increase costs and which don't.

21. *Ignore minor errors.* Don't waste time arguing with a printer about tiny flaws that only you will notice.

22. *Negotiate critical flaws.* If a printing mistake or flaw hinders your newsletter's ability to communicate, or if it detracts from your organization's image and you are on deadline, insist on a price adjustment.

23. *Ensure compatibility.* Check that a service bureau or printer can read your disks before handing over the entire newsletter.

24. *Investigate imagesetting services.* Taking your newsletter directly from disk to film or from disk to printing plate may offer substantial savings when compared to giving camera-ready copy to the printer.

25. *Keep everyone informed.* Ensure that everyone who creates electronic input uses identical fonts and software. Tell the service bureau or printer all of the applications and fonts on a disk.

26. *Learn to do good, fast pasteup.* Think SCAN: square, clean, accurate and neat.

27. *Buy the right tools.* Approximately $100 spent on proper adhesives, rules, blades and other supplies will save you that much in time and fees over just a few days' work.

28. *Preprint boards.* Have your printer make blue line or black line boards to fit your format. Start each paste-up session with these precise guides already made.

29. *Recycle elements.* Use the same type, standing heads or art from mechanical to mechanical.

30. *Use an acrylic fixative.* Laser-printed mechanicals stay cleaner and withstand further pasteup and burnishing when sprayed with fixative.

31. *Keep tight control over electronic files.* As you approach deadline, avoid letting more people than necessary work on last-minute changes.

32. *Involve a printer from the start.* Ask for help in planning all production stages. Build your design around your printer's capabilities.

33. *Use mock-ups.* Make a dummy to plan and show elements such as folds, screens and colors.

34. *Tell the printer how many copies you must have.* Many printers follow the trade practice that allows 10 percent over or under the print order. Don't get caught short. Know that some printers may charge for copies up to 10 percent more than the number ordered.

35. *Plan for colors.* It's expensive to clean presses, so some printers have a certain day of the week for each color, for example, brown on Tuesdays. Plan color printing for the appropriate days.

36. *Reduce your grade of paper.* If you like the feel of 70-pound wove, consider 60-pound vellum; 60-pound matte may do as well as 70-pound gloss. Think about how much quality you really need.

37. *Price your own paper.* For long runs or many issues, consider buying paper separately from printing. Use your printer's regular suppliers to be sure stock is compatible with presses and find out from your printer how much paper your job will require.

38. *Give your printer everything at once.* There's less room for error when everything is kept together in one packet with instructions.

39. *Always have a proof copy.* If your printer does not supply a proof before running the presses, make two photocopies of your pasteup to use as proofs. Give one to your printer.

40. *Inspect proofs carefully.* After printing, compare the proofs to the printed piece. Use proofs to settle any disagreement between you and your printer.

41. *Use the least expensive proof.* If your newsletter has no photos, a pho-tocopy will do as well as a blue line. For color work, overlay proofs are usually as useful as integral or press proofs.

42. *Insist on good work.* Learn to recognize reasonable standards of print quality. You have a right to expect clean pieces that are properly aligned and uniformly inked.

Eight Efficient Distribution Tips

1. *Don't waste newsletters.* Use business reply cards, common sense and any other way you can think of to ensure that newsletters go only to people who want or need them.

2. *Learn correct address formats.* Verify that punctuation, attention lines, capitalization and other aspects of your addresses conform to postal regulations.

3. *Verify addresses.* Use membership information, employee records and other methods to ensure that newsletters go to correct addresses.

4. *Use nine-digit ZIP codes (ZIP + 4).* Address correction services can verify addresses and convert five-digit ZIP codes to nine-digit ZIP codes.

5. *Presort.* Take advantage of discounts in postage offered to mailers who presort.

6. *Try for nonprofit status.* If you qualify for nonprofit status, your postage might be cut in half. (Nonprofit status for mail rates is different from nonprofit status under IRS regulations.)

7. *Consider co-mailing.* Look for opportunities to share postage costs with others, such as including everybody's materials in one envelope.

8. *Use bar codes.* Get additional postage discounts by printing bar codes as part of addresses. Ask your mailing service to include bar codes on address labels or update your address maintenance software so that it prints bar codes.

Chapter 2

Typography

Because your newsletter's ultimate goal is to inform, type is the most important design element. Inappropriate type, such as that that is too small, makes content hard to read and understand; appropriately speced type makes a newsletter inviting and the information accessible.

Eye movement and reading comprehension studies of people at all age levels point to these seven hallmarks of good typography:

• *Consistency.* Good type design uses one or two type families for text, headlines, captions and all other elements. Designers build interest and create emphasis by changing type size and weight, not by switching from one type family to another.

• *Familiarity.* People read by the shape of whole words, not by the form of individual letters. The shape of words, however, depends on letterforms. Familiar letterforms create words whose meanings readers perceive instantly.

Familiar typefaces for body copy promote efficient newsletter reading. Although most designers and editors have dozens of typefaces at their fingertips, there are only eight or ten suitable for most newsletters. This small pool includes typefaces such as Times Roman, Bookman, Optima, Garamond, Palatino, Helvetica and Avant Garde, which have letterforms familiar to most readers.

• *Downstyle.* To aid readers in quickly identifying words by their shapes rather than by the shapes of their individual letters, words that readers expect to begin with lowercase letters should do so consistently. This is especially important for headlines, which are easiest to read when set downstyle so they look like bold sentences.

• *Serifs.* Dozens of research efforts show that readers comprehend text in serif type much more easily than sans serif type. Good design sticks with serif typefaces such as Garamond and Palatino for text and saves typefaces such as the sans serif Helvetica and Avant Garde for headlines.

• *Letter count.* Readers comprehend writing best when lines of type have an average of six or seven words. Because the average word in English has six characters, the most efficient line length is forty to forty-five characters. Good design avoids lines over fifty characters and under thirty-five characters.

• *Alignment.* Ragged vs. justified type does not influence legibility unless it affects space between words. When there is too little space between words, readers cannot distinguish one word from another. When there is too much space, the words become disconnected.

• *Color.* Although many designers feel that printing headlines in color makes readers pay more attention, research shows the opposite. Headlines printed in color slow readers down and reduce comprehension. Effective headlines are printed in the same ink color as text type.

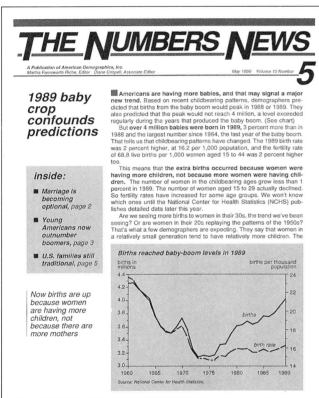

Tips for Improving Readability

The redesign of *The Numbers News* brought four type-related changes to improve readability. It now uses:

- serif instead of sans serif type for text
- headlines over articles instead of in the scholar margins
- arrows to lead from pull quotes into stories. (More pull quotes appear on page 33.)

- bold titles for infographics reversed out of solid rules instead of over printed on tints

The publisher also switched from blue ink to black ink. There is no evidence that blue captures attention better than black.

Name *The Numbers News*

Publisher *American Demographics, Inc., Ithaca, NY*

Purpose/audience *Service to subscribers*

Production *PageMaker on Macintosh*

Printing *Black on white offset paper*

Format *8½-by-11 inches, twelve pages*

Design *Jim Keller, Diane Crispell and Pat Driscoll*

Award *Newsletter Clearinghouse*

Summer, 1991 Vol. XIV; No. 2

*Money*talks

Hemming Morse
Certified Public Accountants and Consultants

*Money*talks

The Long and Winding Road to Work

Finding solutions to the complex, controversial transportation problems in the Bay Area is demanding increased levels of support and involvement from the business community.

Today companies are expected to take an active role in implementing programs that encourage commute alternatives, so that traffic is reduced and air quality is increased. Whether or not businesses have moved into this arena willingly is not at issue: What's critical is that they recognize the problems are reshaping our region and threatening the quality of life in the Bay Area. All of this affects business.

According to the Bay Area Economic Forum, jobs are dispersing rapidly because of the congested state of the roads and the lack of affordable housing. Commuters are moving to outlying areas or leaving the region to get access to the labor they need. Employers worry about retaining and attracting employees who must commute to work from their homes that are located in more affordable areas.

As a region, the failure to solve our transportation problems is costing nearly $2 billion annually, reports the Bay Area Economic Forum. This is partly because residents are collectively delayed in traffic nearly 100 million hours each year.

Business leaders are being asked to
● participate in organizations that support regional planning,
● use their political leverage to back reforms aimed at solving the gridlock,
● work closely with local governments to assess the impact of new development and growth.

Developers in particular are challenged to use vision when planning projects that impact growth and traffic congestion.

"We are not bold enough when it comes to looking at solutions for regional problems," emphasized transportation leader and State Senator Quentin Kopp. To help ease the transportation burden, for example, Kopp advocates evaluating another Bay crossing, bringing BART to the San Francisco Airport and extending CalTrain to downtown San Francisco.

Regarding the issue of air quality, Kopp believes that "most of what can be done in industry has been done. And the biggest area in which we must now secure proper quality of air is motor vehicles."

Indeed, auto emissions are the largest contributor to air quality problems in the Bay Area, and major employers may soon be asked to help clean them up. In an effort to meet the states clean air standards by 1997, the Bay Area Air Quality Management District is considering enforcing regulations that lead to fewer cars on the road. One of these measures would force employers to change employees parking fees.

The Bay Area Council in San Francisco and the Santa Clara County Manufacturing Group support a different option in market-based strategy to reduce single occupancy travel, including methods such as monitoring gas taxes so that people who drive longer pay more and raising vehicle registration fees for heavily polluting cars.

Cities and counties are passing ordinances mandating that businesses concern themselves with curbing transportation problems. Silicon Valley's Golden Triangle Task Force passed an ordinance that requires companies to survey their employees on how they get to work and to name a commute coordinator. The ordinance affects the cities of Milpitas, Mountain View, Palo Alto, San Jose and Sunnyvale. Santa Clara also passed a similar ordinance.

(continued on Moretalk)

I*Computer*talk

Managing Rapidly Changing Technology

Management Information Systems (MIS) are reshaping the business world in an irreversible way. Both large and small businesses have come to recognize new information technology as a source of competitive advantage.

Yet to understand and ultimately exploit technology, companies must first accept that the implementation process is complex, time-consuming, filled with hidden costs and often doesn't work—or doesn't work the way you expected it to. "You have to be willing to keep trying until you get it right," said Suzanna Musick, Manager of the Computer Services Group for Hemming Morse. "But the war will never be won without fighting the battles."

Acting as moderator at a recent forum on "Demystifying Technology," Musick introduced two veterans who talked about their battle scars and victories in applying MIS technology.

The speakers represented two diverse companies: Stephen Levandowski, Vice President of Information Resources at Levi Strauss International, spoke about how a corporate giant manages rapidly changing technology and Lee Tulp, a principal of Abacus, Inc., discussed how a fast growing company handles technological innovation in an entrepreneurial environment.

The forum was sponsored by the University of California's McClaren School of Business and was underwritten by Hemming Morse.

Levi Strauss:

Famous for its blue jeans, San Francisco-based Levi Strauss & Co. is the world leader in the manufacture of commercial apparel. Given the challenges and obstacles Levi faces by operating within 65 countries, Levandowski asked the audience, "How could one manage in this environment, let alone beat your competition, without taking advantage of information technology?"

Levandowski noted within the last 12 months Levi has seen: (1) dramatic growth in the capabilities and utilization of personal computers; (2) the implementation of a global satellite network linking Europe and Asia to the U.S.; (3) the installation of a minicomputer whose performance rivals that of a mid-range mainframe (but at a fraction of the cost); and (4) major advances in software engineering.

At Levi, information technology is part of a strategic business plan that yielded over four billion dollars in 1990. It is involved in virtually every business function and touches every individual at the company. "This includes administrative assistants using personal computers to do word processing or spreadsheet analysis to merchandisers using computer-aided design to develop new products," Levandowski said.

To improve productivity in its critical manufacturing function, Levi recently installed computer systems in its factories which resulted in a dramatic 5% improvement. "This is exceptional when you consider that our factories have been operating for decades and every ounce of productivity has been squeezed out of them," Levandowski said.

Guided by its "corporate vision" and a global strategic business plan, Levi has devised key strategies and organizational changes to turn technological change from a burden into a competitive advantage. "My premise is that a rapidly changing technological environment offers opportunities to those companies that can effectively manage their way through these changes," said Levandowski.

Abacus, Inc.

Abacus, Inc., a women-owned computer retailing company, is listed as 33rd on Inc. Magazine's list of the 500 fastest growing companies in the country, and is the fifth largest computer reseller in the Bay Area. According to Tulp, the axiom "time equals money" is especially true for small companies with limited financial resources. "Information is a resource that must be managed," she said. "Each piece of information must be examined for its value to the company."

Even though harried small business executives tend to feel as though they're "being shot out of a cannon" on a daily basis, Tulp still called zero-analysis "foolhardy" and emphasized the need for taking the time for analysis and planning. She stressed that once a commitment has been made to invest in information technology, then companies must develop a policy and procedure for implementing the system.

For those with limited resources, Tulp advised using an "entrepreneurial, street-fighting mentality"

(continued on Moretalk)

I*Tax*talk

Don't Postpone Paying Payroll Taxes
by Mark Costantini

As a Manager in the San Jose office, Mark Costantini specializes in income tax and business consulting for small to moderate-sized firms.

These are not easy times for many business owners. Because cash flow is tight, many of us are stretched to make ends meet while waiting for one of our customers to pay on an invoice that's long overdue. Maybe you've even been tempted to lighten your load by missing a payroll tax deposit.

Don't do it. And don't expect any sympathy from the Internal Revenue Service (IRS) if you do. This is possibly the greatest sin a business owner can commit in the eyes of the IRS.

Federal taxes must be withheld on salaries and wages paid to company employees. These federal taxes have to be turned over to the IRS—and they have to be turned over promptly.

The IRS takes the position that the withholding taxes you have failed to pay actually belong to your employees and the IRS, not to you. The IRS will go as far as to say that using these funds to finance your business operations is an illegal use of the U.S. Treasury. Maybe you'll go even further when it comes to collecting them.

If you delay (and few excuses will be accepted) in depositing your payroll taxes, the IRS will come after you for the unpaid tax plus penalties and interest.

It isn't only the company that is at risk here—the IRS can also seek payment from certain responsible individuals. This particular provision of the Internal Revenue Code is referred to as the "100% tax penalty," so named because the responsible party's liability is 100% of the amount due. The Code states that any person who "willfully fails" to turn over withheld federal income or Social Security taxes may be held personally liable for the unpaid taxes. Willful failure means that the act was voluntarily, consciously and intentionally done by the responsible party.

The IRS uses specially trained revenue officers within the IRS Collection Division to determine who makes the financial decisions, who is responsible for paying the taxes and who has the check-signing authority. Several responsible parties may be named. And since the IRS wants to increase its chances of collecting, they may go after whoever they think will be easiest to collect from.

The 100% penalty can only be assessed against the undeposited withholding taxes, not against the matching Social Security or unemployment taxes imposed on the employer. But deposits must be made

for both types of payroll tax liabilities and other substantial penalties may apply for late payment or nonpayment, even if the 100% penalty is not assessed. Similar deposit requirements and penalty provisions are imposed by the State of California.

The bottom line is: do whatever you can to pay your payroll taxes on time. Determine your firm's payment responsibility and make timely deposits at your local financial institution that is a federal depository. Fill out a federal tax deposit coupon and submit it, along with your check, to your banker. Ask for a receipt, because even being a day late can mean substantial tax penalties. If you are a responsible party in your company, make sure that you are protected. Mark each payroll due date on your desk calendar, appointment book or other ledger that you refer to frequently. If you designate the responsibility, keep abreast of the collection and payment process. Finally, appoint a back-up in case the person assigned to the job is out sick or on vacation.

If the IRS does notify you of an unpaid payroll tax liability, don't delay. Make an appointment with your tax attorney, CPA or enrolled agent immediately. They can help you determine the appropriate course of action.

Please remember that, even if cash flow is tight, the alternative is much worse and far too serious to even consider. Nonpayment of payroll taxes is one area where the IRS flexes its muscles to the full extent. Putting up with tight cash flow might be burdensome, but it is preferable to being put out of business or even forced to sell your personal assets to meet your payroll tax obligations. ■

Maximizing a Nameplate Design

Each page of *Moneytalks*, with its large drop sink and clever "talk" title, reinforces the nameplate design and creates continuity. Each page features only one article, which is introduced by an understated red headline. The overall effect is sophisticated and conservative without being staid—an appropriate look for affluent individuals and companies.

Name *Moneytalks*

Publisher *Hemming Morse Co., San Fransisco, CA*

Purpose/audience *Service and marketing to clients*

Production *By hand*

Printing *Black and red on white offset paper*

Format *8½-by-11 inches, six pages (six-panel foldout)*

Design *Kale Keating and Dennis Harms*

Award *Communication Concepts*

Creating an Efficient Design

Readers like the summary deck between headlines and lead paragraphs because it captures the essense of the story. Setting the deck in italic gives it a sense of urgency. Using the same typeface for kicker, headline, deck and text gives readers the consistency that aids in quick and accurate comprehension. In this design, only the subtitle appears in a different typeface, lending just the right touch of contrast to that crucial element.

Name *The Service Edge*

Publisher *Lakewood Publications, Minneapolis, MN*

Purpose/audience *Service to subscribers*

Production *PageMaker and FreeHand on Macintosh*

Printing *Black and turquoise on white offset paper*

Format *8 1/2-by-11 inches, eight pages*

Design *Phil Russell, Brian McDermott, Dave Zielinski and Julia Tilka*

A LAKEWOOD PUBLICATION

The Service Edge®

For Creating and Maintaining Distinctive Service

August 1991 — Vol. 4, No. 8

Reward & Recognition Survey

Service incentives: Good performance earns praise, prizes, and cash awards

The sales world has lost its monopoly on performance incentives. In some companies, the trips, cash bonuses, and special parking spots once reserved for salespeople are being shared with the non-sales population for achieving service goals and other quality performance standards — and for good reason.

You can talk about improving service in your organization until the proverbial cows come home, but until you are clearly rewarding workers for their service-related performance, service performance isn't likely to change much.

Clearly rewarding workers means building service performance standards into job descriptions and compensation plans. But it also means finding special ways to recognize and reward people for providing good service, for celebrating service quality in ways that make it a focal point for an entire organization, and for having well-defined plans to make sure all the talk results in some action.

For the purposes of a rewards and recognition survey conducted by *The Service Edge* and *Total Quality* newsletters in cooperation with Maritz Inc., we defined three types of reward plans:

Recognition Plans award a few outstanding performers or teams for unique contributions or sustained performance, and are usually based on subjective criteria.

Activity Award Plans award individuals or teams for specific, predetermined activities related to service quality, such as participating in service research projects or completing related training.

Performance Improvement Plans award individuals, teams, or business units for reaching long-term improvement project goals or milestones, and are based on very specific quantitative *continued on p. 2*

Bob finally gets the recognition he deserves.

Taking Note

Can companies looking at implementing reward and recognition plans tied to service quality expect a solid return on their reward investment?

The Service Edge survey of 179 companies seems to indicate yes, particularly in the area of performance improvement awards, those tied to quantifiable, measurable service standards.

But there are qualifiers. If reward plans aren't carefully managed (read: if chosen rewards aren't constantly monitored for their perceived value by employees) and if the reward process is perceived as partisan, you'll soon discover diminishing returns from recognition plans targeted to the non-sales population.

Perhaps compensation guru Ed Lawler, writing in his book *Strategic Pay*, says it best: "I believe many organizations are more concerned with doing the wrong things right than with searching for the right incentive practices. They have systems driven more by history and what other organizations do than by strategic analysis of their own organizational needs." — *DZ*

Inside this issue...

Service Journal:
High-tech gadgets guide Wal-Mart shoppers through stores' aisles ..**p.4**

Recovery Clinic:
Effective communication only comes from training **p.5**

Inside Feature:
Loosening frontliners' reins boosts satisfaction ratings **p.5**

Questions Readers Ask:
How to simulate partnership for employees 'serving in the dark'... **p.6**

Ideas from Experts:
Service savvy is make-or-break skill in high-tech — *G. Major* ..**p.7**

A Few Last Words: By Ron Zemke
Quality debate needs reason, not venom **p.8**

Lakewood Publications
Subsidiary of Maclean Hunter Publishing Company

Adding Visual Interest to Text

Signature focuses on one lengthy feature article each issue, so the typography uses lots of subheads, sidebars and pull quotes to break up the text and add visual interest. The four-column grid keeps readers moving quickly through the text.

Name *Signature*

Publisher *Griffin Printing, Glendale, CA*

Purpose/audience *Service and marketing to customers*

Production *Microsoft Word and WordPerfect on Macintosh*

Printing *Black and a second color on natural offset paper*

Format *8½-by-11 inches, eight pages*

Design *Tim Coussens and Ernest Weckbaugh*

Awards *Printing Industries of America, Graphic Arts Monthly*

Griffin's

Signature

A NEWSLETTER FOR THE PUBLISHING INDUSTRY

McHUGH ON PUBLISHING

VOLUME 6, NO. 3

SUMMER 1991

Book Publishing and Non-Publishing Organizations
PART II: *Issues, Opportunities and Management*

by John B. McHugh

John B. McHugh

This newsletter is printed on recycled paper.

Part I of this article was in our July/August 1990 issue. Part III will appear in our Fall 1991 issue. A reprint of Part I and/or a copy of the balance of the article (Part III) are available on request.

Unclear and Unspecific Responsibility

Many book publishing executives in a non-publishing organization are unsure about their specific responsibilities and accountabilities. The executive over the book publishing entity and book publishing manager may not have reached agreement on the *objectives* of the book publishing program. In many organizations that sponsor book publishing programs, I find the publishing manager's job description is either outdated or nonexistent. It is important to establish the responsibilities and expectations of the book publishing executive. Much of this organizational confusion and ambiguity will disappear if a book publishing mission statement is prepared by top management. The mission statement should define exactly the expectations of the parent organization when it comes to the operations and results expected from the book publishing entity. What are the expectations for: product support? service to members? generating profits? breaking-even? Unspecified goals will

---

With in-house providers, where is the incentive to please the customer?

---

lead to poor financial performance.

Centralized Promotion: A Concern

Many organizations centralize their marketing and promotion function. The centralized promotion group provides promotional support and services for the *entire* organization.

From an organizational standpoint, centralization makes sense as there are many economies and efficiencies to be achieved. However, there may be drawbacks for the book publisher.

Consider the matter of service. Who gets taken care of first? If the books in production are on schedule and the promotion is not timed with the book production schedule, then book sales will suffer. The book publishing executive is responsible for sales, while someone else, not accountable for either sales or Profit & Loss, can affect the publisher's performance. The promotional group can (and will) bump the book publisher's work for someone else. That "someone else" may be considered more important politically or financially to the organization.

Let's talk about quality and accuracy of the promotional materials. A major problem of being an internal customer is the "forced" use of someone

(Cont'd on page 2)

Laying Out Long Articles

The scholar margin gives ample space for the masthead and the contents on the front page. Inside, the margin allows flexibility with illustrations, photos and captions, while leaving plenty of white space. Sans serif text type is set ragged right with lots of leading to provide an informal sense for this newsletter about financial services. The overall effect is that *Access* has room for long, text-intensive articles, yet retains a light, airy look.

Name *Access*

Publisher *Chase Access Services, Lexington, MA*

Purpose/audience *Service to employees*

Production *WordPerfect, Sicky Business, FreeHand and PageMaker on Macintosh IIx. Format from Wil Sherwood 911 Graphics.*

Printing *Black and blue on white gloss-coated paper*

Format *8 1/2-by-11 inches, eight pages*

Design *Dorothy Quinn*

ACCESS, a newsletter from Chase Access Services, is published four times a year. Please direct all inquiries, including story ideas and requests for additional copies, to Dorothy Quinn, CN 395-8192.

CHASE

ACCESS

Pursuing New Opportunities in 1991

Message from Peter Crowell, President, Chase Access Services Corporation

As 1990 comes to a close, this issue of *Access* reflects the "state of the nation" very well. Chase Manhattan and the banking industry have had a tough year, a situation which has been reflected in our performance and in the actions Chase has had to take. The beat does go on, however. InfoServ International represents a highly profitable core business of the Bank which is vigorously pursuing additional revenue. CAS's role in this pursuit is reflected in a number of articles in this issue. The INFOStation article describes new technology being developed for our customers. The ADP team winning a SWAT award highlights some super performance in pursuit of new business. The Franchise News column mentions several recent franchise wins. Potential CONFEX business, described on page seven, represents a unique opportunity for Chase. CONFEX would expand the types of applications CAS provides as a processor for other banks. Efficiencies in bank system-wide processing have eroded transaction fees. Winning new processing business would create a good defensive position by providing replacement revenues.

Looking forward to 1991, the American banking system is not out of the woods. We will have to continue to look for new opportunities to generate revenue, become more efficient, and encourage innovation. Be more efficient and innovate — is this a contradiction? No. Remember the adage: "Necessity is the mother of invention"? We are often most creative when faced with ambitious schedules and complex problems. Our thoughts by necessity turn to solutions designed to achieve our goals "faster, better, and cheaper". CAS has consistently demonstrated this aptitude for innovation and I know that we will continue to excel in applying people and technology to the challenges ahead.

Thank you for your dedication this year. Have a joyful and peaceful New Year.

CONTENTS

For Internal Use Only

INFOStati[on]

An Interview with Ralph Cutone, Vic[e]

Chase Access Services has been press[ing] for some time to overhaul our microstat[ion] technology. From a technological and marketing perspective, CAS thought it [was] time to develop a consistent, easy to in[stall] micro-based interface for client access [to] help us project the image of 'one Chase' [to] our customers. Last year, Global Secu[rity] Services identified a similar business requirement for a new microstation that [would] support all of their applications. The INFOStation™ is being developed for u[se] throughout the sector and the Bank.

Why are CAS and Global Custody building the INFOStation?

"Historically, Global Securities Ser[vices] has had several separate and distinct systems organizations, each develop[ing] products for its respective market. In[terna]tional Securities markets to clients in United Kingdom, Europe, and Asia. [...] products are developed for the North [...]

Ralph Cutone is the Global Securities Services point man for the INFOStation™. In the following article Ralph describes new business requirements and talks about the technology for this new microstation platform.

News from the Franchise Sales group at Chase Access Services.

FRANCHISE NE[WS]

Facing competition from GEISCO, **Al Salzano** has sealed an agreement [with] Standard Chartered Bank of New Yor[k for] automated treasury management ser[vices.] The deal will generate $25,000 in ann[ual]ized revenue. Standard Chartered ha[s] signed up for Balance and Transactio[n] Reporting Service (TX/BTS), Cash Co[ncen]tration Reporting service (TX/CCR), a[s well] as Chase's Controlled Disbursement [service.] Since CCR will feed Cash Managemen[t and] Electronic Funds Transfer product, th[is] will be additional fee income to Chas[e] beyond the CAS product revenues.

Kevin McNamara has sold intrad[ay] balance reporting to existing client C[entral] Fidelity Bank of Richmond, VA. Cen[tral] Fidelity has been a Treasurers' XCHA[NGE] client since 1984. The new product [will] generate approximately $36,000 in ad[di]tional annualized revenue.

Recently Bank One, Texas moved [...] hardware for transmissions to Los Co[...] Texas. Since Bank One transmits ei[ght?] a day to CAS, we were involved with [...] extensive transmission testing. The f[...]

Kenney Heads to Tallahassee... Barry Kenney...marketing director at Metrozoo...has been appointed director of tourism for Florida's Department of Commerce... Kenney brings lots of experience to job...was past president of Florida Attractions Assn/South Florida Chapter... Bureau President Merrett Stierheim part of selection committee.

Two New Cruise Ships Call Miami Home... "Ecstasy," Carnival Cruise Lines new ship in port mid-May... Royal Caribbean's "Monarch of the Seas" arrives in November.

Miami Looks Toward Far East... May 7–12...Miami's sister city...Kagoshima, Japan bringing delegation to Miami... will attend a "Tourism Idea Exchange" at Bureau's offices.

ITIX & POW WOW... Travel Trade Department attended trade show in April in Las Vegas with worldwide travel agents and tour operators... will attend POW WOW in Denver, Colorado May 11–15.

The Russians Are Coming... Aeroflot launched Miami to Moscow service April 28...twice weekly to Moscow via Ireland.

Spanish Connections... May 23...American Airlines launches daily Miami–Madrid and Cancun–Miami non-stop... expanding Miami hub with four more flights over next two months... April 7 Miami–Houston... Miami–Islip, N.Y.

Bavarian Link... Lufthansa now flying non-stop Miami–Munich...twice a week...started March 31... Alitalia... adding fourth flight to Miami–Rome connection launched in October... Pan Am looking South... building its Latin

Advertising Campaign Underway... Bureau and marketing partners developing marketing campaign... local and feeder market campaigns began in March in Miami, Europe and U.K. Other elements...two-sided poster...TV/Radio Public Service Announcements (PSA)... sales presentation video... sales brochures... Co-op opportunities available to Bureau members.

National Geographic Visits Miami...correspondent and photographer in town doing major piece on Greater Miami for Winter/Spring issue. Watch for it.

Vacation America Television Series...produced half-hour documentary about Greater Miami for The Travel Channel...seen by 46 million viewers...will air nationally more than 12 times during the year.

Caribbean Travel... coming back after a two-month slump... perception that travel to region is expensive delaying recovery... to salvage winter season Caribbean hoteliers are discounting rates to tour wholesalers.

In Europe... tour operators emerging from effects of Persian Gulf War... putting together new travel packages... aiming for summer travel... fear of travel and U.S. recession still having impact on number of Americans going abroad... vacationing in Europe is expensive... may mean more Americans taking domestic vacations.

Warning Lifted... State Dept. lifted worldwide travel advisory warning of possible terrorism against Americans... Advisory had been in effect since Persian Gulf War.

Oil Consumption... U.S. continues to increase oil use...1973 U.S. imported 35%...in 1991 it's 50%... 67%

Economizing Time and Type

By printing text in small chunks, *NewsWire* presents lots of information in a little space without seeming cluttered. Bold lead phrases replace standard headlines. Ellipses supplant words. The simple, two-column grid allows writing, printing and mailing all within a six-day schedule.

Name *Bureau NewsWire*

Publisher *Greater Miami Convention and Visitors Bureau, Miami, FL*

Purpose/audience *Service to bureau members and the media*

Production *QuarkXPress on Macintosh SE/30*

Printing *Black and green on light gray offset paper*

Format *8½-by-14 inches, two pages*

Design *Neil D. Littauer*

AMICUS

Issue No. 9	**McGuireWoods Battle & Boothe**	August, 1989

Bankruptcy and Creditor's Rights

The Final Chapter?

Not Any More.

In the past ten years, creditor's rights has come into its own as the laws governing bankruptcy have turned chapters in the code from corporate swan song to sophisticated business alternative. Though we may represent a debtor or borrower (as is the case with our current representation of Miller &

Rhoads), the firm's main focus is on creditors such as banks, savings and loan institutions and even individuals who have lent money to a faltering entity. The escalated demand from creditors and the new legal challenges created by the relatively recent code changes has brought our bankruptcy and creditor's rights practice from an occasional case to a thriving specialty.

When Lee Mason (T-BUS) told her father, also an attorney, that she wanted to specialize in bankruptcy and creditor's rights a few years ago, he got a strange expression on his face. "He just couldn't understand why I would pursue such an unglamorous area of the law. That was his understanding of it. He didn't realize how much had changed," she said. Mason had been able to see today's brand of the practice area by clerking under Judge Shelley during the Robins bankruptcy proceeding.

Another former clerk for Judge

Shelley is Bruce Matson, who joined us in 1986 from a Norfolk-based firm. Matson's familiarity with the Bankruptcy court's personnel and procedures gives an extra dimension to the practice area.

The image boost for creditor's rights began in earnest with the 1978 enactment of the Bankruptcy Code which turned court appointed referees into bankruptcy judges. In addition, procedural changes and policy additions created a more complicated code, one that made the practice "certainly more intense and created much more opportunity for legal work than existed beforehand," says Slate Dabney (R-BUS) who initiated the bankruptcy and creditor's rights group about four years ago. Tom Geisler (R-BUS) explains that the changes "modernized the Chapter 11 process and made it more attractive to seek relief under the Bankruptcy Code."

As these regulations evolved and *continued on page 2*

Suiting the Type to the Purpose

Elegant serif type dominating the nameplate conveys authority without seeming too formal. Centering the newsletter name adds to the conservative image, while text type set ragged right contributes a friendly feeling. The attorneys and staff that depend on *Amicus* perceive it as highly sophisticated from a production standpoint.

Name *Amicus*

Publisher *McGuire, Woods, Battle & Booth, Richmond, VA*

Purpose/audience *Service and marketing to clients*

Production *PageMaker on AT&T 386*

Printing *Black and blue on white linen text paper*

Format *9-by-12 inches, six pages*

Design *Lisa Cumbay*

Award *Communications Concepts*

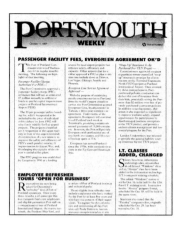

PORTSMOUTH WEEKLY
September 30, 1991 — Port of Portland

PORT'S ANNUAL GIVING CAMPAIGN GETS UNDERWAY

The Port of Portland's Annual Giving Campaign is once again underway, with information orientation sessions now completed in all of the Port's operating areas.

According to Larry Flax, human resources special projects manager, this is the second year the Port has had additional charitable organizations besides the United Way solicit funds from employees through the payroll deduction process.

"This is a convenient way for employees to donate to one or more worthwhile non-profit agencies," Flax said. "Participating charities, generally represented by umbrella organizations such as the United Way or the Black United Fund, offer employees the advantage of making payroll deductions or cash donations through one simple donation form. The lead organization then distributes the funds to specific individual agencies as directed by the donor."

The non-profit organizations involved in this year's Annual Giving Campaign include those represented by the Black United Fund of Oregon, Environmental Federation of Oregon, International Services Agencies, United Way of the Columbia-Willamette, and the Spinal Cord Association.

The donor pledge documents, which were distributed to all eligible Port employees in early September, may be completed and returned to any one of five site coordinators. Site coordinators and their representative areas are: Larry Flax (ext. 7429), Port of Portland Building; Barbara DeJager (ext. 1144), Portland International Airport; Bob Laughlin (ext. 2234), marine terminals; Vicki Mallonee (ext. 3022), Portland Ship Yard; and Judy Johnson (ext. 2200), Engineering. Employees working outside one of these representative areas can submit their completed pledge forms directly to Larry Flax.

The last day to return completed pledge documents is Oct. 11.

PDX SCORES SECON[D] PASSENGER MONT[H]

More than 685,000 passengers traveled through Portland International Airport (PDX) last month, making August 1991 the airport's second best passenger month in its 50-year history.

"While August didn't set a new record, it was a great month!" said Keith Phildius, the Port's aviation director. "We nearly matched the all-time one-month record, which is something I think we can all feel proud of."

Attributing August's high passenger numbers to the strength of the local economy and the attractiveness of the region as a vacation destination, Phildius added that PDX continues to outperform the national aviation

PORTSMOUTH WEEKLY
September 16, 1991 — Port of Portland

PORT COMMISSION OKS NEW MULINO FBO, PDX CONTRACTS

The Port of Portland Commission convened Wednesday for its regular monthly meeting. The following are highlights of that meeting.

Mulino Airport FBO Selected – Cougar Aviation was chosen as the new fixed base operator (FBO) for Portland-Mulino Airport, effective Oct. 1. Replacing Mulino Air Center as the airport's on-site management firm, Cougar will provide aircraft maintenance and flight training to airport customers as well as perform certain airport management duties. Those duties include renting hangar and tie-down space, monitoring airfield operations,

PDX Construction Contracts Awarded – The Commission awarded four construction contracts for work

construction office to the King Interest's Inc. multi-tenant cargo building at Portland International Airport in Airtrans Center. The Port's construction office is being relocated due to the Terminal Expansion North (TEN) project, expected to begin in December.

Currently, construction offices at the airport are in a portion of the Old Maintenance Building, adjacent to the terminal, which will eventually be demolished to make way for the new Concourse E.

changes will fund the design and construction costs according to their respective requests, with expenses for jointly used facilities to be shared by all of the airlines serving PDX.

A $104,176 contract was awarded to Wilsey & Ham Pacific for design of Airtrans Center's N.E. Taxiway and J.W. Presley & Co., Inc. received approval for a $248,834 contract to provide grading to prepare a site for the proposed 2,600-foot taxiway. The N.E. Taxiway provides the only airfield access to several Airtrans Center lease parcels. A majority of the design and grading project costs will be funded through a grant from the Federal Aviation Administration's Airport Improvement Program.

Also approved was a contract with Eagle Elsner Inc., in the amount of $155,526, for utilities and access road construction to serve a new lease site at PDX. The site will be leased by Delta Air Lines for its ground services equipment facility, which will be relocated from the airport terminal building to accommodate the TEN project.

PORTSMOUTH WEEKLY
September 23, 1991 — Port of Portland

USS ORISKANY TRANSFER ENDORSED

A United States House of Representatives subcommittee took action Sept. 12 that clears the way for a major overhaul and conversion of a 41-year-old Navy vessel at the Portland Ship Yard.

Testifying before the Seapower Subcommittee of the House Armed Services Committee, Congressman Les AuCoin said conversion of the obsolete aircraft carrier USS ORISKANY into an American cultural center for placement in Japan's Yokohama Harbor was "a victory for the American economy."

Steve Nousen, Port of Portland government relations manager who attended the crowded Washington, D.C. hearing, said the Seapower Subcommittee's decision "nearly assures that the ORISKANY will come to Portland for conversion at the Portland Ship Yard."

AuCoin said the Japanese non-profit organization "City of America," sponsor of the conversion project, will purchase the ORISKANY from the Navy and repair and retrofit the vessel on the West Coast once the Secretary of the Navy authorizes its release. AuCoin estimated the ORISKANY project will require approximately $30 million in shipyard work and create about 2,000 direct job-years of labor (a job-year is the equivalent of one full-time employee working one year). Much of the work is expected to be concentrated at the Port of Portland's shipyard.

In referring to U.S./Japanese economic relations, AuCoin said the ORISKANY is a "sound visionary proposal" and "a symbol of hope of improving relations." He said the project will "build bridges and reduce friction between the U.S. and Japan."

Before the ORISKANY project can proceed, Congress must formally authorize the Secretary of the Navy to transfer title of the ORISKANY to a non-profit organization – expected to be just a formality now that the Seapower Subcommittee has approved the project, Nousen said.

SHIP YARD EMPLOYEE RECOGNIZED

Michael Malish, a journeyman electrician at the Portland Ship Yard, has been named May 1991's "Employee of the Month" by Bruce Robeson, director of the shipyard.

In a congratulatory letter to Malish, Robeson wrote: "Since you have come to the Port, you have shown yourself to be a very conscientious worker, and any job that you have been assigned has been completed in a very efficient and effective manner. Your interest in wanting to learn more about the equipment and different systems we have here in the shipyard makes you an asset to the electrical shop and the Port of Portland. Thank you."

ART WORK CAPS REMODELING PROJECT

After this week, according to Adella Martell, Port marketing communications manager, visitors to the Port of Portland Building's 13th floor will have more to look at than just a superb view of the city. As the finishing touch to the Port offices remodeling project, three pieces of art have been purchased which will be installed in the 13th floor reception area and the International Conference Room the week of Sept. 30.

A 40" x 60" acrylic on paper, titled "Token Moon" by artist Bill Hoppe, will hang behind the reception room couch. A mixed-media watercolor collage, created by Harry Widman, titled "Kernel," will hang above the reception room writing desk. In the International Conference Room, a mixed-media transfer print, titled "Fin de Siecle Skirmishes" by artist Paul Chojnowki, will be put above the couch.

The Port offices remodeling plan also calls for the use of photographs in the Commission Room and in other public areas of the Port-owned share of the building. The selected photographs will be installed during the next few months.

PORTSMOUTH WEEKLY
October 11, 1991 — Port of Portland

PASSENGER FACILITY FEES, EVERGREEN AGREEMENT OK'D

EMPLOYEE REFRESHER TOURS 'OPEN FOR BUSINESS'

I.T. CLASSES ADDED, CHANGED

Producing Layouts Fast

Meeting a deadline every Friday requires a design that allows fast turnaround. Floating rules and typography that stay consistent issue after issue let layout staff turn word processing files into page design very quickly.

Although capitalized headlines usually don't work well, as with every guideline, rules may be broken in good design. These headlines are short and bold, helping readers get into stories easily.

Name *Portsmouth Weekly*

Publisher *Port of Portland, Portland, OR*

Purpose/audience *Service to employees*

Production *QuarkXPress on Macintosh*

Printing *Blue preprinted and black on natural, tinted fiber offset paper*

Format *8 1/2-by-11 inches, two pages*

Design *Antonia Manda and Sherry Brookshire*

PARENTS ASSOCIATES

PARENTS ASSOCIATES

PARENTS ASSOCIATES

Kerning for Stylish Results

Palatino typeface in the nameplate brings a sense of dignity that fits with the university-wide image identity program. As elegant as Palatino is, however, the letters require careful kerning to yield this stylish result. Examples of Palatino with no kerning (center) and slight kerning (bottom) are shown below the nameplate

Name *Parents Associates*

Publisher *Loyola University Chicago, Chicago, IL*

Purpose/audience *Service to parents*

Production *By hand*

Printing *Blue preprinted and black on white matte-coated paper*

Format *8 1/2-by-11 inches, eight pages*

Design *Downey, Weeks & Toomey—Janice Stockwell*

Award *Communications Concepts*

On June 5, Continental held grand opening celebrations for our new Reservations Centers in Salt Lake City and Tampa. See the June 20 CO Times for more details on these new facilities.

Continental's print advertising campaign, highlighting our summer program, breaks this week in major newspapers in selected markets around the system.

DifferenceMakers: MCO agent helps family

MCO ASA Barbara Engberg recently demonstrated the kind of compassion for and trust in our customers that makes the Continental difference. During check-in for a flight, she noticed that a child had chicken pox in its contagious stage. Of course, the family could not travel, but rather than simply turn them away at the gate, Barbara asked what she could do to help. They had just returned their vacation rental car and had no transportation to bring the child to a doctor. Acting with extraordinary confidence on behalf of these customers, Barbara loaned them the use of her own vehicle.

Summer is special

Last summer Continental began a new tradition with a program called **Continental Summer: We're Ready**. If you don't remember it, don't feel bad, you're not alone. A post summer survey has shown that, while the program was well received by both customers and employees, the number one obstacle to its total success was inadequate communication to the people who matter most, the frontline team.

(See **Summer is special***, pg. 3)*

CO Summer: We make a differenc

An open letter to the Contin from Chairman, President a Hollis Harris:

"It is a pivotal time in th our airline. Despite all the o combined five post-deregula into the nation's fifth largest giant. Despite war and reces moving quickly toward a rec that I believe will serve as a business survival in an indus with failure.

"We have a new identity rapidly gaining recognition f grace and sophistication. We and very apropos theme: On make a difference. Now, as v into the season that means n industry and our bottom line other, we must bring all our and all our skills to bear.

"Summer presents the e industry with a scenario that be described as a crisis. A w philosopher defined a crisis 'dangerous opportunity.' In c opportunity is 'dangerous' o it has the potential to weake strengthen the momentum o improving image. We're willi the risk because, after all the we've been through, our tim I've watched this team in act know your determination an sionalism is second to none. saying that we can make a d during the busiest travel peri year and we're ready to prov

"It's going to be a challe knows better than we how c hectic our airport terminals g heat of the summer. No one ter than we how desperately tomers want their summer tr for vacation or business, to g despite the crowds, the heat general pandemonium. But v travelers get home and call t and relatives with the news t tinental made it happen, we' met our challenge.

"Continental Summer be 14. I'm confident that we've strategy and the best people Together we will make a diff

Downstyling Headlines

Downstyle headlines (setting them like sentences without periods) contribute to the readability of *CO Times*. Research shows that capitalizing a headline's first word and proper nouns helps readers comprehend quickly. The overall pattern of this type, the combination of black and blue ink, and the accented vertical page size convey a sense of quality while allowing the publication to stay within budget.

Name *CO Times*

Publisher *Continental Airlines, Houston, TX*

Purpose/audience *Service to employees*

Production *Ventura Publisher on IBM*

Printing *Black and blue on white offset paper*

Format *8 1/2-by-14 inches, four pages*

Design *Connie Birdsall and Robin Miller*

Award *Newsletter Clearinghouse*

WordPerfect Report
Fall 1991 — Volume V, Number 3

WordPerfect for Windows in the Final Stretch!

As of this writing, WordPerfect for Windows is scheduled to enter Beta testing in July—one of the last required milestones before it ships. We expect the Beta and Beta II testing phase to take two or three months.

Selecting dates for the release of WordPerfect for Windows has been much more of an art than a science. Says Pete Peterson, executive vice president of WPCorp, "When we first set out to produce WordPerfect for Windows, we were not far enough along in the development cycle to accurately predict the Code Complete date—we were very optimistic."

Milestone One: Code Complete Date

Toward the end of developing a software product, we look for five milestones by which we measure our progress. The first of these is called Code Complete. When WordPerfect for Windows was declared "code

three separate print jobs. And they tried printing both portrait and landscape in the same document, another capability unique to WordPerfect printer drivers.

Chuck Middleton, director of WordPerfect for Windows development, says Code Complete also meant an enormous effort was nearing completion. "In about a year and a half," Chuck says, "we completely overhauled WordPerfect for DOS so it would work in Windows while still maintaining the complete feature set and file format which makes WordPerfect for DOS so popular. We also completely redesigned the entire user interface to work in a GUI environment." By the time WordPerfect for Windows ships, an estimated one-quarter-million work hours will have been poured into the project by programmers and in-house testers.

Milestone Two: Alpha Release

...a testing program began May 29,
...Complete. Almost 200
...use WordPerfect for Windows
...to put the program through its

...t anywhere near the polished
...it nevertheless worked. There
...ons, but all in all, it was a

...cess, a battery of tests is set up
...network, and printer

Linking Heads and Subheads

Designers at WordPerfect Corporation rely on their own word processing software to create this effective publication. As their software has evolved, so has their design. The Fall 1991 issue shows the sophisticated power of the software used to put more leading above the subheads than below them, thereby visually linking the subheads to the text.

Name *WordPerfect Report*

Publisher *WordPerfect Corporation, Orem, UT*

Purpose/audience *Service to customers*

Production *WordPerfect on IBM*

Printing *Black and blue on white offset paper*

Format *8½-by-11 inches, sixteen pages*

Design *Randy Nelson*

WPCorp Report

Volume I, Number 1 — Published by WordPerfect Corporation — Third Quarter 1987

WPCorp Report: News, Rumors, and Views

Who would have supposed, when WordPerfect Corporation was only a two-person, single-product operation, that within seven years the company's ledgers would record multi-million dollar profits? Sales continue to grow at a rapid yet steady pace—from $10 million in 1984, to $23 million in 1985, to $52 million in 1986. 1987's year-to-date

figures are following in stride and will foreseeably top $100 million.

How many WordPerfect end-users do these figures represent? Our accounting records indicate a number approaching three-quarters of a million PC users. WordPerfect sales in the VAX, Data General, and Apple II markets account for a noticeable, though smaller percentage of overall sales. WPCorp's other products—PlanPerfect, Word-

line of computers. The $495 list price of WordPerfect 4.2 is unaffected by the media size. WordPerfect Library and PlanPerfect are also available in both 3.5" and 5.25" media. WordPerfect Executive comes with both media sizes in each package.

WordPerfect for the Amiga

The distinguishing advantage of WordPerfect for the Amiga is that it was designed specifically for the Amiga and not simply

THE WPCORP REPORT

Volume IV, Number 2 — Published by WordPerfect Corporation — April 1990

Inside

DrawPerfect—The Presentation Program

Labels can be misleading. For example, when you hear that DrawPerfect is a Business Presentation Graphics program, you may wonder how it could possibly be useful to you. But, if you're ever going to make any kind of presentation, you need the program. In fact, **DrawPerfect's main purpose is to improve any presentation you make.** Some of the most exciting things that DrawPerfect allows you to do are: 1) create overhead transparencies; 2) turn DrawPerfect files into slides; 3) improve WordPerfect documents with visuals; and, 4) create on-screen computer shows.

The ability to make overhead transparencies, slides, or entire on-screen presentations gives you flexibility in your presentation method. For example, in a lecture situation you may want to use overhead transparencies. In a large conference, however, you might need a slide presentation or printed hand-outs. Even when you're given little notice to prepare, you can create visual aids quickly and easily.

Transparencies

With DrawPerfect, turning graphics and text into overhead transparencies is as easy as putting transparency film into the paper bin of your printer, and printing. You can also make transparencies by using a copy machine or a professional service.

Slides

The ability to quickly create slides can be very useful. Suppose, for example that you have a table of sales information that you would like to present to the board of an aerospace company in two days. You can import the table into DrawPerfect and create a bar chart using a variety of colors and fill patterns. To add a creative touch, overlay the chart on top of the airplane image included in the DrawPerfect Figure Library. Once you have chosen the figure, select Export from the File pull-down menu, choose CGM, HPGL, or SCODL as your export format, and enter the filename. Now send the files to a slide service bureau that will turn your illustrations into high-quality slides and return them to you within 48 hours.

On-Screen Presentation

In the example above you could have created an on-screen computer presentation instead of slides. To create a presentation you must first choose the images that will be used.

After you save all the images that you want to use, go to the Presentation feature, found on the File menu. Here you list sequentially the various filenames of the visuals that you want included in your presentation. You can specify the amount of time that each image will display and how it will appear

WordPerfect Around the World

Global Expansion

WordPerfect Corporation is rapidly expanding. At the beginning of this year, the company maintained distribution in 83 countries throughout the world. Now, with organized distribution for Afghanistan, Bangladesh, Ethiopia, Ghana, Nepal, Pakistan, Sri Lanka, Tanzania, and Uganda, WPCorp distributors reach 92 countries.

Currently there are 17 international WordPerfect offices. These offices provide local support and marketing for WPCorp products in their respective territories. As of May, 1991, WPCorp's international offices had 672 employees, an increase of 160 employees since September 1990.

In addition, WPCorp has 26 authorized WordPerfect distributors. These are independent companies which provide WordPerfect support and marketing for their respective regions. Plans are underway to add up to four more distributors by the end of this year.

Capturing the World's Market Place

The number of international product orders is also growing. Sales figures show that WordPerfect is expanding its market share overseas. International sales doubled last year, and have already increased by another 50 percent this year. As a result, international sales amount to more than 20 percent of total WPCorp revenues.

In the United States, DOS WordPerfect claims 60 percent of the PC word processing market. In Europe, WordPerfect has a strong market presence, owning 45 percent of the word processing market. Additionally, WordPerfect had captured 41 percent of word processing sales in South America as of the first quarter of 1991. In the Asia-Pacific region, WPCorp products are also gaining ground.

WordPerfect in Many Languages

WPCorp has released 12 international versions of WordPerfect 5.1: Danish, Dutch, English-UK, Finnish, French, German, Greek, Italian, Norwegian, Portuguese, Spanish, and Swedish.

International versions contain translated software with language-specific spellers, thesauri, hyphenation dictionaries, and in most cases, translated documentation. Development is underway for versions in Afrikaans, Croation, Czechoslovakian, Hungarian, Japanese, Korean, and Russian.

WPCorp also provides 22 Language Modules. In most cases, Language Modules include a combination of speller, thesaurus, and hyphenation dictionary. WPCorp also has Arabic and Hebrew language modules under development which will provide screen font and right-to-left editing capabilities.

International versions of DrawPerfect, PlanPerfect, and WordPerfect Office are available. WPCorp also offers international versions of WordPerfect for the Macintosh, Amiga, Atari, VAX, UNIX, and Data General computers.

Documentation for international products is written at our headquarters in Orem, Utah. More than 120 people in the International Publications Department—each of whom speaks at least one of 22 different languages—work with affiliates all over the world to write, translate, and edit WPCorp's international documentation, pamphlets, and brochures.

International Conferences

In order to keep international affiliates current, WordPerfect Corporation hosts an annual international conference in Orem, Utah. For one week, affiliates attend classes to gain a better understanding of product features and direction; hear lectures from marketing managers on how to help customers fill their needs; and learn from developers what lies ahead in the computer software industry. Participants also have the opportunity to enjoy social activities with their associates from all over the world.

For more information, please call our International Department (see back cover).

"Our goal is to expand our international product line and support capability so customers around the world can benefit from the same level of support and service that customers receive inside the United States and Canada."

—*Bruce Bastian, President of WPCorp's International Division and Chairman of the Board*

WordPerfect 5.1 Makes Its VMS™ Debut

WordPerfect 5.1 for VMS began shipping May 31, 1991. This latest version contains many new features that make WordPerfect even more powerful and easy to use: pull-down menus, context-sensitive Help, Equation Editor, Tables, Spreadsheet Links, and more.

A Closer Look at Equation Editor

The Equation Editor offers the VMS scientific and technical community several important capabilities. These users can now draw from a comprehensive collection of symbols, scientific and Greek characters, and mathematical functions to create and print scientific and technical formulas and equations. WordPerfect will print every character available in the equation palette, as well as any of the 1,500 characters in the WordPerfect character sets. If the symbol isn't built into your printer or included in your soft fonts or font cartridges, WordPerfect 5.1 will automatically print the character as a bit-mapped graphics image. In this way, if your printer supports graphics, you can print every equation you create with the Equation Editor.

Tables

The new Tables feature in WordPerfect 5.1 will prove helpful to users who organize data and work with numbers. Math formulas can be placed in cells so that a table functions as a simple spreadsheet, and Spreadsheet Links can be incorporated with Tables to directly import spreadsheet data from Lotus 1-2-3, 20/20, Microsoft Excel™,

Quattro™, and PlanPerfect. Tables have flexible formatting tools that enable you to create each table precisely the way you need it. Changing the table after it is created is as easy as blocking cells and choosing new format options.

Many aspects of the program have been optimized to be more efficient in the VMS environment, including the installation program, document locking and availability notices, and the number of documents that can be open at the same time (nine).

Documents created using WordPerfect 5.1 for VMS are compatible with WordPerfect 5.1 for DOS. Since more than 50 percent of the terminals connected to VAXes are PCs, the ability to send files from VMS to PC LANS and back with document fidelity intact will be important to many users.

WordPerfect 5.1 for VMS systems requires VMS version 4.7 or later. To install WordPerfect 5.1, a minimum of 35,000 blocks of available disk space, 5,690 global pages, and 46 global sections are recommended. You can significantly reduce the required disk space by installing only the printer drivers you need (over 60 percent of the above mentioned 35,000 blocks are filled with more than 800 different printer drivers!).

WordPerfect 5.1 is priced at $495.US/ $645.CN for a single-user license. Multi-user licenses start at $1,995.US/ $2,595.CN for a 5-user license. Also available are 20-, 50-, and 100-packs. Users can move packs to different machines as long as the original pack (20-pack, 50-pack, etc.) stays intact.

WordPerfect Integration for ALL-IN-1™

Version 2.0.1 of the WordPerfect Integration for ALL-IN-1 is shipping. The new Integration adds support for WordPerfect 5.1, as well as enhancements to installation and setup,

printing, and file access. Licensing for the product will be on a per-user basis. For more information, please call our DEC Products Division (see back cover).

Avoid Jumps and Runarounds

To keep the text layout simple for both reader and designer, *WordPerfect Report* doesn't jump articles or use runarounds. Two columns of text in a three-column grid leave ample room for supporting illustrations and quotes. The bold footer keeps the corporate name in front of readers at all times.

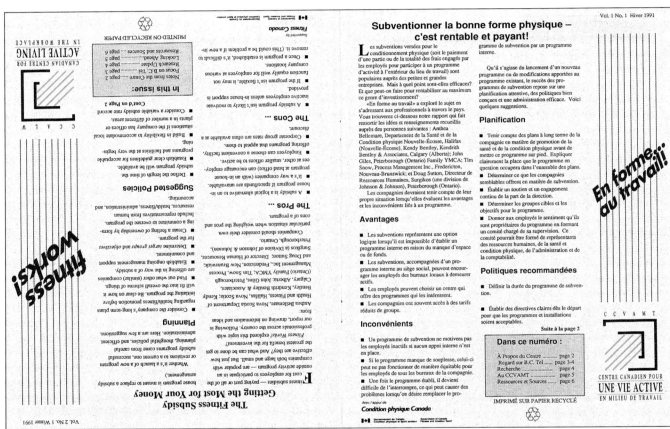

Back-to-Back Bilingual Format

The unusual vertical nameplate works for this bilingual publication because it accents the upbeat slanted title. It also reserves space for six pages of copy in English and six pages in French. Using a back-to-back format begs the question of which language dominates or gets the front page.

Name *Fitness Works*

Publisher *Canadian Centre for Active Living in the Workplace, Gloucester, ON*

Purpose/audience *Service to members*

Production *PageMaker on Macintosh*

Printing *Yellow and green preprinted and black on light gray offset paper*

Format *8½-by-11 inches, twelve pages (six in English, six in French)*

Design *Suzanne Charest*

Weight Loss & Exercise

We're sure that many of you have made New Year's resolutions, including the annual rite of promising to lose weight.

So, to help you accomplish your goals, let's take a short quiz courtesy of Weight Watchers International to test your knowledge of weight loss and exercise.

1. The best type of physical activity for losing weight is: (a) housework; (b) weightlifting; or (c) aerobic exercise.

2. Which of the following is not true about aerobic exercise? (a) it uses large muscle groups, such as leg muscles and large portions of the upper body; (b) it requires a great deal of oxygen; (c) for weight loss, it is best performed at a rapid pace for no more than 20 minutes.

3. Rank the following activities from the highest burner of calories to the lowest: (a) swimming; (b) cooking; (c) light office work; or (d) aerobic dancing.

4. True or false? Exercising before a meal uses more calories than exercising after a meal.

Now the answers!

1 — (c) Aerobic exercise, with its stimulation of the cardiovascular system and use of large muscle groups, is the most conducive to weight loss.

2 — (c) Aerobic exercise is best performed at a low-to-moderate pace for at least 20 minutes.

3 — Swimming: 264 calories
Aerobic dancing: 214 calories
Light office work: 129 calories
Cooking: 94 calories.

All measures based on 30 minutes by a 154-pound person.

4 — Neither. Researchers do not know whether exercising before or after a meal will help you burn more calories. But any exercise burns calories, no matter when it is done.

Dieta y Ejercicio

Estamos seguros que muchos de ustedes han tomado resoluciones de Año Nuevo, incluyendo promesas de perder peso.

Para ayudarles, trate de contestar las siguientes preguntas, cortesía de Weight Watchers Internacional.

1. El mejor tipo de actividad física para perder peso es; (a) tareas domésticas; (b) levantar pesas; o (c) gimnasia aeróbica.

2. De las siguientes preguntas sobre gimnasia aeróbica, diga cual es falsa: (a) usa un grupo grande de músculos, como los de las piernas y el torso; (b) requiere mucho oxígeno; (c) para perder peso, es mejor ejercitar en forma rápida por unos 20 minutos.

3. Liste de mayor a menor cual de estas actividades quema mas calorías: (a) natación; (b) cocinar; (c) trabajo de oficina liviano; o (d) gimnasia aeróbica.

4. ¿Verdadero o falso? El hacer ejercicio antes de las comidas quema más calorías que el ejercicio que se hace después de las mismas.

¡Y ahora las respuestas!

1 — (c) Gimnasia aeróbica; con la estimulación cardio-vascular y el uso de grandes grupos de músculos, es la mejor forma de perder peso.

2 — (c) Gimnasia aeróbica; ejercitada en forma rápida por unos 20 minutos.

3 — Natación: quema 264 calorías
Gimnasia aeróbica: 214 calorías
Trabajo de oficina liviano: 129 calorías
Cocinar: 94 calorías

Basado en 30 minutos y en una persona que pesa 154 libras.

4 — Ninguno. Investigadores no saben con certeza si el hacer ejercicio antes de comer ayuda a quemar más calorías. Lo que sí se sabe, es que el hacer ejercicio ayuda a quemar calorías.

The new CAC Medical Center in North Miami Beach is located at 1701 N.E. 164th Street.
El nuevo Centro Médico CAC de North Miami Beach está situado en el 1701 N.E. 164 Calle.

Have You Had Your Annual Mammogram?

According to the American Cancer Society, the following are the recommended guidelines for screening of breast cancer:

✓ All women over 50 years of age should have a mammogram once a year.

✓ Women 40 years of age and older with prior breast cancer or those with a first-degree relative with a history of breast cancer.

✓ Women 35 years of age with a prior history of breast cancer.

We urge you to contact your CAC Medical Center to schedule a mammogram as part of your preventative health care program.

—Lourdes Agundez, RN
Director of Quality Assurance

¿Se Hizo Usted Su Mamografía Anual?

La Sociedad Americana del Cáncer le ofrece las siguientes pautas a seguir para detectar el cáncer del seno:

✓ Todas las mujeres mayores de 50 años deben hacerse un mamograma todos los años; así como:

✓ Todas las mujeres de 40 años o mayores con historia de cáncer del seno en cualquiera de sus familiares de primer grado.

✓ Mujeres de 35 años o mayores con historia de cáncer del seno.

Póngase en contacto con su centro médico CAC más cercano para hacer una cita para una mamografía como parte del cuidado preventivo de salud.

—Lourdes Agundez, RN
Directora de Seguridad de Calidad

WELCOME NEW DOCTORS
We welcome the following doctors who have joined CAC-Ramsay:

BIENVENIDOS NUEVOS DOCTORES
Los siguientes doctores se han unido a la familia de CAC-Ramsay:

Ray Acevedo, M.D.	María González, M.D.
Rafael Alfonso, M.D.	Rodolfo Gutiérrez, M.D.
Janellie Azaret, M.D.	Luis Hernández, M.D.
María Betancourt, M.D.	Juana Julien, M.D.
James Blair, M.D.	Eduardo Lavado, M.D.
Jorge Caridad, M.D.	Julio Menache, M.D.
José Carreras, M.D.	José Menéndez, M.D.
Mayra Cordero, M.D.	Jack Michel, M.D.
Mario Cuervo, M.D.	Jesús Navarro, M.D.
Jesús Escar, M.D.	José Nieto, M.D.
Yolanda Galarraga, M.D.	Manuel Rodríguez, M.D.
Manuel García, M.D.	Florencio Roig, M.D.

Generic vs. Brand-Name Drugs

(The following questions and answers were designed for our members who receive pharmacy benefits.)

Question: Are companies which produce generic drugs under the same regulations as those which make brand-name prescription drugs?

Answer: Yes. The company manufacturing the brand-name drug has proven to the Food and Drug Administration, which monitors all drugs sold in this country, that the drug is safe. The company distributing the generic drug only has to show the FDA that it has correctly followed the formulation using the same amount of the identical active ingredient.

Question: Are brand-name drugs of better quality than their generic counterparts?

Answer: No. While 80% of the generic drugs sold today are made by the same companies which make brand-name drugs, all companies manufacturing drugs are subject to FDA inspections to ensure that they meet federal guidelines for equipment, workplace environment, drug quality, purity and strength.

Question: Can a patient demand the brand-name drug?

Answer: Yes. A patient always has the right to request a brand-name drug. However, that patient will be responsible for paying the difference in the cost of the two drugs, in addition to any applicable copayment.

Question: Will CAC-Ramsay be adding pharmacy facilities to their centers?

Answer: Yes, in our continuing effort to better serve our members, we are planning to open pharmacies in 4–5 of our centers during the next few months.

Medicinas Genéricas vs. Medicinas de Marca

(Hemos recibido cartas de asociados que tienen beneficios de farmacia con preguntas acerca de medicinas genéricas.)

Pregunta: ¿Tienen las compañías que fabrican medicinas genéricas las mismas regulaciones que las compañías que fabrican medicinas de marca?

Respuesta: Si, porque las compañías de medicinas de marca han probado que las mismas son eficaces y seguras. Una compañía de medicinas genéricas debe ser aprobada por el Food and Drug Administration, (FDA), organización que se encarga de controlar todas las medicinas que se venden en el país. Las medicinas genéricas deben usar la misma fórmula y los mismos ingredientes que las de marca.

Pregunta: ¿Son las medicinas de marca mejores que las genéricas?

Respuesta: Absolutamente no. El FDA inspecciona regularmente las diferentes laboratorios, tanto los de medicinas genéricas como los de marca, para asegurarse que todo esté en perfecto estado de limpieza y calidad.

Pregunta: ¿Puede un paciente especificar que desea solamente la medicina de marca?

Respuesta: Por supuesto. Sin embargo, el paciente deberá pagar la diferencia de precio entre la medicina genérica y la de marca, más el copago cuando sea aplicable.

Pregunta: ¿Tiene CAC-Ramsay planes de abrir farmacias en diferentes centros?

Respuesta: Si, en nuestro continuo esfuerzo por brindar un mejor servicio a nuestros asociados, planeamos abrir farmacias en 4 o 5 centros en los próximos meses.

Just a Reminder...

Always contact your CAC-Ramsay Primary Care Physician or nearest CAC Medical Center for all of your medical service needs.

All Specialist services and hospital admissions must be authorized in advance by CAC-Ramsay.

Carry your CAC-Ramsay membership ID card with you at all times, and present your membership ID whenever you receive medical care.

If you have questions or aren't sure about certain benefits, be sure to call the CAC-Ramsay Member Service Dept., 441-0146 (in Dade) or 1/800-432-1141 (in Broward).

Para Recordarles...

Póngase siempre en contacto con su médico de CAC-Ramsay o con el Centro Médico más cercano cuando necesite servicios.

Todos los servicios especiales y las admisiones en el hospital deben ser autorizados con CAC-Ramsay.

Siempre lleve consigo su tarjeta de socio de CAC-Ramsay y preséntela cuando reciba servicios médicos.

Si tiene preguntas o dudas acerca de ciertos beneficios, por favor llame al Departamento de Servicios de CAC-Ramsay, 441-0146 (en Dade) o 1/800-432-1141 (en Broward).

NEW AFFILIATED PROVIDERS
We welcome these new affiliated providers:

NUEVOS PROVEEDORES AFILIADOS
Bienvenida a los siguientes proveedores afiliados:

Medical Cents of Broward
Alan J. Saltzman, D.O.
7762 N.W. 44 St., Sunrise
Rafiv R. Choksi, M.D.
7741 N. Federal Hwy, #21,
Bldg. A, Fort Lauderdale
Broward Medical Center
Dr. Robert Hunt, D.O.
2601 Davie Blvd., Davie
Marie Adam, M.D.
1011 N.W. 54 St., Miami
Ira Jacobson, M.D.
1190 N.W. 95 St., #401, Miami
John T. McAdory, M.D.
11350 Dunbar Drive,
Richmond Heights
Maritza Diaz, M.D.
900 S.W. 27 Avenue, Miami
North Miami Beach Center
1701 N.E. 164 Street,
North Miami Beach
CAC Kendall Lakes Medical Center
13500 No. Kendall Dr., Miami
Broward Medical Center of Hollywood Hills
Francisco All ttes, M.D.
6100 Hollywood Blvd.,
Suite 106, Hollywood
Pan American Hospital Network –
Primary Care Physicians
Ramón Báez, M.D.
630 N.W. 33rd Ave., Miami
Andrés Cao, M.D.
8782 S.W. 8th St., #21, Miami
Armando Cruz, M.D.
825 S.W. 87th Ave., Miami
René De Laran, M.D.
5799 N.W. 7th St., Miami
976 East 25th Street, Hialeah
Armando Fleites, M.D.
729 S.W. 8th Street, Miami
Carlos O. Ocho, M.D.
1871 Coral Way, #202, Miami
Gustavo Ortega, M.D.
747 Ponce de Leon Blvd., #411,
Coral Gables
Antonio Sar ía, M.D.
7000 SW 97 Ave., #106, Miami
390 West 49th Street, Hialeah
Emilio Trujillo, M.D.
330 S.W. 27th Avenue, Miami
Charles Villacis, M.D.
2075 SW 27th Ave, #100, Miami
Pan Am Health Center,
701 S.W. 57th Avenue, Miami

Side-by-Side Bilingual Format

While difficult to translate and lay out, this side-by-side bilingual format proves more cost-effective than a back-to-back format. The text repeats in each language, but the photos and other visuals are used only once. Text and sidebar directories need two headlines, but only one body of information. This format also gives readers easy access to translation.

Name *Pulse*

Publisher *CAC Ramsay, Coral Gables, FL*

Purpose/audience *Service to employees*

Production *QuarkXPress on Macintosh SE/30*

Printing *Black, red and green on white gloss-coated paper*

Format *8½-by-11 inches, four pages*

Design *Neil D. Littauer*

Aldus Reseller News

June 3, 1991

• • • • • • • •
Silicon Beach Software Products Adopt 'the Aldus Look'

Aldus Corporation and Silicon Beach Software Inc., a subsidiary of Aldus Corporation, are pleased to announce that the Silicon Beach Software product line will begin to assume full Aldus identity.

"This action reinforces the merging of the Aldus and Silicon Beach Software product lines into the most comprehensive product offering from a single software organization," explains Silicon Beach Software Marketing Communications Manager Joanne Rush. "In addition, it communicates our shared commitment of quality to our customers and resellers around the world."

Under this identity standardization, all Silicon Beach Software products will eventually adopt the current Aldus product packaging design, and the Silicon Beach Software shell logo will be replaced with the Aldus logo. Most significantly, their product names will be preceded by "Aldus," and followed by the words by "Silicon Beach Software."

Personal Press 1.0, Digital Darkroom 2.0, and Super 3D 2.5 will be the first to reflect the Aldus identity. The remaining product line will follow. Contact Aldus Sales at (206) 628-2375 for more information.

Aldus Persuasion 2.0

Aldus ships desktop presentations software for Microsoft Windows

The long-awaited desktop presentations software, Aldus Persuasion 2.0 for Windows, is now available for business presenters who wish to make the most of their presentation visuals.

Persuasion has everything your customers need to create overhead transparencies, 35mm slides, speaker notes, and audience handouts quickly and easily. They get a versatile outline processor—just right for typing and organizing their ideas and their information. Persuasion also has charting tools, and a full set of drawing tools for enhancing presentation visuals. Other powerful features include:

► Automatic slide layout
► Import capabilities from word processors, spreadsheets, and graphics programs
► Presentation management tools: visual slide sorter, automatic slide builds, on-screen slide show, speaker notes, audience handouts
► Ability to create color or black-and-white overhead transparencies and paper copies, as well as 35mm slides from Windows 3.0-compatible desktop film recorders and slide-service bureaus

System requirements: 286- or 386-based Windows 3.0-compatible computer (386-based recommended); 2MB of RAM; hard disk; Windows 3.0; EGA or higher video display (VGA or Super VGA recommended); Windows 3.0-compatible mouse.

For more information about Persuasion, see the enclosed literature or call Aldus Sales at (206) 628-2375. To order retail product, call your Aldus distributor at the number below. Suggested retail is $495.

Warning, Customers Ahead!

Aldus is creating customer demand by placing Persuasion 2.0 advertisements in popular computer and business publications: *PC Magazine, BusinessWeek, PC Computing, PC World, The Wall Street Journal, InfoWorld, PC Week.*

Watch for excited customers running to you to buy the hottest desktop presentations software available.

Clinch the sale with the Aldus Persuasion 2.0 video—free to any Aldus reseller by calling Aldus Sales at (206) 628-2375. The Persuasion video explores real-life uses of Aldus Persuasion for both Windows and the Macintosh. Available in VHS only.

Try It, You'll Like It

Aldus Personal Press, the easy-to-use entry-level page layout program, now comes in a trial size!

The Personal Press Trial Size Pack includes a tutorial that guides users through the creation of a one-page newsletter. Users can also explore the program's ample desktop publishing capabilities. To receive free copies of the Trial Size Pack, you and your customers may call Silicon Beach Software at 1-800-888-6293, Extension 8.

Aldus Distributors

Ingram Micro
(800) 456-8000

Merisel
(800) 637-4735

Macamerica
(800) 535-0900

Information at a Glance

Whether reading in English, French or one of the other languages used for *Aldus Reseller News*, readers find very short articles they can grasp at a glance. Small illustrations and lots of color add visual interest. The text type is justified, making body copy seem technical and contrasting to the informal variety of type used for headlines. The French version is printed on A4 paper, the standard European letterhead size. Its four-hole punch fits ring binders used in Europe. See page 39 for another A4 newsletter.

Name *Aldus Reseller News*

Publisher *Aldus Corporation, Seattle, WA*

Purpose/audience *Service and marketing to vendors*

Production *PageMaker and FreeHand on Macintosh IIci*

Printing *Black, light blue, red and gold on white offset paper*

Format *8½-by-11 inches, six pages (six-panel foldout)*

Design *Aliza Corrano, Tom Field and Paul Piacitelli*

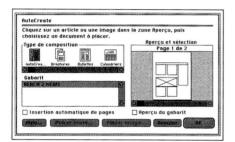

Aldus Actualités
La Lettre Marketing & Ventes d'Aldus

EDITO

Aldus Personal Press : jamais la PAO n'a été aussi accessible …

Huit mois se sont écoulés depuis l'annonce par Apple des nouvelles plateformes "entrée de gamme" avec la série des Classic, LC … Un succès grandissant accompagné de ventes significatives, dont la majorité sont destinées aux nouveaux utilisateurs désireux de réussir leur première informatisation. C'est aussi l'opportunité pour nous d' étoffer notre gamme de logiciels de mise en page en introduisant Aldus Personal Press. Imaginez un instant : un produit facile à apprendre, facile à utiliser dont le prix et les exigences matérielles le rendent performant quel que soit le type de machine ou de périphérique utilisé. Une mise en page toujours réussie grâce au nouveau concept de Maquettes Assistées par Ordinateur. Un produit créatif , amusant, doté de mille et une astuces pour personnaliser et soigner votre publication.
Un produit ouvert …
Vous l'avez compris, Aldus Personal Press et les machines d'entrée de gamme d'Apple représentent la vente facile d'un tandem stratégique, pour guider les premiers pas de vos clients d'aujourd'hui et de demain.
Nous vous invitons sans plus tarder à découvrir à la lecture de cette lettre tous les aspects de ce nouveau produit.

Annie Gesbert - Chef de Produit

Trois raisons qui vous feront craquer !

▶ Le meilleur allié des configurations d'entrée de gamme
▶ Un produit ouvert
▶ Un produit Aldus

Aldus Personal Press fonctionne sur un Macintosh Classic, LC, SE, …
Il est tout particulièrement destiné aux configurations d'entrée de gamme équipées de seulement 2Mo de mémoire vive et de petits écrans

(palettes escamotables).
Selon une étude récente, la part de marché des traitements de textes représente plus de 35% des ventes des logiciels.

Suite en page 2

Son positionnement par rapport à PageMaker

Aldus Personal Press n'est pas un PageMaker "junior" ni un "sous produit" de PageMaker.
Aldus Personal Press est véritablement le produit d'entrée de gamme obligatoire de la PAO personnelle. Son concept lui confère une puissance d'ensemble bien équilibrée, sans toutefois offrir toute la puissance de PageMaker.

Suite en page 2

Trois raisons qui feront craquer vos clients …

▶ La PAO Aldus pour tous
▶ Un produit facile et amusant à utiliser
▶ Des sorties impressionnantes

Aldus Personal Press est le complément indispensable des plateformes "entrée de gamme" d'Apple.

Destiné tout particulièrement aux utilisateurs novices en micro-édition, son prix et ses exigences en matériel rendent la PAO accessible à tous.

Suite en page 3

Aldus vous aide …

Aldus met à votre disposition de nombreux outils d'aide à la vente autour desquels vous pouvez articuler votre stratégie commerciale :

▶ Les outils d'aide à la vente
Brochure commerciale : vous pouvez la commander auprès de notre service commercial, elle est destinée à fournir une information complète au client sur le produit.

Une autodémonstration du produit pour animer votre vitrine ou tout simplement pour présenter rapidement et facilement le produit (bientôt disponible).

Un scénario de démonstration contenant des fichiers d'exemples.

Suite en page 4

Edition Personal Press - Hors série

Septembre 1991

Creating a Classy Image

To enhance a positive attitude toward financial success, rules and dingbats are printed in gold metallic ink on a creamy coated paper that feels like cashmere. Readers like the gold touches, the format of lead stories and the "nutshell" boxes. Elegant headline type, set downstyle to be most readable, complements the classy image by matching type used for the text. Summary decks are set even bolder than in *The Service Edge* on page 10.

Name *Think & Grow Rich Newsletter*

Publisher *Imagine, Inc., Clemson, SC*

Purpose/audience *Service to subscribers*

Production *PageMaker on Macintosh IIx*

Printing *Black and bronze metallic on cream dull-coated paper*

Format *8½-by-11 inches, eight pages*

Design *Jane Dorn and David Bill*

PMA principles work—even on a cop's beat

Police Chief Reuben Greenberg brings PMA to his job.

beat her and took their baby to his parents. The parents refused to give the baby up.

Social service agencies were of no help; the father had as much right to custody as the mother. Greenberg knew that since this was a civil matter his department had no jurisdiction. But looking at the tear-stained face, he knew he had to do something — NOW.

Discovering that the man was driving with a suspended license, Greenberg had two detectives go to his favorite hangout. As soon as he drove off in his

If there's one thing Reuben Greenberg can't stand, it's to hear a police officer say, "There was nothing I could do."

Wrong! says the colorful, controversial and highly successful chief of police of Charleston, S.C. There's always something you can do. The Napoleon Hill success rules of "Do it now!" and "Always go the extra mile" are evident in the way Greenberg does his job.

A case in point:

Shortly after coming to Charleston in 1982 Greenberg was flagged down by a desperate young woman. She told him she had decided to leave her abusive boyfriend and take their two children to her relatives in New York. But when she told the man she was leaving, he

We want your story

We want your story!

Many of our readers have written to tell us how the success principles articulated by Napoleon Hill have contributed to their achievement, both personal and professional.

Have the work and words of Napoleon Hill had a significant influence on your life?

If so, we'd like to hear about you so that we can share your story in these pages with other achievement-minded people.

Please address your letter to:
Think & Grow Rich Newsletter

The 3 D's of work

How you perceive your work affects how well you do it and how the work affects you.

One day psychologist and author Paul Pearsall was sitting at his word processor at home when his concentration was broken by a loud buzzing noise outside.

He stepped outside and saw that the septic tank for his home was receiving its biannual cleaning. Three workmen were standing by a large truck and watching as hoses vacuumed the system.

In *Super Joy: In Love with Living*, Pearsall relates how he joined them, and one man said, "Well, Doc, how would you like to be doing this all day? . . . Some job, eh."

Before he could answer, a second man smiled, "That's the doc's job. He's an author."

Everyone laughed, and the worker continued, "This isn't so bad. I'm getting decent money, so I can send my daughters to college. Everyday working is a day for them in college."

The third man adjusted a valve on the truck and said, "We have to keep a better eye on the pressure. We don't want any fumes escaping. You know, this work saves the environment. None of these homes could be here if we didn't have this equipment and do this job. It's a small thing, but at least I'm doing more than talk about a clean world. The good doctor here couldn't live way out here in the country and write his books if somebody didn't do this."

The three men had exactly the same job, but very different views of their work. Which is most like yours?

Are you working because you have to, because you're helping yourself and your family grow, or because you have a vision or belief that what you do matters in the overall scheme of things?

Pearsall says all three perspectives are important. He calls them the three D's of work.

First, there is "Demand." We must execute tasks that keep the world moving and functioning. We must balance our consumerism with our own contributions.

Second, we must "Develop," see ourselves and our families enhanced by our efforts.

Third, we must have a work "Dream," an image of our overall purpose and contribution to the world that transcends simple execution and the daily barter of survival.

Few people give sufficient thought to the last "D"—a meaningful vision of the purpose of their work.

Those who do tend to perform it best and enjoy it most.

IN A NUTSHELL . . .
■ *Energize yourself by keeping in mind the three D's of work.*

Drag and lift

From an experience in Marine Corps preflight school comes a principle that explains why selling is like flying an airplane.

Before beginning his career in show business, the Tonight Show's Ed McMahon was a fighter pilot for the U.S. Marine Corps and then a salesman.

A principle from preflight school helped his sales work enormously: "No plane can fly if drag exceeds lift."

McMahon found when the drag of his doubts exceeded the lift of his preparation and confidence, he didn't get off the ground.

Drag comes from jumping to negative conclusions. Say Jack's first sales appointment on Monday is at 11:00 a.m. He wants to use his time well, so he precedes it with a few cold calls.

At the first place everyone is at a meeting. At the second, the receptionist holds him up. At the third,

he finally sees a prospect, but the man snarls and tells him to get lost.

Jack feels unhappy about how things are going, and concludes that making calls on Monday is a bad idea. He decides, "That's that—no more Monday prospecting calls for him!"

Jack had one bad Monday, and he came away with a theory about selling that hurt his chances of success. His conclusion about not making cold calls on Monday will reduce his income by 5%.

Over the course of his career, the three rejections he got that one gray Monday will cost him thousands of dollars.

Of course, we must learn from experience. It's dumb to touch a hot stove more than once. But what we learn should be tempered by our goals.

If the "lesson" would set you back from achieving your goals, remain open to new facts and to revising your theory. For example, if Jack's goal was to make as much money as he could, he might have said to himself:

"Boy, I love Monday cold calling. People cranky about being back at work make me earn my keep. The whole thing is a kind of refresher course in the fundamentals of selling. Rejection? Sure, there's rejection, but so what. I'm a heavy hitter, and I expect heavy rejection. I never let it bother me. I enjoy the challenge!"

Notice the lift in Jack's message, no drag. That's the kind of positive theory that should automatically pop up when cold calls must be made on Monday.

(Thanks to Ed McMahon, author of Ed McMahon's Superselling Performance Techniques for High Volume Sales, Prentice Hall.)

IN A NUTSHELL . . .
■ *To add more "lift" to your attitudes, examine any negative theories you have and create positive new theories to replace them.*

Using Type in Calendars

Because Christie's buyers are interested in specific kinds of art, the calendar is organized first by genre, then by topic and only then by date. The eye of the reader can go immediately to events of interest. See more calendars on the next two pages.

Name *Auction News*

Publisher *Christie, Manson, and Woods International, Inc., New York, NY*

Purpose/audience *Service and marketing to customers*

Production *QuarkXPress on Macintosh IIcx*

Printing *Four-color process plus fifth color on white gloss-coated paper*

Format *9-by-12 inches, twelve pages*

Design *Stillman Designs—Linda Stillman and Connie Circosta*

Calendar of Future Sales

Park: 502 Park Avenue, 212/546-1000   **East:** 219 East 67th Street, 212/606-0400

AMERICAN DECORATIVE ARTS

Fine American Furniture, Silver, Folk Art & Decorative Arts	June 25, 2 p.m.	Viewing from June 20-24 at Park

BOOKS

The Stuart B. Schimmel Collection of the Book Arts	May 17, 10 a.m.	Viewing from May 10-16 at Park
Printed Books & Manuscripts including Americana	May 17, 2 p.m. & May 18, 10 a.m.	Viewing from May 10-16 at Park

CARS

Important Motor Cars & Automobilia	May 20, 2 p.m.	at the Vintage Car Store, Nyack, NY

CHINESE ART

Fine Chinese Paintings & Calligraphy	May 29, 10 a.m.	Viewing from May 25-28 at Park
Fine Chinese Ceramics & Works of Art	May 30, 10 a.m. & 2 p.m.	Viewing from May 25-29 at Park

COINS

Ancient, Foreign & United States Coins & Important World Banknotes from the Archives of The American Banknote Company	June 5, 10 a.m., 2:00 p.m. & 6 p.m.	Viewing from June 1-4 at Park

EUROPEAN FURNITURE

Important French Furniture, Porcelain, Sculpture, Clocks & Tapestries	May 8, 10 a.m.	Viewing from May 4-7 at Park

GENERAL SALES

Nineteenth-Century English & Continental Furniture, Decorations & Porcelain	May 14, 10 a.m.	Viewing from May 10-13 at East
English & Continental Furniture, Decorations, Porcelain, Paintings & Oriental Works of Art	June 11, 10 a.m.	Viewing from June 7-10 at East

JEWELRY

Important Jewels	June 11, 10 a.m. & 2 p.m.	Viewing from June 7-10 at Park
Antique & Fine Jewelry	June 13, 10 a.m. & 2 p.m.	Viewing from June 8-12 at East

PAINTINGS, DRAWINGS & PRINTS

Contemporary Art (Part I)	May 1, 7 p.m.	Viewing from April 26-May 1 at Park
Contemporary Art (Part II)	May 2, 10 a.m.	Viewing from April 26-May 1 at Park
Modern and Contemporary Paintings, Watercolors, Drawings & Sculpture	May 7, 10 a.m.	Viewing from May 3-6 at East
Impressionist & Modern Paintings & Sculpture (Part I)	May 8, 7 p.m.	Viewing from May 3-8 at Park
Impressionist & Modern Paintings & Sculpture (Part II)	May 9, 2 p.m.	Viewing from May 3-8 at Park
Impressionist & Modern Drawings & Watercolors	May 9, 10 a.m.	Viewing from May 3-8 at Park
Old Master, American, Modern & Contemporary Prints	May 14, 10 a.m. & 2 p.m. May 15, 10 a.m. & 2 p.m.	Viewing from May 10-13 at Park
Haitian Paintings from the Collection of Angela Gross & Latin American Paintings, Drawings & Sculpture	May 15, 10 a.m.	Viewing from May 11-14 at East
Latin American Paintings, Drawings & Sculpture	May 15, 7 p.m. May 16, 10 a.m.	Viewing from May 11-15 at Park
Nineteenth-Century European & American Paintings, Watercolors, Drawings & Sculpture	May 21, 10 a.m. & 2 p.m.	Viewing from May 17-20 at East
Important American Paintings, Drawings & Sculpture of the 19th & 20th Centuries including Paintings from the Collection of Mrs. George Arden, Part I	May 22, 10 a.m. & 2 p.m.	Viewing from May 17-21 at Park
Barbizon, Realist & French Landscape Painting	May 23, 10 a.m.	Viewing from May 18-22 at Park
Nineteenth-Century European Paintings, Drawings, Watercolors & Sculpture	May 23, 10 a.m.	Viewing from May 18-22 at Park
Important Paintings by Old Masters	May 31, 10 a.m.	Viewing from May 25-30 at Park
Old Master Paintings	May 31, 2 p.m.	Viewing from May 25-30 at Park

STAMPS

Important United States Stamps & Covers	June 12, 10 a.m. & 2 p.m. June 13, 10 a.m. & 2 p.m.	Viewing from June 7-11 at Park

TWENTIETH-CENTURY DECORATIVE ARTS

Art Nouveau, Art Deco & Arts & Crafts	June 6, 10 a.m. & 2 p.m.	Viewing from June 1-5 at East
Important Twentieth-Century Decorative Arts, including works by the Tiffany Studios, American Arts & Crafts, & Architectural Designs and Commissions	June 8, 10 a.m. & 2 p.m.	Viewing from June 1-7 at Park

WINE

Fine & Rare Wines	June 15, 10:30 a.m.	in Chicago

Viewing: Tuesday–Saturday, 10 a.m.–5 p.m.; Sunday, 1 p.m.–5 p.m.; day preceding a sale, 10 a.m.–2 p.m.; Monday, 10 a.m.–5 p.m.; by appointment. Schedule subject to change–refer to catalogue. Call 212/371-5438 for more information.

Catalogue information: To order a catalogue or to obtain a subscription, please call 718/784-1480 or write to Christie's Publications Department, 21-24 44th Avenue, Long Island City, NY 11101

11

WINE INSTITUTE
WineEvents

April 5–10 Vin Italy, Verona, Italy. Contact 212/775-1050.

April 11 Strategic Agribusiness Marketing, UC Davis Extension, 9 A.M.–4:30 P.M., Holiday Inn, Holidome, Sacramento, 916/757-8639.

April 20 - 21 Santa Barbara County Vintners' Festival, Flag is up Farm, Solvang. Pam Maines Ostendorf, 805/688-0881.

April 21–24 "Hostex '91," Canadian Restaurant and Foodservice Association Trade show, Exhibition Place, Toronto, Canada. Contact: 1-800/387-5649 or 416/923-8416.

April 27–28 Temecula Wine Country: Spring Fest '91, 1–4 P.M., 714/699-6444.

May 3 Hambrecht & Quist Wine Industry Forum, St. Francis Hotel, San Francisco, Contact: Nora McKamey 415/576-3470.

May 3 Eastern Canadian Wine Fair, Toronto. Contact: Steve Burns, 415/512-0151.

May 4 Sierra Showcase of Wine, Amador County Fairgrounds, 209/274-4766.

May 4 Eastern Canadian Wine Fair, Ottawa. Contact: Steve Burns, 415/512-0151.

May 4–5 Farmers Fair of Riverside County Wine Competition, University of California, Riverside, 714/657-4221.

May 6 Eastern Canadian Wine Fair, Quebec City. Contact: Steve Burns, 415/512-0151.

May 7 Eastern Canadian Wine Fair, Montreal. Contact: Steve Burns, 415/512-0151.

May 8 Eastern Canadian Wine Fair, Halifax. Contact: Steve Burns, 415/512-

May 11 Friends of the Carmel Fundraising Auction. Contact: 963-3104.

May 14–16 London Wine Tr Steve Burns 415/512-0151.

May 15–18 4ᵗʰ Asian Internal Hotel & Catering Systems, Su Food & Drink, Hong Kong Co Exhibition Centre, 415/433-30

May 18–19 9ᵗʰ Annual Paso F Festival, City Park, 12–5 P.M.

May 24–26 Wine Japan, Tok Burns, 415/512-0151.

May 31 Intervin, International Awards Presentation, New Yo

June 9 9ᵗʰ annual Polo, Wine Sonoma County Wine Library Rosa Polo Fields in Oakmont, 433-9104.

June 10–14 International Fe & Spirits General Assembly, C Jerry Vorpahl at Wine Institute

June 10 Wine Institute Trade Hamburg, Germany. Steve Bu

June 12 Wine Institute Trade Tasting, Munich, Germany. Contact: Steve Burns, 415/512-0151.

June 14 Wine Institute Trade Tasting, Brussels

Label... *from page 1*

"I am pleased that we have come to a resolution of this critical issue," commented Wine Institute President John De Luca. "While religious terms have been deleted, as the son of Italian immigrants, I certainly can identify with, and embrace, the family reference permitted in the statement."

The revised label reads: "Wine has been with us since the beginning of civilization. It is a temperate, civilized, romantic, mealtime beverage. Wine has been praised for

centuries by statesmen phers, poets and schol: moderation is an integ family's culture, herita gracious way of life."

Mail... *from page 1*

cases per month per ad cluding a joint address also prohibits the deliv to any person under 21 stipulates that the wine used for resale or any (

Page 12

MAY CALENDAR

3-5 Atlanta Storytelling Festival
Bring the family for a weekend of storytelling! Headliners include Celestine Sibley and Betty Talmadge on Friday at 7:30 p.m.; Jay O'Callahan on Saturday at 7:30 p.m.; Janet Kiefer on Saturday and Sunday at 4:00 p.m.; and the Georgia Sea Island Singers on Sunday at 5:00 p.m. Eighteen of the nation's best storytellers are featured on Saturday and Sunday from 10:00 a.m. to 4:00 p.m. in three spacious tents, plus a lying contest on Saturday at 5:00 p.m., a Saturday morning storytelling workshop, and four films running from 10:00 a.m. to 4:00 p.m. both days in McElreath Hall.
Day tickets for AHS and SOS members are $8 adults; $6 seniors 65+ and students 18+; $4 ages 6 to 17; and free for children under 6. Weekend passes are available at $12, $8, $6, and free for children under 6. Evening concerts are $8 per person, regardless of age. Workshop tickets are $20. Day tickets and passes do not include evening concerts or workshop. Tickets may be purchased at the door. The festival is presented by the Society and the Southern Order of Storytellers (see p. 1). *Atlanta History Center, day events, 10:00 a.m.-6:00 p.m.*

8 Members Guild Meeting
The guild meets to install new officers and discuss upcoming projects. If you would like to join, call Reg Bridges at 351-8850 (see p. 4). *Home of Mrs. Betsy Switzer, 1665 West Wesley Road, 10:00 a.m.*

Nina Totenberg, May 9

9 Alston Lecture
Nina Totenberg, National Public Radio's award-winning legal affairs correspondent, whose reports air regularly on "All Things Considered," "Morning Edition," and "Weekend Edition." She will speak on "Covering the Courts: Cases, Convictions, and Confirmations. *Georgia-Pacific Center Auditorium, 133 Peachtree Street, noon. Free.*

Betty Friedan, May 13

13 Livingston Lecture
Betty Friedan, pioneer of the women's liberation movement, founder of the National Organization for Women, and author of *The Feminine Mystique,* speaks on "The Twentieth Century: Was It a Woman's Century?" *Woodruff Auditorium, McElreath Hall, 8:00 p.m. Doors open at 7:00 p.m. Free for members–please bring your membership card. $5 nonmembers.*

15 Double Discount Day
Members receive a 20 percent discount on all Museum Shop purchases, excluding books, from 11:00 a.m. to 4:00 p.m. You must present your current membership card. *McElreath Hall.*

Volunteer Appreciation Luncheon
All Atlanta Historical Society volunteer staff are invited to the annual volunteer appreciation luncheon. Call 261-1837 by May 1 to make your reservation. *Members Room, McElreath Hall, noon-1:30 p.m.**

29 Volunteer and Member Tour to Rome
Volunteers, members, and guests are invited to travel to Rome, Ga., for this one-day tour. Highlights include a guided tour of the Historic Victorian River District and the Chieftan's Museum, a visit to Berry College, and tour of Oak Hill (Martha Berry's home) and its museum. $49 includes motorcoach, lunch, and all entry fees. Reservations are limited. Call Dot Evans, 238-0652, for information or registration. *

"Life in the Great Houses of Ireland"
This symposium features five lecturers on the architecture, paintings, gardens, and decorative arts of Ireland and includes lunch (see p. 1). *McElreath Hall, 10:00 a.m.-3:00 p.m. $45.**

Current Exhibits
Atlanta Resurgens, permanent exhibit
Atlanta and the War, 1861-1865, permanent exhibit, Mr. and Mrs. Clyde Lanier King Gallery
The Atlanta Historical Society: A Family Album, Atrium
The Atlanta Historical Society Plans for the Future, Atrium
Philip T. Shutze Collection of Decorative Arts, Swan House*

Atlanta History Center Downtown at 140 Peachtree Street
Monday-Saturday, 10:00 a.m.-6:00 p.m.
Exhibit, The Real Peachtree: Past and Present

Upcoming Events
Swan House Ball, June 1; Swan Song Sale, June 2; and a recertification course for teachers, "Local History Resources at Your Doorstep," June 17-28.

> *Preregistration or tickets required. For more information on any program or event, call 261-1837.

7

Creating Calendars That Work

Some people read a newsletter mainly for its schedule of events. No other publication has such a specialized listing.

A calendar is one of the most demanding design tasks. It should be easy to assemble and proofread, efficient to read and conservative of space. It should appear in the same place each issue and not have other important items placed so they'll need to be clipped out from its opposing side.

Begin designing a schedule of events for your newsletter by asking what readers want to know. Try to make the calendar's design help answer their questions. Here are some possibilities.

• *Location.* If you're announcing activities at branch libraries or a series of public hearings, readers probably want to know only about locations they find convenient. Put the place first or in bold type, then tell dates and details.

• *Activity.* If you're listing a variety of events, group them into categories that make sense to your readers. Don't make people who care deeply about one kind of event fight their way through the list of everything else to find the information they want.

• *Date.* If you're presenting a variety of dates for the same event such as a stage play, let your design highlight dates instead of the program or performers. You don't need to repeat the name of the event next to the date for each performance.

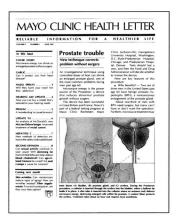

Use a Standard Typeface

Skilled designers often use simple typography. The Optima family of typefaces used here works equally well for text, headlines, captions and nameplate. As elegant as the June issue is, however, notice two slight improvements for December. The December subtitle is letterspaced to eliminate the gaps between words in the June version. And the "In this issue" column for December uses downstyle instead of all capitalized headers.

Name *Mayo Clinic Health Letter*

Publisher *Mayo Foundation, Rochester, MN*

Purpose/audience *Service to subscribers*

Production *PageMaker and Windows on IBM*

Printing *Four-color process on natural offset paper*

Format *8½-by-11 inches, eight pages*

Design *George E. DeVinny and David E. Swanson*

Awards *National Coalition for Consumer Education, Newsletter Clearinghouse*

MAYO CLINIC HEALTH LETTER

RELIABLE   INFORMATION   FOR   A   HEALTHIER   LIFE

VOLUME 9   NUMBER 6   JUNE 1991

In this issue

COVER STORY
Microwave energy can shrink an enlarged prostate without surgery.

GARLIC 2
Can it protect you from heart disease?

NASAL SPRAYS 3
Will they harm your nose? Are they addictive?

HEARING AID UPDATE 4
Now you can buy a model that's tailored to your hearing needs.

PROZAC 5
A 'wonder drug' or cause for worry?

UPDATE '91 6
An analysis of McDonald's new **McLean Deluxe** burger. Improved treatment of **rectal cancer.**

HEPATITIS C 7
New methods of detection enhance the safety of donated blood.

SECOND OPINION 8
Can **sexual activity** continue in later years? Will **skimming fat** from chilled leftovers help reduce **blood cholesterol?** Can **age-related tremors** be cured? Are **anal cramps** a cause for concern?

Coming next month

Skin wrinkles: Can moisturizers reduce signs of aging? How are wrinkles treated? **Fiber supplements:** To avoid constipation, are they your best option?

Prostate trouble

New technique corrects problem without surgery

An investigational technique using controlled doses of heat can shrink an enlarged prostate gland, one of the most common problems facing men past age 60.

Microwave energy is the power source of the Prostatron, a device

Clinic Jacksonville; Georgetown University Hospital, Washington, D.C.; Rush-Presbyterian Hospital, Chicago; and Presbyterian Hospital, Denver. Tests should last a year, and then the Food and Drug Administration will decide whether to license the device.

Here are key features of this procedure:

■ *Who benefits?* — Two out of three men in the United States past age 60 have benign prostatic hy-

MAYO CLINIC HEALTH LETTER

RELIABLE   INFORMATION   FOR   A   HEALTHIER   LIFE

VOLUME 9   NUMBER 12   DECEMBER 1991

In this issue

COVER STORY
Today there are more treatment options for people with Parkinson's disease.

Lifestyle changes 3
If you can't live by yourself, should you move in with your kids?

Chest surgery 4
New video technique reduces hospital time, recovery and cost.

Alcohol and your heart 6
Moderate drinking may help protect you from heart disease. We'll show you how to weigh the benefits and hazards of alcohol.

Update '91 7
Exercise: A little can mean a lot. **Television:** How much you watch may affect what you weigh.

Second opinion 8
Is dried, flaked **coconut** high in saturated fat? Can **stretch marks** disappear? What is **Schamberg's disease?**

Coming in January

How much do you weigh? How much would you like to weigh? How much should you weigh? With holidays past and resolutions still intact, our article on **healthy weight** explains why you shouldn't take weight charts too seriously. **Burning feet** is a common complaint. We'll address causes and offer self-help measures.

Parkinson's disease

A drug called selegiline is enhancing traditional treatment

For more than 20 years, the drug L-Dopa has been the cornerstone of treatment for Parkinson's disease. Today, another medication is broadening treatment options. Called selegiline, it is marketed under the brand name Eldepryl.

Selegiline, used in Europe and Israel for more than a decade, is gaining acceptance in the United States.

Selegiline can enhance the effectiveness of L-Dopa.

If you take selegiline at an early stage of Parkinson's disease, the drug often delays the onset of disabling symptoms.

And selegiline shows promise as a way to perhaps even slow the disease process by preventing the death of brain cells associated with Parkinson's disease.

What is Parkinson's disease?
Parkinson's disease is a central nervous system disorder. It is caused by the accelerated death of a small group of brain cells called the substantia nigra. These cells produce a chemical called dopamine.

Your brain needs dopamine to send correct signals to your muscles. Without enough dopamine, your brain has trouble transferring movement messages to your body.

If you have Parkinson's, your brain

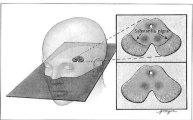

Parkinson's disease is linked to the accelerated death of a small group of brain cells called the substantia nigra. The substantia nigra, meaning "black substance," is situated deep in the brain. Top inset shows normal brain tissue. In Parkinson's disease (lower right), the black substance is missing.

Communiqué

March 1991

Minorities hit glass ceiling

Racism still prevalent in media industry

Minorities still do not have a significant voice in the media, despite efforts over the last 25 years by the media industry to improve racial diversity in the profession as well as in coverage.

At a panel discussion held on Jan. 30, *Newsday* reporter Evelyn Hernandez of the National Association of Hispanic Journalists said that minorities have made advancements into newsrooms, but they have not made inroads into boardrooms. "A lot of mi-

ing especially prevalent in the cable industry. "Seventeen percent of the cable industry is made up of minorities, but most are in entry-level posi-

tion, said *Ms.* Managing Editor Helen Zia of the Asian-Ameri-

Racism still plays a role in recruiting and retention of minorities, said *New York Times* reporter Tom Morgan of the National Association of Black Journalists. "Racism is present in the newsroom when during a recession one of the first areas that is cut in the budget is minority-recruiting efforts," Morgan said. "I think that minority hires are seen as 'extra' hires, as 'luxury' hires."

There is a strong correlation, said *Ms.* Managing Editor Helen Zia of the Asian-Ameri-

Communiqué

Tracing the roots of communication studies

Histories are by nature selective versions of the past. They are fashioned in relation to the goals and interests of those who organize them. They are not, therefore, simply the recounting of "facts," which are themselves subject to interpretation.

Historiography, or a "history for," acknowledges this act of interpretation and employs a method of problem-solving that is evidence based. It critically examines original sources, traces the genealogy of ideas and creates narrative that synthesizes individual events into interpretive wholes.

Senior Fellow Gertrude Robinson is pursuing this objective for North American communications studies, a relatively young field often noted for its interdisciplinary approach. Robinson, whose own interdisciplinary academic training is rooted in philosophy and political science as well as communications, says her primary goal is to "write a history of the field of

selves within universities or institutes.

Within this framework, Robinson places the beginnings of U.S. com-

Gertrude Robinson

munication studies in the 1890s with the "Chicago school," where the notion of communications as a social process by which society is built and maintained was first studied by such noted scholars as George Herbert Mead, John Dewey, Robert Park and

paying special attention to radio.

Lazarsfeld's redefinition of social communication studies from issues involving groups to a focus on media and individual effects, Robinson says, is closely linked to the rise of market and radio research in the '30s.

"Privately owned newspapers and radio stations were searching for advertising sponsors and the competitive advantages of messages transmitted by radio or print. As a consequence research agendas were redrawn and explanatory paradigms changed."

While in New York, Robinson will concentrate her research on the Lazarsfeld archives at Columbia University and the New School of Social Research. Her greatest interests center on Lazarsfeld's collaboration both with Merton and emigré colleagues, and the research activities of the Bureau during World War II.
—*Jeanne Sahadi*

Communiqué

Staff notes

Everette E. Dennis' op-ed piece "No, TV Has Not Killed the Print Media" appeared in the Feb. 7 issue of *Newsday*. He also wrote the article "New News Technology: Death Knell or Challenge?" which was published in *Television Quarterly*, Vol. XXV, No. I, 1991.

John V. Pavlik is a panelist for a session on media technology and ethics at the Columbia Scholastic Press Association/College Media Adviser conference, in New York City, March 22. He will also moderate a panel on "Electronic Journalism: Investigative Reporting Through Computers" for the conference of the National Association of Hispanic Journal-

Consequences of technology raise ethical and legal concerns—*cont'd. from page 1*

that has entered my life since my children," Jennings said.

He recalled his days as a foreign correspondent when information traveled much more slowly. "Reporters are able to move around so quickly," Jennings said, "that there is little time to do any real reporting. There is also a power struggle between producers, who have the capacity to get the news on the air fast, and reporters."

Moreover, he said, broadcasting at all hours leads to more raw, unanalyzed coverage and less actual, original reporting. This, according to Jennings, is one of the worst results of poorly managed technology.

In addition, Jennings spoke of the increasing disparity between knowledge and information dissemination, noting that there are young people

working and living in the midst of it."

Other speakers, including journalism professor and former Fellow Elliot Jaspin and Greystone Communications Director John Carey, also expressed both optimism and concern about technology's repercussions on the media profession.

In presenting the time and cost savings as well as the artistic possibilities of the new digital systems used to edit photographs, Professor Shiela Reaves of the University of Wisconsin discussed the potential violation of trust between reader and journalist given the capability of these technologies to alter photographs.

Anne Branscomb, a research affiliate at Harvard University's Program on Information Resources Policy and former senior fellow, raised questions about intellectual property rights for

Use Familiar Layouts

Following the familiar, comfortable newspaper-style layout, the designer uses floating rules to separate text columns and lead the eye into the main photos. I like the small door that invites readers inside. Printing on light gray paper further adds to the air of comfortable wisdom.

Name *Communique*

Publisher *Gannett Foundation Media Center, New York, NY*

Purpose/audience *Service to members and friends of the center*

Production *PageMaker on Macintosh*

Printing *Dark red nameplate preprinted, plus black on gray offset paper*

Format *8½-by-11 inches, six pages*

Design *Craig LaMay and Jeanne Sahadi*

Award *Newsletter Clearinghouse*

Merchandise Advertising Technology™

V O L . 1 N O . 1

A digest of advancements in wholesale and retail advertising technology from BESTINFO, Inc., the leader in merchandise advertising systems.

INSIDE THIS ISSUE

Desktop publishing *vs.* electronic publishing: What's the difference?

Desktop systems serve single-user environments well, but merchandisers need a system that lets all participants in advertising materials production work together.

MOST people today are more familiar with the term desktop publishing than they are with the term electronic publishing. Still others use the two terms synonymously. While both technologies flow from traditional typesetting, and both now operate from the same platforms (personal computers), they have moved in very different directions: desktop publishing toward small, convenient, single-user systems, and electronic publishing toward extremely powerful, multi-user systems that support professional publishing organizations.

The distinction is important. Many organizations assume that the efficiency of desktop publishing at producing short documents for single users carries over into volume production in a multi-user environment. Unfortunately, the inherent assumption behind

Cont'd on p. 8

Mapping the new world of market-driven advertising

By Jim Bessen
President
Bestinfo, Inc.

IN 1991, copywriting, design, copy editing, typography, page composition, image scanning, stripping, and film output are no longer discrete activities but part of a continuum, an ongoing electronic process.

It's hard to believe, but the integration of these steps in the publishing cycle occurred only within the past five years. And we at Bestinfo were pleased to play a leading role in creating the new world of multi-user, workgroup publishing technology.

Many catalog producers and publishers now use Bestinfo systems to produce better quality publications at far less cost. These systems go beyond desktop publishing's merging of text and graphics to include integration of project management, marketing and electronic pre-press activities.

Linking electronic publishing and merchandising technologies

Linking these technologies offers merchandisers greater benefits than the sum of their parts. Linking text/image/design databases to price/inventory/demographic information not only allows for faster, more substantial last-minute changes to pages, but creates substantial competitive advantages as well.

In recent years, merchandisers have made greater and more productive use of integrated extensions of MIS systems—incorporating point-of-sale scanning, and Electronic Data Interchange (EDI) with suppliers. By maintaining constant information on inventory levels and communicating that information electronically with supplier distribution centers, quick-moving items can be constantly restocked—making products available for sale much faster, and at much more competitive pricing.

However, while Quick Response (QR) or Just-In-Time systems have given them the ability to quickly react to changed market conditions, merchandisers have often lacked a similar ability to respond anywhere nearly as quickly with supporting advertising, signage, and promotion.

Typically, ad production times range from 48 hours for grocery ads, to six weeks for retail ads and inserts. Catalogs take months. And it can take two to four weeks to produce in-store signs.

In every case, merchandisers are in the awkward

Cont'd on p. 2

1

Efficient Use of Type Space

The two columns on this front page use space efficiently by confining the nameplate to the top of only one column. Note that the subtitle not only describes the newsletter, but adds a sales phrase at the end. Nice touch. The whole effect of the left column leads the eye from nameplate through the list of contents directly into the first article. Compare the summary deck at left to those on pages 10 and 24.

Name *Merchandising Advertising Technology*
Publisher *Bestinfo, Inc., Media, PA*
Purpose/audience *Service to customers*
Production *Bestinfo software on IBM*
Printing *Black and dark blue on light gray felt text paper*
Format *8¹/₂-by-11 inches, eight pages*
Design *Steve Smith and Jim Morris-Lee*

Marketing Briefs

Signs of tight times for the airlines: With the escalation of fuel prices and sluggish traffic growth in certain sectors come news of the reaction of four major carriers. Air France is cutting service on certain routes because of sluggish traffic growth, it was reported in *The New York Times*. Yes, but this applies only to North Africa and French West Indies routes,a company spokesman then quickly tells us. Nevertheless, there are belt-tightening measures, including a hiring freeze for all non-navigational personnel, deferral of all nonessential work on buildings and informational systems, delay of all non-aircraft investments and the phasing out of chartering planes from other airlines. Meanwhile, Northwest Airlines has cut a half a billion dollar deal with Airbus Industries and General Electric for the purchase of 75 A320's at favorable rates. While the arrangement helps Northwest purchase needed aircraft at a time it is still $1.7 billion in debt from last year's $3.65 billion acquisition by Alfred Checchi, with the rising fuel costs and declining ridership, some observers question whether such financing by the foreign government subsidized Airbus represents unfair competition to U.S. airframe manufacturers, such as Boeing and McDonnell Douglas. Next, Donald Trump has declared he will not meet a $1.1 million loan payment on the Trump Shuttle. Here again, the international bankers who hold the $245 million loan fault fuel and ridership, rather than management, for the carrier's problems. The fact is that the entire Northeast shuttle market is off 16% this year. (Pan Am may also sell its East Coast shuttle operation to raise much needed funds.) And finally, U.S. Air has suspended its 3-cent quarterly stock dividend and has delayed indefinitely delivery of new aircraft. Chairman and president Edward Colodny blamed "the nation's economy and its effect on air travel."

International revenue passenger miles by U.S. carriers grew 16.7% in August, compared to a domestic rpm growth of only 1.4% for the month. Year-to-date load factors for domestic service is down to 61.7%, while it is up to 71.2% on international routes.

U.S. citizen visits to Europe this year will easily top 7 million, a new milestone. Last year (1989), there were 6.9 million visits. Off-season travel (October through April) was 10% ahead from a year ago. On a calendar year basis, the increase is 14.4% through May. Although firm DOT figures will not be available for the peak third quarter for several months, early indications are that activity has held up well. Going into the off-season again, the European Travel

Commission (ETC) is running full page advertising in the October issues of 10 upscale consumer magazines (*Smithsonian* and *The Atlantic*, for example) offering the booklet, *Planning Your Trip to Europe* . Certainly with the weaker dollar and U.S.economy, and the skittishness among travelers prompted by the crisis in the Middle East, there could be more challenging days ahead—which prompts the theme of this November's New York City ETC marketing conference (see calendar on page 14), "Facing Up to the Challenge of Change."

The challenge for all travel marketers is not just the weakening U.S. economy, but the general ebbing of consumer confidence. For the second straight month (September), the Conference Board's Index of Consumer Expectations is in a depressed range not seen since the recession of 1982.

The U.S. recorded a balance of travel payments surplus of $2.1 billion for the first half of this year, according to Rockwell Schnabel, chief of the U.S. Travel and Tourism Administration (USTTA). This surpasses the surplus for the entire 12 months of 1989, the first year in which a surplus was achieved. A plus balance was recorded for Canada and Japan, whereas a minus balance was recorded for Europe and Mexico. Schnabel projects a $4.9 billion surplus for the year, but all bets are off, he says, if we have a shooting war in the Persian Gulf.

Should travel writers accept freebees? Attendees at the annual SATW (Society of American Travel Writers) September meeting in St Johns, Newfoundland, informally debated the issue at length. Paul Grimes of *C.N. Traveler*, backed by the well-heeled Condé Nast organization, might be called the knight errant in the "crusade of the unsullied scribes." American Express's *Travel and Leisure* does not permit its writers to accept free travel, either. But the debate ranged on in St. Johns, as it does elsewhere, because many travel publications, especially the trades, simply cannot afford to pay for all of their writers' travel, a necessity for their doing business.
But where should writers and editors draw the line?
Even the most Simon-pure publications occasionally must buy free-lance stories based on free travel.

You might ask, is a free lunch at a pricey New York restaurant allowable? Quiet, now. *That* isn't supposed to count.

Color such areas gray, rather than black and white. Regarding the free lunches, "a little bit pregnant" is heard more and more these days among groups of travel writers debating the is-

sue. But discussions or not, for most it is business as usual, and the integrity of their bylines, not who bought lunch, is their moral mentor.

Incidentally, this reporter traveled free all the way from JFK to San Juan, Puerto Rico, recently in the back of the American Airlines plane, sitting next to a squalling baby sitting on his mother's lap. No matter how hard we might try, it would be difficult to portray this as a positive travel experience.

Edwin Cooperman and G. Richard Thoman jointly will take over the reigns of the American Express Travel Related Services Company from Aldo Papone, who becomes senior adviser to AmEx's overall chairman, James D. Robinson 3rd.

Speaking of American Express, *Travel & Leisure* sports a new look—"a bold new logo and design," according to publisher Jim Berrien. Says Editor-in-Chief Ila Stanger: "Our aim is to present everything we do with a heightened sense of style, strength and timeliness." Starting in the October issue.

Associate Publisher Doria Cacciotti tells us that the magazine also is sponsoring the "Travel & Leisure Mark of Innovation Award ." The program will recognize product/service innovation in the context of one or more of these areas: service, value, safety, health and the environment. Entries due December 15 must demonstrate a breakthrough in one of four categories: lodging, transportation, tourism or travel-related products. Winners in each category will be announced at a gala New York dinner and in an extensive public relations effort, while having the privilege of carrying the "Travel & Leisure Mark of Innovation" symbol in their advertising and promotion.

Bed and Breakfasts (B&B's) are having their effect felt in the lodging industry. Although there is not enough data to say just how much, they tend to thrive more in tertiary markets where the larger operators find it hard to make a profit, and return on investment is slim until the operation gets over 20 rooms, at which point it is really an inn. All of this information comes by way of a study by Pat Hardy of the Professional Association of Innkeepers International of Santa Barbara, and presented at the TTRA Annual Conference. The report concludes, "Bed and breakfast is here to stay—but we will all be better off if we never say just 'Bed and Breakfast'—add 'home' or 'inn' after it." The home with six bedrooms and shared baths, run by a semi-retired couple "doing their thing" by being with people and making a modest profit, is just not the same thing as a professionally managed

inn with private baths and TV in the rooms and making 20+% return on investment.

Naturally your next question would be, " So what about Bed and Breakfasts in the U.S.S.R.?" No problem. AMICO INTERNATIONAL of Silver Springs, Maryland has a program "from European urban apartments of Moscow, to the traditional homes of Central Asia ." They now accept bookings in Moscow, Tbilisi and Tashkent. Leningrad, Kiev and Sochi will be offered in the near future. The Russian B & B's are "...ideal for the business traveller who ...wants to have the freedom of holding meetings late into the night without the hotel curfew restrictions," says the brochure.

More Information, Please

U.S. media advertising spending in 1989 for airlines, cruise lines, foreign and domestic destinations totaled $1.2 billion, up 8% from 1988 , according to the study just released by Ogilvy & Mather.

Veteran travel industry researcher Ed Berrol, who is responsible for the study at the advertising agency, says the biggest gain came from U.S.destinations outside of the state tourism office category, namely U.S. possessions, convention and visitors' bureaus, regional associations, etc. Labeled "Other U.S.," Puerto Rico led this classification in spending at $8 million—which in fact was greater than the highest spending U.S. state, New York ($6 million). Moreover, this "Other U.S." category surged ahead 21%, while the states increased 8%. "What we are seeing," Berrol says, "is a spreading of advertising and promotional activity. The number of destinations in this category which spent over half a million dollars rose from 20 to 30."

Total airline advertising increased by 7% to $753 million, with U.S. carriers showing an 8% increase and foreign carriers just 1%. American Airlines again led the domestic group with over $95 million, and British Airways, although showing a decline, still led the foreign carriers.

Cruise line expenditures also increased 8%, totaling $180 million for the year. Royal Caribbean Cruise Line (RCCL), with $38 million in measured media expenditures, took over the number one spot from Carnival Cruise Lines, which had $22 million.

Newspapers and TV were still the top media categories. Magazine expenditures, nevertheless, grew to $195 million, up 22%. Cable TV (including The Travel Channel) grew by 64% to $17 million for the year.

-8-   -9-

Keeping the Editorial Timely

Many readers feel that copy that looks typewritten seems fresher than typeset copy. They infer that typewriting involves up-to-the-minute information. Using this approach, the marketing briefs in *The Travel Market Leader* appear up-to-date. They are, of course, typeset.

Name *The Travel Market Leader*

Publisher *Coalition of three magazines and a cable TV channel, Darien, CT*

Purpose/audience *Service to the press and others interested in travel marketing*

Production *PageMaker and Illustrator on Macintosh IIcx*

Printing *Black and green on gray offset paper*

Format *8½-by-11 inches, sixteen pages*

Design *Kenneth Shafton*

Combining Tints and Pull Quotes

The background tint on page one sets off photos and illustrations without the cost of a second color. The pull quotes are especially striking. Note how using bold type for pull quotes and putting the quotes in boxes offset from the column makes the pull quotes seem to jump from the text. *Graff Paper* reflects a personality that is more enthusiastic than objective, on the informal side but very informative, professional and stylish within a budget.

Name *Graff Paper*

Publisher *Graff Advertising, Inc., Palo Alto, CA*

Purpose/audience *Service and marketing to clients*

Production *PageMaker on Macintosh IIx*

Printing *Black on light gray text paper*

Format *8 1/2-by-11 inches, four pages*

Design *Michael Craft*

GRAFF PAPER — Vol. I Issue 3 Winter 1990 — Nº 3

Which Came First, the Chicken or the Egg?

This age old question was the basis for a recent Fuji ad that not only demonstrated the latest technology in medical imaging, but pushed the limits of advertising technology as well.

Site for Sore Eyes—an Eye-Catching Campaign

The scenario

New client, Site for Sore Eyes wanted to promote their annual Half Price Sale (buy one pair, get 1/2 off the second pair), using radio and newspaper. They also wanted to stand out from a big competitor who holds their half price sale at the same time. The key difference about Site for Sore Eye's sale is that it allows the two pair to be purchased by different people. So one can therefore go with a friend to take advantage of the sale.

Do it with a friend

Half Price Sale

(Continued page 3)

GRAFF PAPER — Vol. I Issue 2 Summer 1990 — Nº 2

Introducing Graff-Sherman Advertising, Inc.

In the photo at right, Lloyd L. Graff and Donald J. Sherman sign the documents creating the new entity we now know as Graff-Sherman Advertising, Inc.

Who?

Graff-Sherman Advertising, Inc. is the result of a merger between Graff Advertising, Inc. of Palo Alto, CA—a nine year old business-to-business agency noted for its creative work in print advertising and collateral materials—and Donald J. Sherman & Associates, Inc.—a 10 year old firm from San Jose with a reputation for strong media buying capabilities and a primarily consumer based clientele.

What?

Sherman & Associates had projected billings at five million dollars for 1990. Graff estimated seven million. Now, as the "fullest" of full-service ad agencies, we have total billings of $12 million, moving to among the top five full-service agencies in Santa Clara County. What's more, we will be one of only nine Santa Clara agencies who are members of the AAAA. (see page 2)

How

How will this merger provide any benefits to our present and future clients and vendors? Probably no one knows all the answers to that question, but here a few ideas.

Clients of the former Graff agency will benefit from a stronger, larger and more experienced media department, an expanded capacity for broadcast advertising and video production, plus a wealth of information and resources for successful merchandising and promotional ideas.

"Our name may have changed, but we still hold strongly to the philosophy that creativity is the ability to develop uncommon solutions to common problems."

Lloyd L. Graff

GRAFF PAPER — Premiere Issue Spring 1990 — Nº 1

Graff Acquires Two New Clients

High Technology

Design of this trade ad by Creative Director, Mikey Craft, kicked off Graff's media advertising campaign for our new client, Plasma Science. The Graff team is excited and challenged by the creative possibilities presented by Plasma Science's unique treatment process of the modification of polymer (plastic) surfaces.

In the ad pictured, Plasma Science created a bonding process for a prosthesis in which the bond will last for up to four years, instead of the previous period of several months utilizing another treatment process. Plasma Science manufactures and markets equipment for accomplishing the process. Founded in 1985 by Stephen Kaplan, Plasma Science is a subsidiary of HIMONT Advanced Materials Group, HIMONT U.S.A., Inc.

Breaking New Ground

With the addition of a new food produce client, the Graff Team 'breaks new ground' in the agricultural area to promote the sales of mushrooms. Our new client is the Western Mushroom Marketing Association (WMMA), an enthusiastic and growing new agricultural association. WMMA is a group of member mushroom growers of the western U.S. whose purpose is the promotion of the western mushroom product.

Our challenge is literally to get western mushrooms 'off the ground, into the stores and onto people's plates.'

Designing a new logo to identify members of the association was our first project. Created by Mikey Craft, the personalized logo pictured below also will be used for WMMA's packaging and letterhead.

Our next opportunity is the creation of a trade and consumer summertime promotion.

"The addition of these new companies demonstrates the wide spectrum of our full service capabilities," commented Jim Marble. "One of our greatest strengths is the ability to individualize our talents to this widely varied client base."

WESTERN MUSHROOM MARKETING ASSOCIATION

Marble Named VP

With over 26 years as a publishing, printing and advertising executive under his belt, James M. Marble, 54, has joined Graff Advertising as vice president, account services. Responsible for the smooth operation of the account services department, Jim will draw on his 15 year career in publishing with Lane Publishing Company (*Sunset Magazine* and *Sunset Books*), where he supervised a 10-million dollar worldwide advertising and sales service budget.

Jim's background with Hudson Publishing as national sales manager, adds to the depth of his background, along with Jim's most recent nine year experience with two major bay area printing companies in the areas of sales, consultation and production.

"Jim brings a level of experience and knowledge we've been seeking in order to serve our clients with the high professionalism we have established over the past nine years," said Lloyd Graff. (cont'd page 4)

Long Joins Graff

An impressive professional and educational background precede Kelly A. Long, 26, in her new position as production coordinator. Kelly comes to Graff from Lutat, Battey in San Jose where she served as account coordinator, traffic manager and proof-reader. Previous to this, she was an editorial assistant at *The Independent Newspaper* of Santa Barbara. (cont'd page 4)

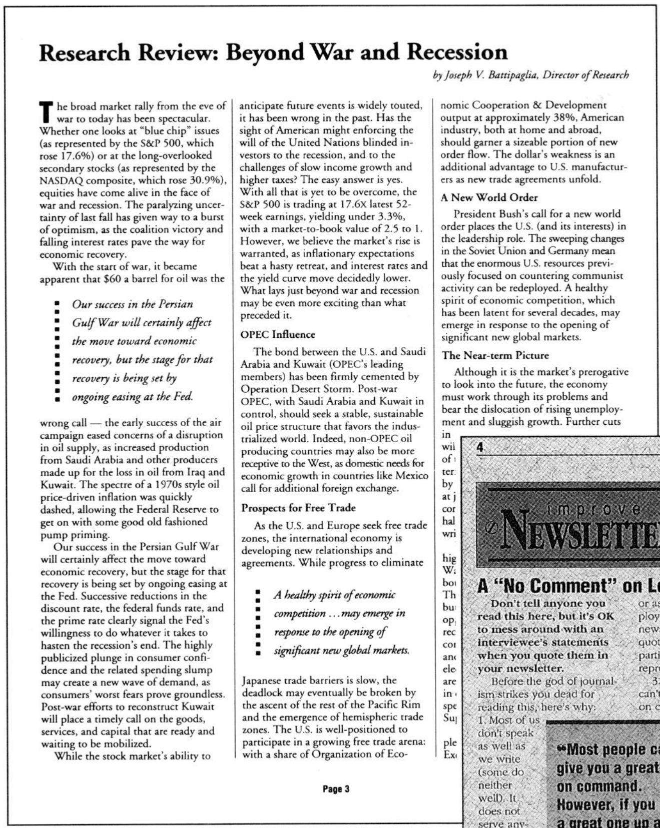

Research Review: Beyond War and Recession

by Joseph V. Battipaglia, Director of Research

The broad market rally from the eve of war to today has been spectacular. Whether one looks at "blue chip" issues (as represented by the S&P 500, which rose 17.6%) or at the long-overlooked secondary stocks (as represented by the NASDAQ composite, which rose 30.9%), equities have come alive in the face of war and recession. The paralyzing uncertainty of last fall has given way to a burst of optimism, as the coalition victory and falling interest rates pave the way for economic recovery.

With the start of war, it became apparent that $60 a barrel for oil was the

> *Our success in the Persian Gulf War will certainly affect the move toward economic recovery, but the stage for that recovery is being set by ongoing easing at the Fed.*

wrong call — the early success of the air campaign eased concerns of a disruption in oil supply, as increased production from Saudi Arabia and other producers made up for the loss in oil from Iraq and Kuwait. The spectre of a 1970s style oil price-driven inflation was quickly dashed, allowing the Federal Reserve to get on with some good old fashioned pump priming.

Our success in the Persian Gulf War will certainly affect the move toward economic recovery, but the stage for that recovery is being set by ongoing easing at the Fed. Successive reductions in the discount rate, the federal funds rate, and the prime rate clearly signal the Fed's willingness to do whatever it takes to hasten the recession's end. The highly publicized plunge in consumer confidence and the related spending slump may create a new wave of demand, as consumers' worst fears prove groundless. Post-war efforts to reconstruct Kuwait will place a timely call on the goods, services, and capital that are ready and waiting to be mobilized.

While the stock market's ability to anticipate future events is widely touted, it has been wrong in the past. Has the sight of American might enforcing the will of the United Nations blinded investors to the recession, and to the challenges of slow income growth and higher taxes? The easy answer is yes. With all that is yet to be overcome, the S&P 500 is trading at 17.6X latest 52-week earnings, yielding under 3.3%, with a market-to-book value of 2.5 to 1. However, we believe the market's rise is warranted, as inflationary expectations beat a hasty retreat, and interest rates and the yield curve move decidedly lower. What lays just beyond war and recession may be even more exciting than what preceded it.

OPEC Influence

The bond between the U.S. and Saudi Arabia and Kuwait (OPEC's leading members) has been firmly cemented by Operation Desert Storm. Post-war OPEC, with Saudi Arabia and Kuwait in control, should seek a stable, sustainable oil price structure that favors the industrialized world. Indeed, non-OPEC oil producing countries may also be more receptive to the West, as domestic needs for economic growth in countries like Mexico call for additional foreign exchange.

Prospects for Free Trade

As the U.S. and Europe seek free trade zones, the international economy is developing new relationships and agreements. While progress to eliminate

> *A healthy spirit of economic competition ... may emerge in response to the opening of significant new global markets.*

Japanese trade barriers is slow, the deadlock may eventually be broken by the ascent of the rest of the Pacific Rim and the emergence of hemispheric trade zones. The U.S. is well-positioned to participate in a growing free trade arena: with a share of Organization of Economic Cooperation & Development output at approximately 38%, American industry, both at home and abroad, should garner a sizeable portion of new order flow. The dollar's weakness is an additional advantage to U.S. manufacturers as new trade agreements unfold.

A New World Order

President Bush's call for a new world order places the U.S. (and its interests) in the leadership role. The sweeping changes in the Soviet Union and Germany mean that the enormous U.S. resources previously focused on countering communist activity can be redeployed. A healthy spirit of economic competition, which has been latent for several decades, may emerge in response to the opening of significant new global markets.

The Near-term Picture

Although it is the market's prerogative to look into the future, the economy must work through its problems and bear the dislocation of rising unemployment and sluggish growth. Further cuts in

Page 3

Getting the Most From Pull Quotes

The *pull* in *pull quotes* has a double meaning. You pull the quote out of the story. The quote pulls readers into the story. Effective pull quotes capture the essence of the story using the words of one of its main speakers. Massive, ornate or colored quote marks signal that the item is a quotation, not a headline or an excerpt. Design elements such as rules or screen tints separate the quote from the story in which it is embedded.

4

improve your NEWSLETTER TIPS

A "No Comment" on Loose Quotes

Don't tell anyone you read this here, but it's OK to mess around with an interviewee's statements when you quote them in your newsletter.

Before the god of journalism strikes you dead for reading this, here's why:
1. Most of us don't speak as well as we write (some do, neither well). It does not serve anyone's interest to embarrass them — no one's ever sued over having all of their "ums" and "ahs" edited out.
2. Newsletters are usually friendly publications — intended as a marketing tool

or as information for employees. Even subscription newsletters score by making quotes sound intelligent — particularly when they represent "the opposition."
3. Finally, most people can't give you a great quote on command. However, if you make a great one up and ask them if it's OK to say they said it, most interviewees agree.
4. Quotes are a more comfortable

> "Most people can't give you a great quote on command. However, if you make a great one up and ask them if it's OK to say they said it, most interviewees agree."

editor, co... or some o... print the ... in an edit...

Condense!

You may find this newsletter a bit chatty, but that's our style. Most of the time, readers prefer brief, well-written tidbits to in-depth discussion. In fact, you can increase the response to the information contained in your newsletter if you stick to the highlights, but give people a chance to request a more complete report.

— Edit newsletter articles by thinking "How many of these ... can I elim... to tighten... More cond... out withou...

What Your Act Needs is a Gimmick

Anything which will differentiate your newsletter from the rest of the mail will dramatically increase readership and response rate. For example, we make a point of mailing *Newsletter Nameplate* in less common ways (in a plastic bag, in a colored mailing tube, etc.) to attract attention (it worked, didn't it!).

One consulting client sent its newsletter both in printed form and on diskette. We've seen newsletters mailed with five cent goldfish (fishing for sales leads?), pens, scratch pads, rocks (a solid bar-

gain), posters, calendars, and magnifying glasses (a big value!).

Our sales increased three-fold when we began offering free books, catalogs, posters, etc. to our readers, but our costs increased only marginally. How's that for first-hand advice!

... extra for a special ink or paper when they would have been just as happy with something standard.

For example, most paper comes in widths that are divisible by 11 or 11½.

(Cont'd on page 4)

3

time, showed between 10,000 to 15,000 backorders. Mind you, the Interscience product line at that time was one of 20 product lines at Wiley.

In publishing, an unpublished book is launched months before it is actually out. Result: pre-pub or backorders. Later the book is successful and you sell at your first printing. It takes two to three months for a reprint. What happens in between the time you run out and the availability of the reprint? . . . backorders!

I believe, under postal regulations, if you take money, you must ship within 30 days or advise the customer that you cannot ship in 30 days and give the customer an option of a refund or later shipment.

As a book publisher, you may find yourself wrestling with top management who will resist backorders. This attitude will hurt your sales and hinder your success!

Inventory Space

Consider inventory space. You may be in an organization with no experience in managing an inventory and, consequently, unable to forecast inventory space needs. You must

> **Use an order key or code so that you can determine the effectiveness of a mail list.**

and what promotions didn't work.

If the organization's order takers do not view the need to track orders as a priority, then you may have some unpleasant surprises. What you might take for granted in an organization devoted exclusively to publishing books is really an exception to another department's work routine. Your needs as a book publishing company are an additional headache for some other manager to worry

important principles of direct-mail promotion is to always use an order key or code so that you can identify the source of an order to determine the effectiveness of a particular mail list. Once the orders arrive, you track the source of as many as possible so that you have a statistically reliable sample out of a population of orders. From that data, you can make inferences as to what promotions worked,

outlandish or excessive advances. Most association acquisitions editors are deluged with excellent proposals that fit right in the mainstream of their editorial strategy from their own members.

Visibility and Reputation

An extraordinary advantage is the fact that the book publishing company will come to the marketplace with credibility in the field because of the association with the parent organization. There are related items of interest to sell to the audience, i.e., periodicals that will reinforce the book publisher's credibility. The parent organization most likely will have the most responsive mail list available for use in promoting books.

Editorial Development

Experts in the field will review your manuscripts. Many association and periodicals have editorial review boards that help run the editorial portion of the program. The members of these editorial review boards will often read manuscripts for a modest honorarium.

'Profits' Are Tax Free

For a tax exempt association, there are also two other significant financial advantages.

First, no taxes are paid on those monies earned by the book publishing subsidiary. Generally speaking, the product or service must be substantially related to the organization's function. If this is not the case, then such income can be classified as unrelated business income (UBI). UBI will then be subject to regular corporate income taxes. (For an excellent discussion of UBI, see *Profit Making by Non-Profits*, The Grantsmanship Center, Department DD, P.O. Box 6210, Los Angeles, CA 90014.)

The second advantage of tax-exempt status is that of the low not-for-profit mailing rates. With the recent increase in postal rates, the growing attractiveness of this benefit is obvious. The not-for-profit postal rate decreases the cost of promotion. Consider the fact that most of these

(Cont'd on page 4)

3

7

now offer custom-tailored newsletters for their individual subscribers via computers and fax machines. Pinpoint Publishing of suburban Washington D.C. offers daily, fax-delivered newsletters for and about the computer industry which are customized to each subscriber's specific needs.

With the development of its own software to handle the daily production of hundreds of newsletters, press releases are first gathered from all over the country along with the latest news from wire services and trade periodicals. An editorial staff then indexes and categorizes each story which are assigned keywords to make the custom newsletter approach possible. Then, the machines take over.

Lists are maintained of what each subscriber would like to have in his newsletter. Computers then compare a client's preferences with that day's selections and choose appropriate stories, averaging a story's relative importance as a whole by using rankings assigned by the editorial staff and comparing them to a client's stated priorities. The newsletters are then delivered by fax before 7 a.m.

With a client list of 300 and subscriptions costing $1,800 a year, Pinpoint Publishing's operation shows just how profitable and imaginative a newsletter can be. "The cost is pretty low for a daily service," said Harvey Golomb, firm president, "and if you're in a competi-

tive industry, you need competitive information."

Of course, most subscription newsletters are not produced with all of this technological wizardry. *The Old House Journal*, a $16-a-year monthly on home restoration, was created by Clem Labine without fancy gadgetry. In March 1984, *Money* reported that Labine's publication grossed almost $900,000 annually.

This type of astronomical success helps drive the expanding $2 billion-a-year world of newsletters. Almost one half of the commercial newsletters in the country are less than 10 years old according to *Money*.

Naturally, no newsletter is guaranteed success. Being dependent on one particular

person can be dangerous for a publication as it was for the *I.F. Stone Weekly* which quickly folded after its namesake left it to pursue other projects.

While some newsletters have a lengthy or indefinite life span, others run their courses. "A lot of newsletters don't last forever," remarked Kenneth Kaufman, President of Newsletter Services Inc., which produces, prints and mails 500 newsletters in the Washington D.C. area.

"You see a new area crop up, then comes a shakeup and then consolidation,"

Kaufman stated. He cited the fate of a score of publications relating to energy which proliferated during the energy crisis of the '70s and subsequently died out.

Marketing Letters

Newsletters used for marketing date back to the 1880s. Most of the more than 100,000 newsletters currently published in the United States fall into this category.

These newsletters include everything from the in-house publication employees get with paychecks to medical bulletins from your doctor to a business or association's latest news about its products and services.

Publications which focus on their function as mar-

> **Newsletters used for marketing date back to the 1880s. Most of the more than 100,000 newsletters currently published in the United States fall into this category.**

keting tools are usually the most successful. Whether produced from scratch or canned, every headline, article, graphic, photo, and design element has a marketing function. Every newsletter has a purpose and point of view to convey to its specialized audience.

Ronald Skinner, a customer service specialist, wrote in *Fuel Oil & Heat* that "professionally produced newsletters can create the exact image you want for your company. It's the simplest, most cost effective means to keep customers

informed and make them feel valued."

"People are creating newsletters to sell their own products, build credibility, make their company names known and attract new customers," wrote Art Spikol in the *Writer's Digest* column, "Non-Fiction."

Marketing newsletters demand that you target a specific audience. They let you to reach the people you want to contact while making the exact impression that you wish to convey. As George Griffin wrote in the *Graphic Arts Monthly* of July 1989, "Newsletters should function as a salespeople."

Doctors are one of the 1990's hot growth areas for newsletters. A recent survey in *Forbes* showed 32% of 500 physicians asked nationwide expressing an interest in newsletters. "My newsletter lets me create an expert image," said Dr. Ira Bloomfield who runs a clinic in Miami and mails a four-page newsletter to select local zip codes. Dr. Brent Laing echoed that sentiment, "I'd rather give up my listing in the Yellow Pages before I'd stop using my newsletter."

Other subjects considered to be good growth areas for newsletters include travel, wine, biotechnology, mutual funds and health and fitness for senior citizens.

> **Next Issue:** More on marketing, the plight of the editor, technology, and problems for the future.

Ruddle & Associates Publishing 408-452-0120

Chapter 3

Graphics

Newsletter graphics express, organize or enhance thoughts, ideas and information. They include design elements, shown in this chapter, illustrations and infographics, shown in the next chapter, and photographics, shown in the last chapter.

Design elements are rules, screen tints, reverses and bleeds. All help organize information into efficient visual layouts.

Rules. Good newsletter design uses rules extensively to organize information. Whether subtle or bold, rules keep the eye of the reader focused on the page and direct the reader's attention from one element to the next.

Screen tints. Also known as shadings and fill patterns, screen tints highlight blocks of type such as mastheads and sidebars. They organize data within calendars and diagrams and, in the hands of experts, add dimension and depth to illustrations.

Unlike rules, to select screen tints you must consider the paper and the printing process. Uncoated paper calls for coarse screens having 85 or 100 lines per inch. Photocopy reproduction also calls for coarse screens. Coated stock allows for finer 120- or 133-line screens. Offset printing can be used to reproduce finer tints.

Reverses. Because the eye is accustomed to seeing dark type against a light background, reversed type (sometimes known as knockout type) commands special attention. It also presents special problems. Text type or other copy requiring more than a few seconds to read should never be reversed, nor should type smaller than ten points or with fine serifs. Reverses call for strong contrast with the background, so should not be used with screen tints of less than 50 percent. When used as a bold design element, as shown on the following pages, a reverse enhances the effects achievable with a single ink color and arrests the eye of the reader for a dramatic moment.

Bleeds. Printing ink up to the edge of the page, that is, "bleeding it," magnifies the advantage of color and provides a canvas for other graphic elements, such as tints and rules. Because they require slightly oversized paper and, in some cases, larger presses, bleeds also increase costs.

Good designers use graphic elements consistently. Newsletter readers see them on front pages and meet them again on inside pages, and learn to recognize these visual cues that indicate important information. Caution: Using a great variety of elements, while easy to produce, may lead only to reader confusion. Employ these four elements—rules, screen tints, bleeds and reverses—with care. They often work better in color than black, lending themselves to preprinting. See pages 76-77 for examples.

RESOURCE PERSPECTIVES™

HR Council to Guide Editorial Focus

We believe that the management of human resources is a vital link to achieving corporate success in the 1990's. "Resource Perspectives" is intended to stimulate discussion of important business issues as they relate to the effective management of human resources in the corporation.

To help us tap into the most significant concerns of human resource executives, we've formed the Human Issues Midwest Advisory Council. Members of the Advisory Council, all top executives in the HR function, will provide advice and counsel for the coming year.

"The executives we've selected are all plugged in to the best resources in the HR industry," notes Heidrick and Struggles Managing Partner Charlie Ratigan. "Their insights will help us focus on those parts of the human equation that make a real difference."

We are pleased to welcome the members of the 1991 Advisory Council:

Richard J. Darlington — Vice President of Human Resources at The Northern Trust Company in Chicago, in charge of the Recruiting Division. Prior to joining Northern Trust, Mr. Darlington was Senior Vice President-Human Resources, Operations and Customer Service of Carson Pirie Scott

The Quality Challenge: Making a Case for HR Leadership

Blame it on Japan. Slavish dedication to quality improvement took hold there in the 1950's. But complacent American companies, for the most part, went on with business as usual until it became painfully obvious how much of an impact quality could have on market share.

Even now, in many companies, "quality" is just the latest buzzword, perceived as another passing management fad. As a result, according to Joseph Juran, one of Japan's first quality gurus, American businesses are now further behind Japan's than they were in 1980.

"That's because quality is hard," declares Larry McMahan, Vice President of HR Development at Federal Express, winner of the prestigious Malcolm Baldrige National Quality Award in 1990. "There is simply no formula for creating an atmosphere where customer satisfaction is everyone's ultimate goal."

Of course, a commitment to total quality cannot take hold without the passionate support of senior management. The cultural transformation that must be implemented is simply too extensive. But in that process, human resources can be an important catalyst for change.

A sense of what HR can do to help raise quality standards can be found in the guidelines for the Baldrige Quality Award. Companies must be able to measure, for example, the effectiveness of team efforts

and employee empowerment, as well as continuous quality training. And all employees are expected to participate in the process of discovering and implementing a shared definition of quality.

At Motorola, a Baldrige Award winner in 1988, a massive quality training program earned high marks from the judges. Over 100,000 employees have been trained worldwide, at an estimated cost of $50 million, or 2% of total compensation.

While many companies would see such extensive, ongoing training as an unacceptable hefty addition to expenses, Motorola considers it a necessary investment, even in difficult economic times. "If companies don't have the skills to adjust to competitive conditions, very little else matters," says Joe Miraglia, Senior Vice President and Assistant Director of Personnel.

Motorola's focus on quality, dating from 1979, initially targeted a 10-fold reduction in defects and concentrated on statistical methods training. By the time the company won the Baldrige Award, defects had been reduced by a factor of 100.

"We believe that quality improvement comes from making sure that everybody has the same approach to quality and has the appropriate skill level to achieve it," Miraglia continues. "Every

Continued on other side

RESOURCE PERSPECTIVES

Resource Perspectives is published by Heidrick and Struggles, Inc.

Midwest Offices:

HEIDRICK AND STRUGGLES, INC.
125 South Wacker Drive
Chicago, IL 60606
312/372-8811
Charles C. Ratigan, Managing Partner

1470 Interchange Tower
600 South Highway 169
Minneapolis, MN 55426
612/544-0316
David D. Healey, Managing Partner

1991 Human Issues Midwest Advisory Council

Richard J. Darlington
Vice President, Human Resources
The Northern Trust Company, Chicago, IL

John M. Eiden
Vice President, Human Resources
Lutheran General Hospital, Park Ridge, IL

James M. Sweet
Vice President, Personnel
W.H. Brady Co., Milwaukee, WI

© Copyright 1991, Heidrick and Struggles, Inc.

Reversing Out Nameplates

One-page newsletters call for inspired design techniques that make them stand out from other one-page documents. The three-inch flap along the left edge folds out to show the nameplate reversed out of burgundy, creating an impressive entrance to the newsletter itself by lending a sense of luxury. Printing on top quality, 80-pound cover paper, using rich corporate colors, and exaggerating space between lines of the elegant type all contribute to the air of authority.

Name *Resource Perspectives*

Publisher *Heidrick and Struggles, Inc., Chicago, IL*

Purpose/audience *Service and marketing to clients*

Production *PageMaker on Macintosh SE/30*

Printing *Black and burgundy on gray linen cover paper*

Format *8¹/₂-by-11 inches, two pages*

Design *The Newsletter Group, Inc.*

Clever Graphics

Cute! Putting the dateline in the red postal indicia reminds the reader that the newsletter carries timely information. The publication is printed on a 14-by-34-inch sheet that folds to eight 8½-by-14-inch panels. Every page uses standing headlines reversed out of ³⁄₈-inch red rules to create a consistent visual cadence as readers unfold the newsletter. Typography for standing heads, article headlines and subheads is consistent throughout, making it easy for readers to jump into stories that interest them.

Name *The Smart Mailer*

Publisher *Pitney Bowes Co., Stamford, CT*

Purpose/audience *Service to Pitney Bowes customers*

Production *PageMaker on Macintosh IIcx*

Printing *Black, gray and red on white gloss-coated paper*

Format *8½-by-14 inches, eight pages (eight-panel foldout)*

Design *Charles Lanza and Gordon Diamond*

Award *International Association of Business Communicators*

Interchange

A Newsletter for the Employees of the Department of Transportation · February 1991

Budget Tops Priority List for 1991 Legislative Session

Giving Your Nameplate Impact

A dynamic nameplate can be reproduced in one color and in smaller versions elsewhere in the publication. Gradual transition from dark to light stripes gives a three-dimensional feel to the design and reinforces the concept of transportation, which is the topic of the newsletter. Reproducing the graphic element in the masthead and on the address panel keeps readers focused on the title of this source of news.

Name *Interchange*

Publisher *Washington State Department of Transportation, Olympia, WA*

Purpose/audience *Service to employees*

Production *Microsoft Word, PageMaker and FreeHand on Macintosh IIci*

Printing *Black and dark red on light gray offset paper*

Format *8¹/₂-by-11 inches, twelve pages*

Design *Marc Livingston*

Interchange

A Newsletter for the Employees of the Department of Transportation | February 1991

Budget Tops Priority List for 1991 Legislative Session

During this year's legislative session the top concern is the department's 1991-1993 budget request.

Even with our state's impressive transportation network, improvements must be made to support future growth and maintain existing service levels. This in turn will require increased investment in order to continue providing a transportation system that is safe, efficient, dependable, and environmentally responsive.

The 1991-93 budget request totals $1.9 billion. The largest part of this request is to provide for continuation of the current level of operation. After taking inflation and workload increases into account, the request reflects a minimal increase of 1.7 percent.

The budget includes several policy emphasis areas such as the update of highway preservation needs for roads and bridges, a proposal for an advance right of way revolving fund, adjustments to marine services, and requests for increased training, research and assistance to local governments. Changing emphasis areas, such as environmental concerns, will also impact the department's operation. The department is ready to face these and other challenges and takes pride in its 1991-93 budget request which is responsible and yet requests sufficient funding to carry out our mission.

In addition to the budget, topics such as growth management, salary increases for engineers, and environmental issues are also of concern to the department this session.

Growth Management

The State Transportation Commission passed a resolution supporting the recommendations made by the Growth Strategies Commission last year and is supporting the Growth Management bill being prepared by the Department of Community Development (DCD) on behalf of the Governor. "The DCD bill implements the recommendations made by the Growth Strategies Commission very well," said **Charlie Howard,** Manager for the Transportation Planning Office.

Four primary proposals contained in the legislation that will impact the department:

1. State agencies are brought into the planning process ensuring that all development plans are consistent with state goals and local plans.

2. A Growth Management Board of six members appointed by the Governor is established to function only as an appeal board to resolve land use planning disputes.

3. DCD will review all local land use plans to ensure they coincide with state goals.

4. An interagency group is established to develop the state's open space plan. WSDOT hopes to participate because of the department's scenic highway program and the role our highway system will play in creating scenic vistas between urban growth areas.

Engineer Salary Increases

Engineers and general technicians are the department's largest occupational group with 1,800 individuals working in this job series. Over the past two years, there has been a dramatic increase in the resignation rate of these individuals. "We're losing many very capable people," said **Bob Hahn,** Engineering Review Manager. "The resignation rate among junior engineers averages about 8 percent in the engineering market place, WSDOT's is doubled at nearly 16 percent." In studying the loss of these employees and the negative effects on the department, Hahn found that in two-thirds of the cases where engineers resigned department salary was the primary reason.

Unable to compete with salaries provided by other employers in the job market, WSDOT is missing out many of the most qualified graduates. "Fifty-five

(Continued on page 2)

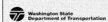

Inside

...reason, I'm really proud to ...d with WSDOT," the

...chwartzman was one of ...s who battled terrible ...ditions to provide ferry ...n assistance to the

...y arrived in the bay area, ...n and the others were ...to share their expertise and ...perators. For nearly ...owing the quake, the ...the rest of the group helped ...ancisco's water ...needs.

...ptain points out, the ...f his job continue and a ...oncern is dealing with ...r concerns voiced by ferry ... With complaints ranging ...sfaction with ferry ...d ferry runs to complaints ...rvice on the ferries, the ...ssed the difficulties he and ...e in keeping the public ...'e do our best to please ...t that's not always ...d Schwartzman. The on-...enges keep the Captain ...r more. He admits that at ...ds a break from it all and ...e to enjoy hunting, fishing ...et Sound, and boating.

Call 022-CAn3

For Seattle Area Freeways
Monday-Friday
6:00am to 7:00 pm

 Washington State Department of Transportation

Interchange

The *Interchange* is published monthly for employees, retirees, and friends of WSDOT. Comments, suggestions and questions are welcome. Travice Apple, Editor. Call 753-2150, SCAN 234-2150

The *Interchange* is printed on recycled paper.

---

transportation in Washington. The success of WSDOT's intermodal transportation program is largely due to the efforts put forth by Lenzi.

Areas most noticeably benefiting from his efforts include the State Transportation Policy Plan, establishment of regional transportation planning, strengthening the department's relationships with rail and motor carrier groups, and legislative success on transportation issues.

Working on coordination between various modes of transportation and pursuing funds for such projects have

been issues Lenzi actively ...the past year. His involve... intermodal transportation... all made significant advan... towards encouraging peo... their automobiles and int... systems so that the state i... more efficiently move gr... of people.

The Seattle-Tacoma (S... Carrier Study and a Wash... Ports Study, which must... connections between two... different means of transpo... areas Lenzi has played a...

Interchange

 Washington State Department of Transportation
Transportation Information Office
Transportation Building, 3D20
Olympia, Washington 98504-5201

COMLEARN

NEWS PUBLICATION OF THE COMMONWEALTH OF LEARNING

SEPTEMBER 1990
VOL.1 NO.2
SPECIAL EDITION

Quality through distance

trained teachers, more adequate supplies of teaching and learning resources, improved infrastructure and related factors have all been identified as necessary in the search for qualitative improvements in education. Each of these has further financial implications for countries in which education already takes a significant part of the national resources. Efforts must continue in each dimension but realism suggests that progress will be slow unless truly imaginative and creative ways can be found to address the already well documented problems.

Against this background distance education and the approaches and techniques with which it is associated merit close consideration. It is not a panacea. It is not even an alternative but wisely used, and integrated into overall systems, it can contribute significantly to better training for large numbers of teachers and to making available teaching and learning resources - better tools with which to tackle the formidable challenges. Its potential in increasing access has already been acknowledged. Now we need to explore its potential in the search for quality and more importantly to ensure that that potential is realised.

Can distance education

COMLEARN

ate of COL Activities

GUYANA - Agreement has been reached with University officials on the Guyana Distance Education Communications Network (GDECN) project. The project which is to be implemented as a series of sub-projects over a one to one-half year period commencing November 1990. It will provide the Institute of Adult and Continuing Education (IACE) at University of Guyana with the necessary communications infrastructure to develop and deliver by distance a pre-university entrance course in Science, Maths and English, as well as a programme to upgrade teachers in schools.

SAINT LUCIA - COL, in cooperation with North Island College (NIC), and with assistance from CFTC, has arranged for the secondment for one academic year of a lecturer from NIC to Sir Arthur Lewis Community College in Saint Lucia. The COL fellow will assist the College in establishing a distance teaching infrastructure and delivery system, and have at least one outreach centre operational before the end of his assignment.

The COL/AIDAB project which provided an initial training workshop in the adaptation of teaching materials for the Centre has been completed. The project was undertaken under the management of the Adelaide College of TAFE A full report has been completed, and a small fund has been set aside to provide the Tonga Centre with course materials identified from suitable Australian sources.

Visits, Consultations

· visits to COL (and attendant consultations) were undertaken by the Principal, Open Polytechnic of New Zealand, representatives of Monash University (Australia) and staff of USP's Extension Services Course Development Unit;

· representatives of Otago University and USP attended a workshop in Jamaica concerned with developments in teleconference teaching;

Improving Quality through Materials

Whatever else distance education has done it has undoubtedly highlighted the critical importance of good teaching-learning materials to the quality of education. The constraints imposed by distance and by studying in isolation have resulted in the development of courses whose content, structure and presentation have been designed to guide, encourage and motivate individual study. Adopting the view that the effectiveness of instruction is likely to be influenced more by the quality of the instructional message than by the particular characteristics of the instructional medium, not excluding the human medium at that, an important principle followed by distance educators in the area of

the fact of being able to call upon the services of experts wherever they can be located. This means that once a course is developed it is more than likely to have encapsulated the latest developments in the field, as interpreted and articulated by the experts themselves. The materials thus offer, albeit indirectly, some of the best attributes of team teaching.

The need for appropriate materials of quality to serve the needs of both pupil and teacher at all levels is a reality that is recognised in many countries, and access to good, relevant teaching-learning materials has become one of the recurrent items on the educational agenda of many countries. In proposing the establishment of The Commonwealth of Learning, the Expert Group on Commonwealth Co-operation in Distance Education attached the greatest importance to cooperation in the production and sharing of essential educational materials. They saw both the exchange of existing materials, and the cooperative development of new materials, as necessary to realise significant economies of scale and to yield particular benefits for new institutions and small states.

COMLEARN

Linking Nameplate and Editorial

Three rich ink colors boost the effectiveness of this two-column design and allow for the bold reverse in the nameplate. Broad bands of color in the nameplate repeat alternately at top and bottom of inside pages. The gold ink in the nameplate repeats in the huge, raised caps that signal the entrance to each story. Printing on A4 paper (8¼-by-11⅝ inches) gives *Comlearn* the international flair that its publisher wants. See page 51 for another example of repeating the nameplate theme and page 22 for another A4 publication.

Name *Comlearn*

Publisher *The Commonwealth of Learning, Vancouver, BC*

Purpose/audience *Service to members*

Production *By hand*

Printing *Black, purple and gold on white offset paper*

Format *A4 (8¼-by-11⅝ inches), eight pages*

Design *E.A. Sommerville*

Using Graphics for Visual Flair

Financial publications often seem dry and formal. In *Outline*, the calligraphic nameplate creates a friendly first impression. Ample white space surrounding the nameplate fosters easy segue into the copy. The market rate chart and list of articles put the most useful information on page one. On the inside, the square bullets that are used to end articles and the set-in columns that are used to identify pull quotes also appear in a line to set off the standing head on page five.

Name *Outline*

Publisher *Gruntal & Co., Inc., New York, NY*

Purpose/audience *Service and marketing to clients*

Production *PageMaker and Illustrator on Macintosh IIfx*

Printing *Black and dark red on natural offset paper*

Format *8¹/₂-by-11 inches, six pages*

Design *Mary Jane Harris*

Market Rates *as of March 19, 1991*

PRIME RATE	8.75%
DISCOUNT RATE	6.00%
FEDERAL FUNDS	5.94%
6-MO. TREASURY BILLS	5.85%
1-YR. TREASURY BILLS	5.97%
30-YR. TREASURY BONDS	8.32%

A Message to Our Clients

from Howard Silverman,
Chairman and Chief Executive Officer

On February 13, 1991 The Home Insurance Company and Gruntal Financial Corp. were sold by AmBase Corporation for approximately $1 billion to Home Holdings Inc. We are very

position and record of growth. A recent publication of the Securities Indus-

Research Review: Beyond War and Recession

by Joseph V. Battipaglia, Director of Research

The broad market rally from the eve of war to today has been spectacular. Whether one looks at "blue chip" issues (as represented by the S&P 500, which rose 17.6%) or at the long-overlooked secondary stocks (as represented by the NASDAQ composite, which rose 30.9%), equities have come alive in the face of war and recession. The paralyzing uncertainty of last fall has given way to a burst of optimism, as the coalition victory and falling interest rates pave the way for economic recovery.

With the start of war, it became apparent that $60 a barrel for oil was the

- *Our success in the Persian*
- *Gulf War will certainly affect*
- *the move toward economic*
- *recovery, but the stage for that*
- *recovery is being set by*
- *ongoing easing at the Fed.*

wrong call — the early success of the air

anticipate future events is widely touted, it has been wrong in the past. Has the sight of American might enforcing the will of the United Nations blinded investors to the recession, and to the challenges of slow income growth and higher taxes? The easy answer is yes. With all that is yet to be overcome, the S&P 500 is trading at 17.6X latest 52-week earnings, yielding under 3.3%, with a market-to-book value of 2.5 to 1. However, we believe the market's rise is warranted, as inflationary expectations beat a hasty retreat, and interest rates and the yield curve move decidedly lower. What lays just beyond war and recession may be even more exciting than what preceded it.

OPEC Influence

The bond between the U.S. and Saudi Arabia and Kuwait (OPEC's leading members) has been firmly cemented by Operation Desert Storm. Post-war OPEC, with Saudi Arabia and Kuwait in control, should seek a stable, sustainable

nomic Cooperation & Development output at approximately 38%, American industry, both at home and abroad, should garner a sizeable portion of new order flow. The dollar's weakness is an additional advantage to U.S. manufacturers as new trade agreements unfold.

A New World Order

President Bush's call for a new world order places the U.S. (and its interests) in the leadership role. The sweeping changes in the Soviet Union and Germany mean that the enormous U.S. resources previously focused on countering communist activity can be redeployed. A healthy spirit of economic competition, which has been latent for several decades, may emerge in response to the opening of significant new global markets.

The Near-term Picture

Although it is the market's prerogative to look into the future, the economy must work through its problems and bear the dislocation of rising unemployment and sluggish growth. Further cuts

•••••••••••••••••••••••••••• INVESTMENT BRIEFS ••••••••••••••••••••••••••••

CD Update
Do you have a bank CD coming due soon? Don't just roll it over—come to us. Gruntal has available certificates of deposit, insured by the BIF or SAIF for $100,000 per depositor. Both the BIF and the SAIF are administered by the FDIC. The following is a sample of CDs and their yields as of March 19, 1991—yields change every Tuesday. Additional maturities are available.

3-mo	6.60%	3-yr	7.50%
6-mo	7.00%	5-yr	8.00%
1-yr	6.80%	10-yr	8.40%

Gruntal's Insured Deposits Account
(I.D.A.) allows you to receive FDIC insurance coverage for up to $500,000. I.D.A. offers competitive monthly yields with interest compounded daily. Free check writing (limit of three monthly and each check must be for a minimum of $100.00) is available when you maintain an average minimum monthly balance of $5,000. If you choose, cash balances in your Gruntal brokerage account can be automatically swept into I.D.A. so your money is insured and

view these shares as an attractive opportunity for investors seeking to outperform the rest of the utility group.

For a complete copy of this report, please contact your Gruntal Account Executive.
*Price as of March 19, 1991.

The Sterling Advantage:
Quality and Service
If you have a minimum of $100,000 in cash or securities, Sterling Advisors (a division of Gruntal) can offer you professional management services usually reserved for wealthier individuals and large institutions through its Sterling Advantage Account. Each portfolio is maintained individually, tailored to accommodate your investment needs and goals, and can be modified at any time. And you are never charged brokerage commissions, no matter what the level of activity in your account.

Professional management is not beyond your reach — consider the Sterling Advantage today!

Reduce Your Tax Liability
Did you know that you may qualify for a credit against your Federal tax bill? Fed-

through the use of credits, so your savings could be substantial. The tax savings provided by this type of investment is equivalent to tax-free cash flow; tax credits represent spendable income.

Federal Tax Credits are generated by "affordable" housing — one of the few economic issues to receive favorable treatment by legislators over the years. For complete information concerning tax credit investment opportunities, and to see if you qualify, call your Gruntal Account Executive today.

Are You About to Change Jobs?
Are You About to Retire?
If you are you have an important decision to make. Should you pay taxes now on your retirement plan distribution perhaps at favorable rates, or pay taxes later at ordinary rates, after your distribution and its earnings accumulate tax-free? This is a critical question that Gruntal can help you answer with our personalized computer illustration that will enable you to determine which option is better for you.

Tax Deferral With a *Plus*

September/October 1990

the
travel
market
leader

THE JOURNAL OF
TRAVEL MARKETING
DANIEL NESBETT, EDITOR

BULK RATE
U.S. Postage
PAID
Stamford, CT
Permit No. 35

Provided as an industry service by *U.S. News & World Report, European Travel & Life, Smithsonian, The Travel Channel*

From the 1990 Caribbean Tourism Conference

SOFTER U.S. MARKET PROMPTS REASSESSMENT OF STRATEGIES.

OTHER ISSUES INCLUDE GROWTH FROM EUROPE, ECO-TOURISM AND MAKING THE PRODUCT MORE COMPETITIVE.

Destination countries such as Jamaica, Aruba, Bermuda, Cayman Islands and Grenada are continuing to enjoy double-digit growth in arrivals this year. Others, such as The Bahamas, St. Lucia, Curacao, St. Maarten and Puerto Rico are seeing growth—but in single digits—while negative growth is being experienced in the Virgin Islands (due largely to Hurricane Hugo), Barbados, Antigua and Barbuda.

crisis, prompted concern among delegates. How could the conference's theme itself, "Competing in the 1990s," then have been more apropos in its challenge to the Caribbean community to carefully review future strategies ?

The conference officially opened on the evening of September 13 amid the polished marble and crystal chandeliers at the Antiguo Casino in Old San Juan, and the colorful presenta-

Route to: **See page number:**

IN THIS ISSUE:

Selling to Seniors   **6**

The Rewards of Historic Preservation   **7**

Extra Placements from P.R. "Takes"   **11**

Creating a Graphic Theme

The nameplate doubles as the address panel, keeping page one face up when the newsletter arrives in the mailbox. Clever! Subscribers get more for their money when they use the routing instruction box. Although difficult to see in this reproduction, the routing box frames a 10 percent screen tint of black ink that looks very businesslike on the light gray paper. The business form theme extends to the calendar, reproduced on page 27.

Name *The Travel Market Leader*

Publisher *Coalition of three magazines and a cable TV channel, Darien, CT*

Purpose/audience *Service to the press and others interested in travel marketing*

Production *PageMaker and Illustrator on Macintosh IIcx*

Printing *Black and green on gray offset paper*

Format *8½-by-11 inches, sixteen pages*

Design *Kenneth Shafton*

Director's News
By Michael Taves

The Graphic Nameplate

The reference card, printed on coated cover paper using the same ink colors as the newsletter, makes it handy for students to keep information about the computing center at hand. The vertical nameplate leaves plenty of room for copy while serving to shorten lines of type that would otherwise be too long in a one-column format. Thin vertical rules accent the orientation of the nameplate. Inside the designer runs breakout quotes in the margin introduced by the nameplate.

Name *On-Line*

Publisher *Ithaca College, Ithaca, NY*

Purpose/audience *Service to users of academic computing services*

Production *PageMaker on Macintosh IIfx*

Printing *Black and red on white gloss-coated paper; insert: two colors on C2S card stock*

Format *8½-by-11 inches, four pages*

Design *Dave Well*

REFERENCE CARD
Academic Computing Services - Ithaca College - February 1991

Computer Lab Hours - Spring '91
January 28, 1991 - May 5, 1991

Muller Center (1)

ACS Offices - Rm. 102 (274-3030)
- Open 8:30am - 5pm, Monday - Friday
- Additional offices are located in Friends 110

VAX Complex - Rm 101 (274-3093)
- 35 VAX terminals, 3 highspeed printers
- Room is open daily 8am - midnight, longer if occupied
- Consultant is duty Monday - Thursday 10am - 11pm, Friday 10am - 5pm, Sunday 2pm - 11pm

Friends Hall (2)

Friends Microcomputer Complex - Rm. 110 (274-3379)
- 37 MS-DOS computers, 18 Macintosh computers
- Free laser printing, WordPerfect, Quattro Pro, etc
- Open Monday - Thursday 8:30am - midnight, Friday 8:30am - 5pm, Saturday 11am - 6pm, Sunday 11am - midnight

Math/Computer Science Lab - Rm. 207 (274-1277)
- 30 IBM PS/2 Computers, WordPerfect, Quattro Pro, etc

Hill Center (4)

Hill HPER Lab - Rm. 54 (274-3197)
- 9 IBM, 1 Macintosh and 8 Apple IIe computers
- Open Monday 2pm - 11pm, Tuesday - Thursday 1pm - 11pm, Friday 2pm - 4pm, Sunday 4pm - 11pm

Gannett Center (5)

Library VAX Lab - Rm. 500 (274-3646)
- 5 VAX terminals
- Open library hours

Williams Hall (6)

Science VAX Lab - Rm. 113 (274-3993)
- 5 VAX terminals
- Open building hours

Roy H. Park School of Communications (7)

Journalism Lab - Rm. 219 (274-1015)
...omputers, WordPerfect, Quattro Pro, etc
& Wednesday 6pm - 11pm, Tuesday &
... - 11pm, Saturday 11am - 5pm,
... - 11pm
...ometimes reserved for classes

...ab - Rm. 273 (274-1332)
...n 210 computers (IBM compatibles),
...Quattro Pro, etc
... - Thursday 6pm - 11pm,
...n - 5pm, Sunday noon - 11pm
...ometimes reserved for classes

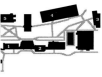

...r current hours

Director's News
By Michael Taves

As I mentioned in my last column, a number of plans to add to or improve our systems were coming to fruition, and I indicated that I was hoping to report some concrete progress in the near future. Well, at least *some* of the future has arrived. We were able to complete some purchasing decisions over the break, and made substantial progress on some other projects — e.g. communications between Novell network computers and our VAX 11/785 — which will still require much further work before we are comfortable with a solution. So here's some news on what we have accomplished so far.

Sun SPARCstations for Computer Science

As I have mentioned before, we have been planning for some time to upgrade our VAX 11/750 to some newer platform for providing UNIX-based services. We have decided to purchase seven new Sun SPARCstation IPC color workstations for this purpose. Each of these UNIX workstations will have 8 megabytes of memory, a 16" color monitor, a 207 megabyte internal hard disk and a 1.44 megabyte floppy disk drive. We are also purchasing a CD-ROM drive from Sun for software distribution to the network of SPARCstations. In addition, as part of this purchase, Sun Microsystems is donating the operating system software, the "C" and "C++" languages, and a Sparc laser printer. These machines will arrive sometime in early March and will, for the time being, be installed in faculty offices for curriculum development, before being made available to Computer Science students at a later date. These machines will be combined with, and networked to, the Sun Sparc 4/280 network server which we received as a grant from Sun a few months ago.

UNIX workstation networks are rapidly growing in importance in computer science. These facilities will serve our Computer Science faculty and students well — they will now have access to a truly up to date UNIX workstation network for their curriculum. I want to give special thanks to Prof. Eric Robinson, Chair of the Mathematics & Computer Science Department, for his superb leadership and extraordinary effort in helping ACS complete this decision in cooperation with the faculty.

Continued on page 2

The Media-Research Lab — A lab with some unique features
By Wendy Shutter, Systems Manager

While you may think that the Media Research Lab, located in Park 273, is just like all of the other MS-DOS microcomputer labs on campus, it is actually the first lab of its kind on this campus. What makes this lab unique is that in addition to having access to the usual array of MS-DOS software, such as WordPerfect and Quattro Pro, and you can also access any of the academic VAX computers.

These machines are able to use most of the microcomputer software that we support. Currently, the Media Research Lab is running WordPerfect, SPSS/PC+, Dr. Halo, Black Magic and a radio tutor program. Quattro Pro (a Lotus 123 spreadsheet look-a-like) is scheduled to be installed soon. You access these computers the same way that you access any of our microcomputers — by turning on the machine and typing: LOGIN GUEST.

What makes this lab different from the other PC labs on campus is that you can also use these machines to connect to the academic VAX computers (Ithaca, ICunix, ICcomm). To get to the VAX instead of the PC network, use the "sethost" command.

Continued on page 2

ACS On-Line
February '91 ∎ Vol 3.3

Inneraction — A MONTHLY FORUM

THIS MONTH: RECYCLING PAPER BY SKIP BOYER

PAPER CHASE

There's nothing new about the concept of recycling paper. Americans have been doing it since 1690, the year the first colonial paper mill was built. Recycling was the foundation of making paper in the beginning.

Of course, things changed. In colonial times, paper was made exclusively of fiber taken from cotton and linen rags. The result was a very high grade, long-lasting paper. This was fine until the demand for paper jumped.

That happened during the Civil War. The demand for news meant more newspapers, which meant more paper. The result was the introduction of wood fiber into the papermaking process. We still call it newsprint.

By 1904, 60 percent of all American paper was made from wood fiber. By the 1930s, recycled fibers had just about disappeared from the mass paper market. Nearly all paper was made from virgin resources.

The impact of that should be obvi-

out recovery systems. More than 42 million tons was simply destroyed in municipal solid waste systems.

And what happened to the 32 percent we saved? It was recycled.

More than 21 million tons became new paper products. Six million tons were exported to other countries as raw material for their recycling mills. The rest was used to make cellulose insulation, packing materials, etc.

The entire 27.6 million tons of paper waste represents about 25 percent of the total paper fiber used by paper mills in the United States. The other 75 percent is, of course, virgin fiber.

Why don't we do more?

Well, the answer, according to the American Paper Institute, is that it just isn't all that easy.

Here are a few questions and answers from a conversation with the American Paper Institute, one of the nation's leaders in encouraging paper recycling.

The first question is basic. Why aren't we doing more to recycle paper?

The potential for recycling paper, by definition, is limited by the ability to recover usable waste paper. A partnership between the public and private sectors is essential to achieve the ambitious goal of 40 percent recovery. If this goal can be achieved, the total recovery of recyclable waste paper will increase by nearly 50 percent, to more than 40 million tons annually.

What are the biggest problems in increasing paper recycling?

Increased recycling is dependent on expanded market demand for the finished products that can be made from waste paper. It is also dependent upon the availability of a quality waste paper supply. As the demand for a product increases, industry will meet that demanded—provided the grades of waste paper needed to make the product are available. The principal barriers include uneven population distribution, which restricts potential waste paper recov-

(continued on the next page)

Inneract BEST WESTERN
A BEST WESTERN EMPLOYEE PUBLICATION

APRIL 19, 1991

Looking for a way to the top? Try Innside Line

You've been working on it for months and you've finally figured out a way to power the Best Western reservations system for a full year using only 30 large white mice and 600 tons of oat bran. Think of the money you'll save the company.

Or you've been reading **Interact** stories about Best Western recycling programs and it dawns on you that **Interact** isn't printed on recycled paperstock. Some hypocritical commitment, you decide.

Then what?

What happens to your good idea or your real concern with a management issue?

Try **Innside Line**, your hotline to Best Western management.

You'll find Innside Line boxes and forms for both the suggestion program and employee concerns at several locations throughout Headquarters and the Beardsley Center. There are two ways you can use Innside Line:

If you have an idea or suggestion that can save Best Western time and money (nothing involving white mice and oat bran), you'll find a Suggestion Form near the Innside Line box.

Your suggestion will be evaluated by a management committee. If your suggestion results in a tangible

savings to Best Western, you will receive one-tenth of the first year net savings, up to $2,000. If the results of your suggestion can't be measured from the standpoint of dollars saved, but still have a significant impact on Best Western, the committee may offer awards up to $100. Guidelines for submitting suggestions are printed on the back of each Suggestion Form.

While your suggestions may earn you money, the second way to use Innside Line may only earn you peace of mind.

If you have a concern or comment you want to share with Best Western management, but would prefer not to discuss it directly with your supervisor or a Human Resources representative, use Innside Line.

Your comments may be anonymous or you may sign your name and request a direct response. If the issue which concerns you also concerns others at Best Western, your comment and a response may appear in **Interact**. Responses can also be kept confidential, at your request.

Innside Line will be coordinated jointly by Corporate Communications and Human Resources Management.

Tush is Wichita ACE winner

MARY TUSH

Mary Tush is the 1990 A.C.E. Award winner in Wichita. And, though she had won the monthly A.C.E. award in the past, the yearly honor came as a surprise. The shocked Tush received the news, complete with candy, balloons and the congratulations of Center Manager **Ron Trog** and Special Services Manager **Gary Doyle**.

A member of the charter training class at the Wichita Center, Tush has

been with Best Western nearly three years. She helped establish the Special Services department in Wichita before moving into the International area.

A cat and Nintendo lover, she is also active in Wichita community theater productions. Co-workers describe her as "unique, outgoing, upbeat and a team worker." She describes herself as a "fiercely loyal native Kansan."

SWEET TOUCH

A recent Headquarters bake sale to benefit the Make-A-Wish Foundation drew an enthusiastic crowd of staff members, including Paula O'Connor, left, who couldn't wait.

Tints as Graphics

Both type and design unify the newsletter with its insert *Innteraction*. Using a 20 percent screen tint of black for the words "Best Western" in the nameplate allows the name of the newsletter to leap forward. Horizontal rules printed in the same 20 percent tint maintain a crisp theme throughout the publication. Readers benefit from news in the insert and can also copy it for distribution with regional newsletters. The newsletter and insert are 9-by-12 inches, which gives both an extra feeling of authority.

Name *Innteract*

Publisher *Best Western International, Inc., Phoenix, AZ*

Purpose/audience *Service to employees of Best Western*

Production *By hand*

Printing *Black on white matte-coated paper*

Format *9-by-12 inches, six pages*

Design *William H. Skip Boyer*

Awards *International Association of Business Communicators, Editor's Forum*

The Shaker

School Review

Shaker Heights
City School District
Shaker Heights, Ohio
January 1991

Shaker Students Earn National Honors

Each year, students from around the country pat themselves through perhaps one of the most difficult academic challenges of their school years when they take the Preliminary Scholastic Aptitude Test/National Merit Scholarship Qualifying Test (PSAT/NMSQT).

The National Merit Scholarship Corporation sponsors the test and awards the top one-half percent of all high school seniors who took the test with citations as National Merit Semifinalists and Commended Students, National Achievement Semifinalists and Commended Students, and National Hispanic Scholar Award Program Semifinalists. In the Spring of 1990, over one million students from 19,585 schools took the 1991 test.

Since the inception of the test more than 30 years ago, Shaker High School students have constantly ranked among the best in the state. This year Shaker ranks in the top two percent of all private and public schools nationally, based on its number of National Merit Semifinalists. Twenty-three Shaker Heights High School students earned these national honors.

The Shaker Heights City School District recognizes the following students for being named either National Merit Semifinalists and Commended Students, National Achievement Semifinalists and Commended Students, and National Hispanic Scholar Award Program Semifinalists.
— continued on page 6

THE SHAKER HEIGHTS CITY SCHOOL DISTRICT

VOL. 1, NO. 1

MATHEMATICS REFORM: Challenge for the 90's

by Lynn Cowen and Ovella McIntyre

How educators respond to the research and recommendations made in the NCTM report, for too long, students and teachers have been "prisoners" of textbook curriculums. American students have traditionally learned mathematics via textbook pages and worksheets, doing problem after problem, filling in the blanks, and relying narrowly on drill, practice and rote memorization - all unreflective of mathematics in the real world.

this decade will help determine the health of this nation as we enter the 21st century. Recent public criticism of schools is certainly less than

the real world of mathematics that includes statistics, probability, estimation, measurement, geometry, patterns, graphs, functions, numbers, calculators and computers.

Many Shaker educators concur with the research and recommendations made in the NCTM report. For too long, students and teachers have been "prisoners" of textbook curriculums. American students have traditionally learned mathematics via textbook pages and worksheets, doing problem after problem, filling in the blanks, and relying narrowly on drill, practice and rote memorization - all unreflective of mathematics in the real world.

at a "grass roots" level. Initial efforts began in the mid-80's when a team of kindergarten teachers started using and adapting a "hands-on" program specifically tailored to the developmental learning stages of young children, called *Math Their Way*. In this program, real materials familiar to students (buttons, lids, shells, keys, etc.) are used to develop mathematical concepts. These materials provide motivation for learning, and at the same time provide the tools for exploring mathematical ideas and engaging in problem solving. Most parents whose children have attended kindergarten in the Shaker schools know how

teaching mathematics has become popular, non-threatening and fun with an endless variety of concrete materials such as colorful uncooked pasta, blocks, puzzles, color tiles, teddy bear counters, geoboards and food (edible data).

At Boulevard Elementary School, first grade students are involved in a program called *Explorations*. Young children learn mathematics by manipulating concrete materials and interacting with teachers and other children in an environment where problem solving is interwoven with numbers, operations, measurement, geometry, statistics and graphing. In *Explorations*, students also

STUDENTS IN THE NEWS

Ohio's first place winner in the sixth grade category of the 1990 Invent America Contest is Shaker's own Christopher T. Hill. Hill's invention, a device which aids in filling a high-hanging bird feeder, impressed judges from the United States Patent Service and earned him top honors in his grade category. The contest rewards students who demonstrate innovative thinking and analytical problem-solving skills. Hill is currently a seventh grader at Shaker Heights Middle School.

Shaker Heights High School's spirited varsity and junior varsity cheerleaders began the year winning top honors at the Universal Cheerleader Association's Cheerleading Camp held in August at Kent State University. In addition to winning superior and excellent ribbons for daily evaluations, the team earned trophies for outstanding cheers and sideline chants. The group also received the camp's most prestigious award, the Master Key Plaque—an award presented to the most spirited squad. There were over 450 cheerleaders from across Northeast Ohio competing for this top honor. The 1990 Shaker Heights High School Varsity cheerleaders are: Mokita Baskerville, Ayesha Bell, Melissa Collins, Katie Fox, Colette Jones, Tisha Norman and Charmaine Spearman. The Junior Varsity Cheerleaders are: Meredith Albert, Jennifer Bohl, DeMeka Embry, Amy Minkowetz, Crystal Patrick, Emily Seppelt, Vellice Sims and Halley Smith. The adviser to these squads is Shaker Middle School science teacher Susan Landi.

Also at the Universal Cheerleader Association Camp, senior Melissa Collins and junior Tisha Norman earned spots on UCA's All-Star Team which is scheduled to perform in London, England, this month in the Lord Mayor of Westminster's New Year's Parade. UCA selected the top one-percent of more than 100,000 cheerleaders from across the United States to comprise the 1990 All-Star Team.

Fifteen Shaker Heights High School musicians were selected to perform in the Cleveland Youth Wind Symphony. Once again, Shaker is proud to have a large group of students audition and earn positions in this prestigious group. Congratulations go to

Treasurer's Report

Daniel L. Wilson

The Shaker Heights Board of Education recently approved the 1990-91 budget. The adoption of this balanced budget allows for the continuation of high quality educational programming in the Shaker schools. The budget was approved and was based on the current three-year financial projections developed for the board of education.

The educational reform movement in Ohio has had very little positive impact on the problems of funding public education. The possibility of legal challenges to the current school finance structure and a movement to redistribute educational funding within the state are viewed as detrimental to our school district.

In 1989, the state legislature passed and the governor signed into law the Omnibus Education Reform Act and Accountability (Senate Bill 140). This major piece of educational reform contains significant unfunded new mandates which are to be phased-in over the next several years. With the exception of a $9,194 in-state grants (less than $1 per student) funding has not been provided to implement these new mandates.

In addition to the legislated mandates, the board of education continues to cope with impossible restrictions on income that effectively prevent any reasonable growth to pay for normal inflation in the cost of operating the school district. The state budget provides for very little growth in basic aid from the state and House Bill 920 continues to effectively freeze local tax collections at current levels.

The 1990-91 budget will receive full benefit from the May 1989

school levy and represents the majority of growth in income. It is anticipated this year's general fund budget will receive $41,282,241. A total of $39,973,143 is budgeted for expenses; the planned carry-over balance being used to help fund next year's operating budget. The budget also reflects the benefit of the May 1990 bond issue which provides funds for capital repairs, renovations and improvements to the district's facilities and for the acquisition of major equipment.

The budget continues to be attacked by the pressures of new expenses. The phase-in of the Medicare tax will add an additional $107,815 in expense this budget year. If Congress mandates full compliance for Medicare taxes, an additional $656,818 will be required out of the annual operating budget.

Additionally, money has been budgeted to comply with Federal EPA Guidelines to continue to implement the 10-year Asbestos Management Plan adopted by the board. Money has also been budgeted to test for Radon gas, lead in the drinking water and the condition of underground storage tanks.

Other expense pressures include the continuing health insurance crisis. This budget is impacted greatly by a 14 percent increase in health insurance costs over last year bringing the increase to $329,800.

On the plus side, the upgrading of the district's phone system has saved the budget $40,100 this year. The district will continue to explore ways to improve other operations with the hope of saving additional monies.

The entire budget book is on file in the Treasurer's office and is available for review. A limited quantity is available for distribution upon request. If you have any questions concerning the 1990-91 budget, please contact the Treasurer at 295-4316. ∎

seniors Christopher Ackerman, alto saxophone; Christopher Anderson, trombone; David Conner, percussion; Andrea Conrad, E-flat clarinet; Jennifer Shapiro, clarinet and Alisa Warshay, clarinet; juniors Theodore Folkman, trumpet; Erica Jacobs, oboe; Rachel Lowenthal, flute; Joshua Moskowitz,

oboe and Daniel Sorin, clarinet; sophomores Thomas Finch, bassoon and Matthew Freeman, French horn; and freshmen Elise Collin, clarinet and Katherine Doll, French horn. High school instrumental music instructors are Hans Bohnert and Darryl Gregory.
— continued on page 3

2 School Review

January 1991

1989-1990

Annual Report

Shaker Heights
City School District
Shaker Heights, Ohio

Message from the Superintendent

As in recent years, debate about the quality of education in America continued to rank high on national, state and local agendas. National summits redefined public education goals while legislative mandates, intended to improve the quality of education, affected school operations. In the midst of these initiatives, the status of the Shaker Heights City School District remained academically and fiscally sound.

Throughout the 1989-90 school year, diligent efforts to maintain and improve our instructional program continued. New courses of study were devised and approved by the board of education. Other courses of study were updated and appropriate revisions made to the instructional program. Teachers participated in these efforts through an expanded summer writing program which resulted in 30 significant curriculum projects affecting grades kindergarten through 12. The district also invested in technology by purchasing Macintosh computers for the computer labs at the high school. In addition, new computers for clerical use were added to enhance district operations.

The board maintained its practice of recognizing student and staff achievements both in and out of the classroom at its monthly meetings. Over 300 separate honors were earned for projects, contests and events in English, the fine and performing arts, foreign language, language arts, mathematics, science and social studies. The board was pleased to recognize 47 members of the Class of 1990 who were named National Merit and National Achievement Commended Students and Semifinalists. That number placed Shaker first in Ohio and in the top 10 nationally among all public schools.

Other accomplishments included the successful signing of our secretarial and custodial unions' contracts, and the development of extensive inservice and continuing education opportunities for our staff. The district also created a task force to address gang activity and youth violence. This task force focused on inservice activities which covered compassionate communication, cultural diversity, racism and oppression.

Plans were made to improve physical facilities throughout the district. A facilities study was

conducted to identify and prioritize capital improvements and maintenance projects. In addition, a study of the district's physical assets resulted in a long-term model for repair and renovation of the school facilities.

These studies preceded the district's successful efforts to gain public approval of a $10 million bond issue. Voters supported this issue by a 63 percent approval rate. A portion of the monies was targeted for the addition of a classroom wing to both Boulevard and Onaway schools. The additions will ease the pressure of increased enrollments while updating these buildings. Other portions of the bond issue will go to relieve the general operating budget of costs to repair and maintain facilities, and to purchase equipment and furniture.

Board members and administrators continued to closely monitor the budget, in hope of deferring the next operating levy until 1992. Additional revenue sources were sought at both the local and state levels, and every effort was made to ensure collection of all revenue due the district.

Initiatives were taken to strengthen the cooperative relationship between the city and the school district. Numerous individual and group meetings were held, involving school board members, school administrators, the mayor, city council, city staff and the library board. A better understanding of the school district's and the city's goals and needs emerged from these discussions. One result of this master planning was a decision to consider relocating the public library into the Moreland school building.

As we enter a new decade, we will maintain our focus on the mission of the school district to ". . . nurture, educate, and graduate students who are civic-minded and prepared to make ethical decisions; who are confident, competent communicators, skillful in problem-solving, capable of creative thinking; who have a career motivation, and a knowledge of our global and multicultural society." In doing so, we are confident that Shaker students will be prepared to face the challenges of an ever-changing world.

Mark Freeman

Creating Visual Texture

The annual financial report and the special report about math reform inserted with the newsletter form a unified package of information. A variety of textures, both visual and physical, contribute to a contemporary sense. "Academia," the occasional special insert, looks upbeat and modern, and, according to its designer, draws an overwhelming response from the staff and the public.

Name *The Shaker School Review*

Publisher *Shaker Heights City School District, Shaker Heights, OH*

Purpose/audience *Service to residents of the city of Shaker Heights*

Production *By hand*

Printing *Black and red on white laid text paper; inserts: two colors on white gloss-coated paper*

Format *8½-by-11 inches, eight pages*

Design *Ballash Press—Kathleen Donchess*

Award *National School Public Relations Association*

Designing With Clip Art

Using clip art effectively calls for consistency of style and production. By placing clip art graphics reliably at the bottoms of pages, this design uses art to frame as well as enhance the stories. Placing pictures of people at the bottom of the page also gives them a base to stand on. Instead of floating in space, the images rest on the strong rule that surrounds the page or story.

Name *Lamplighter*

Publisher *Town of Leesburg, Leesburg, VA*

Purpose/audience *Service to residents of Leesburg*

Production *By hand*

Printing *Black and burgundy on white gloss-coated paper*

Format *8 1/2-by-11 inches, fourteen pages*

Design *Custom Graphics, Inc.*

Awards *City Hall Digest, National Association of Government Communicators*

Leaf Collection Schedule Announced

The town will begin its annual fall leaf collection through Grayson's Refuse Service on Monday, October 23.

Leaf collection days will depend on the quadrant in which you live. King and Market Streets are the quadrant dividers. Leaves will be collected on Mondays, Wednesdays and Thursdays based on the following schedule:

■ Southwest quadrant - Monday

■ Northwest and southeast quadrants - Wednesday

■ Northeast quadrant - Thursday

Leaves should be raked to a distance of about four feet from the edge of the curb by the evening of the day preceeding your collection day. On those streets without curbs, leaves should be placed as close as possible to the property line. Leaves can also be bagged and placed with your regular trash for pick-up.

Brush pick-up can be requested by calling the town office on Wednesday prior to pick-up on Thursday. Inclement weather may require a temporary change in the schedule.

If leaves are not collected on the scheduled day, contact Mary Frye at the town office, 777-2420. The last day for leaf collection will be Friday, December 8.

■ Eliminate automobile sales from the B-2 zone and create a new B-4 zone for by-right auto sales and other related uses.

■ Establish "white collar" research and development as a by-right use in the B-2 zone, while laboratory and production would remain a special exception use.

■ Change the by-right maximum square footage from 100,000 square feet to 250,000 square feet for commercial centers in the B-3 zone.

■ Increase residential height in some zones.

■ Make child-care centers by-right uses in most zones, subject to limitations.

"I hope the Town Council will find our recommendations useful," said Citizens Advisory Committee Chairman Fred R. Williams. "Our thorough examination should assist the Council in producing an effective ordinance."

"One of the most enjoyable (as well as productive) aspects of our meetings was our ability to sincerely listen to each other's point of view, and I think we all learned from each other," he added.

11

■ Wear light-colored clothing or reflective tape so you can be seen after dark.

■ Carry a flashlight for visibility and to light your path. Walk on sidewalks, not in the roadway.

■ Wear makeup instead of a mask for better vision.

■ Avoid long costumes that may cause you to trip or fall. Wear fire-proof costumes.

■ When trick or treating with friends, tell your parents where you plan to go and do not change your route. Return home on time.

■ Visit only familiar neighborhoods.

■ Only go to homes with the porch light on.

■ Before eating any candy, let Mom or Dad check it. Do not eat anything that appears tampered with! These should be immediately turned over to the police with the address where they were offered.

Reminder: The maximum age for a child to trick or treat is 12. The trick or treating curfew is 10 p.m.

The 23rd annual Leesburg Kiwanis Halloween Parade (longest-running parade east of the Mississippi) will begin at 6:15 p.m. at the corner of King and North streets and end at Market Station, where Leesburg's Parks and Recreation Department will have plenty of fun in store. Have a happy and safe Halloween.

Going, Going... Gone

Auctioneer Craig Damewood (second from left) works his way through a row of abandoned bicycles during the town's annual sale of surplus and unclaimed property held on October 4 at the public works facility. Twenty-six bidders registered for the auction, which netted $2,849 for the town. The bicycles sold for $2 to $25.

13

Add Pizzazz With Line and Color

Newsletter Trends features a new look each month. Each issue, however, sticks to proven typographic rules, such as serif body copy and down-style headlines. In the three nameplates above, the designer keeps the typeface and sizes consistent for the titles, using ink color, paper color and rules to create variety. The March issue is all black; the May nameplate is reversed out of blue; and the April nameplate is printed black between violet rules on light violet paper. Using screen tints and different colors of paper, the designer generates a wide color palette for each issue from only two ink colors.

Name *Newsletter Trends*

Publisher *Sterling Communications, Inc., Toronto, ON*

Purpose/audience *Service to subscribers*

Production *QuarkXPress on Macintosh*

Printing *Varies from issue to issue*

Format *8¹/₂-by-11 inches, eight pages*

Design *Barbara A. Fanson*

Manipulating Graphics

In these three issues, Barbara Fanson manipulates rules, type and color to produce different graphic effects. February and June rely on strong horizontal rules, while August uses fine, floating rules between columns and a light rule to enclose all the copy.

Trends

Vol. 1, No. 2   *The newsletter about newsletters*   February 1991

How to survive during the recession

By Barbara A. Fanson
There are certain traditional patterns that accompany a downturn in the business cycle. Companies may cut back on general expenses such as advertising, marketing and training.

Employers often look at departments that do not directly impact the bottom line. Unfortunately, newsletters may be their target.

But there are ways to survive. Here are some suggestions to reduce costs without sacrificing the quality of your publication.

existing clients or new business efforts.
Discounts
• Take advantage of suppliers' discounts.
• Offer clients a discount upon prompt payment.
• Stay on top of accounts receivable by telephoning outstanding accounts frequently.
• Hire freelancers or temporary placement agencies instead of hiring new staff.

• Avoid making capital expenditures and incurring long-term debts during the recession.
• If you have a subscription newsletter, try new tactics for renewing subscriptions.
• Determine your most effective promotional and informational campaigns.
• Initiate a productivity drive to increase efficiency.
• Implement suggestions and you'll survive this recession.

Adding color without adding expense

f a large block of color for a special effect. **Make certain that your type is large enough and will not fill in when reversed.**

By having bold, dark type and grey body text, you can achieve various colors or shades of black.

Thick and thin rules can also create the same impression. Thick black rules are dark and add graphic appeal to a layout.

There are many graphic tools available, but don't overdo it.

Inside

NEWSLETTER TRENDS
A newsletter about newsletters

Volume 1, Number 8   August 1991

Seminars can provide editorial material

Attending an industry seminar or presentation can provide excellent material for your next newsletter, especially if you can obtain a quotation from one of the guest speakers or promoters. Best of all, most seminars have a showguide or course manual to assist in writing the story.

In recent editions of *Newsletter Trends*, guest speakers and industry events have been covered to provide readers with information they may have missed.

Your newsletter may include details of training or night courses related to your industry. Perhaps the instructor will provide a quotation on a related topic. If you hear a presentation on advertising, and you happen to be in the automobile industry, you could ask the

speaker for a view on upcoming trends in car advertising, or which method of promotion is best for automobiles.

Sometimes, an article idea may come from the unlikeliest places or at the most awkward of times. A trade publication

may have a story of interest to your readers; you could use the article as a guide or ask for permission to reprint it.

The front page will determine

Portable computer sales increase

Portable computer sales accounted for over 14 per cent of the total PC market in 1989 and by the end of 1991, they are expected to account for over $996 million in revenues, according to Evans Research Corp.

NEWSLETTER Trends

Volume 1, Number 6   A newsletter about newsletters   June 1991

Ergonomics at Work

Comfortable work space helps eliminate fatigue and may increase productivity

In the last few years, computers have evolutionized the newsletter publishing industry. Computers have proven to be fast and efficient at providing solutions.

Safety and health hazards related to computer usage must also be addressed. Many companies obtain quotations and

service contracts for software and hardware equipment, but is the furniture adaptability equally investigated?

Ergonomics is defined as fitting the workplace and the job design to the characteristics, abilities and limitations of human beings. Here are some guidelines for maximizing your comfort:

• top surface of the space bar on the keyboard should be no higher than 2.5 inches above the work space.
• while keying, the forearm and upper arm should form an angle of 80 to 100 degrees, the upper arm almost vertical.
• the wrist should be relaxed and not bent. Wrist rests are recommended if the wrist is not supported.
• keyboard should be directly in front of the operator.
• keyboard should be detachable.
• leave a large area free for documents and other work materials.
• use an adjustable copy stand or document holder. Place it next to the screen, at the same height.
• change the copy stand from one side of the screen to the other side periodically, so that some neck muscles are not overused. If you do a lot of typing, the copy stand should be directly in front of you, with the screen off to the side. This may reduce neck strain and pain.
• top of screen should be eye level.

Ergonomics in the workplace will help reduce fatigue, injuries, eye strain, and perhaps, absenteeism.

Illustration by Drummond Hayes

In this issue
2 The Write Side of the Brain
Don't get stuck in 5 W's rut
3 Designing with DTP
All type must be legible
5 Graphic Tips & Techniques
Initial caps for attention
6 Copyright Protection
Protecting your newsletter

Using Subtle Graphics to Enhance

Graphics are often very subtle for the enjoyment of readers and the amusement of designers. This designer's favorite touch is the screw top that holds down the nameplate, standing headlines and rules at the top and bottom. Mine is the desktop pattern behind the photo. Positioning a photo at an angle always invites a close look.

Name Newsletter Nameplate

Publisher Ruddle and Associates Publishing, Milpitas, CA

Purpose/audience Service and marketing to clients

Production PageMaker and CorelDRAW on IBM

Printing Black and burgundy on light gray offset paper

Format 8¹/₂-by-11 inches, eight pages

Design Henry Ruddle

Award Newsletter Clearinghouse

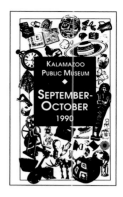

SATURDAY SPECIALS

Nanabozho!

The legends of Nanabozho, playful god of Great Lakes Indian tribes, come alive in a performance by the String Puppet Theatre marionettes. The String Puppet Theatre combines hand-carved wooden marionettes, colorful costumes, and hand-painted scenery to recreate the ancient Nanabozho legends. The afternoon will provide an entertaining glimpse of Indian legends and the art of puppetry. **Saturday, September 22, 2:00 p.m.**

Festival of Indonesia: Sounds of the Gamelan

Celebrate the culture of Indonesia and the opening of the new traveling exhibit **Song of Bali** with a very special presentation by the University of Michigan Gamelan Ensemble. Composed of unusual string and percussion instruments, the gamelan will perform the music of Central Java. A solo female singer and a male chorus accompanies the gamelan. Well-known throughout the United States, the University of Michigan Gamelan Ensemble is one of the few performing gamelans in the midwest. Their performance at the Public Museum is funded by a grant from the Irving S. Gilmore Foundation. Join us to learn about the musical traditions of Java and then enjoy special

refreshments from Indonesia.
Saturday, October 13, 2:00 p.m.

Festival of Indonesia: Traditional Arts

The music, dance, puppetry, and folk art traditions of Indonesia are among the richest in the world. You're invited to explore the culture "up close" with many hands-on activities. Make shadow puppets, costumes for dance, traditional games and masks. A special hour-long film, **Miracle of Bali: Midday Sun**, tracing gamelan, dance, mask-making and religious traditions, will be shown at 2:30 p.m.
Saturday, October 27, 2-4 p.m.

EXHIBITS

Song of Bali

The Public Museum celebrates Indonesia's diverse cultural heritage with **Song of Bali**, toured by Exhibits USA, a national division of Mid-America Arts Alliance. Planned in honor of the year-long Festival of Indonesia, **Song of Bali** portrays the richness and complexity of traditional Balinese life through more than a hundred artifacts. Dance costumes and textiles, baskets, musical instruments and elaborate puppets are included. Balinese masks, used by dancers in festival and ritual celebrations, are an important feature of the exhibit. Browse through **Song of Bali**, and catch a glimpse of the mystery and magic that is Indonesia.
September 22 - January 13

Faces of Kalamazoo: Portraits from the Collection

Sarah Austin, Bazel Harrison, and Dr. Augustus Crane all shared in the life and history of the Kalamazoo area. Their portraits and others, painted from the mid-19th to well into the 20th century, present a very personal view of the people of this community. Selected from the Public Museum's collection, **Faces of Kalamazoo** includes work by Benjamin Cooley and W. W. Gibbs. Join us to see the faces of Kalamazoo through an artist's eyes.
September 15-January 6

MUSEUM ADVENTURES

Museum Adventures provide hands-on learning experiences for preschoolers and their parents. Class size is limited to 15 preschoolers (accompanied by a parent) who are at least three years of age. **Adventures** are free to residents of the Kalamazoo School District, and $1 per preschooler for non-residents. You must pre-register to attend, and may do so by calling the museum at 345-7092. The **Adventure** for October is:

A Potawatomi Day

Preschoolers explore daily life among the Potawatomi of Southwest Michigan, and learn about Indian villages, homes, customs, and food. Hands-on activities include using traditional games, toys, and tools, musical instruments and more.
Friday, October 19, 10-10:45 a.m.

PLANETARIUM

Haunted Skies

Are the skies haunted? Do we see objects in the night sky that aren't really there? This planetarium program especially for children, explores visible objects in space that are "almost nothing at all." Learn about nebulae, the tails of comets and aurorae.
Saturday and Sunday at 1:30 p.m
Free admission

Stargazing

Learn about the stars, constellations and planets visible in the early autumn skies over Kalamazoo. A free monthly star chart will help you identify stars when you go home.
Wednesday at 7:00 p.m.
Saturday and Sunday at 2:30 p.m.
Free admission

Life Beyond Earth

Are we alone in the cosmos or is the

Islands in the Sky

Follow the paths of early oceanic navigators as they traveled thousands of miles across the Pacific in tiny canoes. A detailed knowledge of the sun, wind and ocean currents, and the practical use of the stars as a compass, guided these early travelers on their incredible migration throughout the Pacific. This multi-media planetarium program takes us along on a colorful, exciting journey through the islands of the Pacific.
Wednesday at 8:00 p.m.
Saturday and Sunday at 3:30 p.m.
(October only)
Admission charge

MUSEUM NEWS

Are you on our mailing list? Each year, the museum distributes the September/October brochure through the schools in the Kalamazoo area in hopes of making families aware of the museum programs and resources. If you would like to receive the bimonthly brochure in your home, please fill out the form below and return it to the Interpretation Department, Kalamazoo Public Museum, 315 S. Rose, Kalamazoo, Michigan, 49007.

Volunteers are an important part of the museum... a week... collecti... assist... you ca... tion ab... Public... Jennes...

Be su...

to see the new fall selection of gifts from around the world. For your convenience, the...

KALAMAZOO PUBLIC MUSEUM

315 South Rose Street
Kalamazoo, MI 49007

Hours:
9-5 Tuesday through Saturday
9-9 Wednesday
1-5 Sunday
Closed Monday

Phone:
616/345-7092
24-hour information line:
382-MUSE

Nonprofit Org.
U.S. Postage
PAID
Kalamazoo, MI
Permit No. 1425

Song of Bali

September 22-
January 13

Photos as Graphics

Each issue of news from the Kalamazoo Public Museum uses a different vibrant ink color and features an image from the current exhibit on the address panel. The three-fold format splits information up into boxed material two columns wide. Heavy rules around each box of text become bars from which to reverse the standing headlines. Equally important, the finished size mails for letter rate, not the rate for flats that applies to 8½-by-11-inch publications.

Name *Kalamazoo Museum*

Publisher *Kalamazoo Public Museum, Kalamazoo, MI*

Purpose/audience *Members and friends of the museum*

Production *PageMaker and FreeHand on Macintosh SE using Radius two-page monitor*

Printing *Black and a second color on white gloss-coated paper*

Format *5½-by-9½ inches, six-panel foldout*

Design *Jean Stevens*

Capturing a Look With Graphics

FM's new nameplate makes a statement with simple, bold typography reversed out of a 40 percent screen of black. The second color is gold, used at 100 percent in the nameplate, screen tints and initial caps. With a trim size of 11-by-14 inches, the overall effect of this design is the look of a newspaper—exactly what the designer wanted.

Name *Financial Marketing*

Publisher *Financial Institutions Marketing Association, Chicago, IL*

Purpose/audience *Service to members*

Production *PageMaker on Macintosh IIci*

Printing *Black and gold on gloss-coated paper*

Format *11-by-14 inches, twelve pages*

Design *The Newsletter Group, Inc.*

(Sample newsletter — September–October 1991, Volume 27, Number 5)

Financial Marketing
Published by Financial Institutions Marketing Association

New Services, New 'Look' Highlight 'New' FIMA

Home Equity Loans: Everybody Wins

(Sample newsletter — July-August 1991, Volume 27, Number 4)

Financial Marketing

Savings, Like Politics, Is Ultimately Local

FIMA, AMA To Form New Alliance

Drogos   *Heilbrunn*

Time to Re-price the Passbook?...

New Logo Gives New FIMA A New Look

FIMA's new logo has been created to give the "new" FIMA a new bold visual identity to reflect the new products and services being created for its enhanced value membership.

Emphasizing the words "FIMA" and "Marketing," the new logo also incorporates a bar graph inside the FIMA "I" that is intended to demonstrate the new FIMA's positive outlook toward itself and the financial services industry.

"The design is simple and strong," said Thomas M. Drogos, FIMA president. "It communicates who we are. By itself, the new logo is little more than a promise of things to come. But we expect it to come to reflect the 'added value' we are building into FIMA membership."

Inside *Communiqué*

Coming in January

How much do you weigh? How much would you like to weigh? How much should you weigh? With holidays past and resolutions still intact, our article on **healthy weight** explains why you shouldn't take weight charts too seriously. **Burning feet** is a common complaint. We'll address causes and offer self-help measures.

mayo

Keep Tables of Contents Simple

The table of contents, sometimes called the index, is a thumbnail review of what readers will find inside the newsletter. Always placed on the front page, this element shows names and page numbers.

Design elements, such as rules, a screen tint or a reverse, help readers distinguish the contents box from other items on the front page. Keep the information very simple to ensure that readers take time to grasp its meaning.

Chapter 4

Illustrations

esigners and editors use illustrations in newsletters to touch emotions, establish an overall image and convey information. Clip art and infographics are two common types of newsletter illustrations.

• *Clip art*, a popular form of illustration, was first developed for display advertising in newspapers, not for accompanying editorial matter in newsletters. Used sparingly and placed carefully, clip art can enhance writing. Several newsletters in the following pages reveal expert use of clip art. Desktop publishing software can enable you to transform clip art into unique images, using the original art only as a starting point. Many illustrations in this section reveal that capability, redefining the meaning of art and the function of the artist.

• *Infographics* are the most important form of illustration for newsletters. Charts, maps and diagrams portray key data far more efficiently and memorably than verbal descriptions can. Infographics in the following pages show the influence of newspaper design and the skills that many newsletter editors have with slides, flip charts and other media useful for business presentations.

SMOKE GETS IN YOUR EYES -- AND LUNGS

Call it what you will: second-hand smoke or passive smoke. The smoke puffed into the air by cigar, pipe and cigarette smokers hits kids the hardest.

Because youngsters breathe in more air for their body weight than adults do, they can be especially susceptible to diseases caused by second-hand smoke, according to Joel M. Seidman, M.D., chief of Pulmonary Medicine at Memorial.

Dr. Seidman conducts annual anti-smoking programs for youngsters in local schools and has spoken before the Westborough School Committee on the benefits of smoke-free schools.

It's a sensitive issue, Dr. Seidman acknowledges, but adds, "Last year, 600,000 Americans died from smoking-related illnesses. For every pack of cigarettes sold, it cost the taxpayer $2.17 for medical care."

Dr. Seidman urges that it's time to clear the air -- and schools are an excellent place to start. Today's children face a number of health risks from exposure to second-hand smoke, and the truth about the diseases and complications that can result are frightening--

* Toxic effects of passive smoke are transmitted to unborn children by *both* parents. A pregnant woman who smokes passes toxic chemicals directly through her bloodstream to the fetus, which can result in low birth-weight, congenital malfor-

As a leader in health care, The Medical Center of Central Massachusetts seeks a healthy environment for all patients, visitors, employees, staff members, volunteers and students, and has become "smoke free" as of 1990. Smoking is the leading preventable cause of death and disease in America, and a fire and safety hazard. Smoking is recognized as having potentially damaging effects not only to the smoker but to those exposed to tobacco smoke.

To learn more about smoking cessation classes, call Public Relations, 792-8587.

mations and even death. A man who smokes in the presence of his pregnant partner (even if she *doesn't* smoke) also increases these risks.

* Mothers who smoke have a greater negative effect on the health of their children than fathers who smoke because they generally spend more time together.

* There is a strong correlation between children under the age of two hospitalized for pneumonia and the number of smokers in a household.

* Children exposed to second-hand smoke experience a higher number of chest illnesses (pneumonia, bronchitis and other respiratory tract diseases) than children in non-smoking households.

* Exposure to passive smoke negatively affects a child's normal pulmonary function, increasing

wheezing, allergies to smoke and aggravating already existing conditions such as asthma.

* Children of a parent who smokes have been found to have more colds than those who live with non-smokers, which often results in more missed school days.

* Up to 36% of middle ear infections in children four years old and younger are attributed to passive smoke exposure.

Let's clear the air and do something about passive smoking -- before our children's health goes up in smoke.

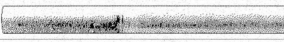

3

Art That Enhances News

In a perfect blend of size and placement, the drawing of the cigarette enhances the story and helps frame the page. Letting the smoke drift up into the rule and type puts action into the art—and leads the eye right to the sidebar that invites readers to learn how to quit smoking. Notice also the headline type that uses large and small caps to create a sophisticated look.

Name *Progress Notes*

Publisher *The Medical Center of Central Massachusetts, Worcester, MA*

Purpose/audience *Service to the community and the media*

Production *PageMaker on Macintosh*

Printing *Green preprinted and black on light gray offset paper with green tinted fibers*

Format *8½-by-11 inches, four pages*

Design *Susan Rich and Ann Godd*

Award *American Society for Health Care Marketing and Public Relations*

58 *Newsletter Sourcebook*

Visuals That "Sing"

Weaving small illustrations throughout text helps break up type as well as convey information, especially when the subject matter is technical. The navy blue and dark salmon-colored inks sing on the felt-textured cream paper, giving the entire publication a rich feel.

Name *Seafood Source*

Publisher *National Fisheries Institute, Arlington, VA*

Purpose/audience *Service to press and educators*

Production *Ventura Publisher on IBM*

Printing *Blue and red on ivory felt text paper*

Format *8½-by-11 inches, eight pages*

Design *Emily Holt and Susan Cole*

Award *American Society of Association Executives*

SEAFOOD SOURCE

SEAFOOD: THE RAW FACTS

by Anne Fletcher, M.S., R.D.

Page 2

Continued from page 1.

tle, WA says, "cooking fish to an internal temperature of 145 degrees F and/or until it loses its translucence and flakes easily is adequate." (When microwaving fish, be sure that all sections are thoroughly cooked. Refer to page 4 for the feature on microwaving.) Marinating, on the other hand, will not destroy parasites if they are present.

Consumers who are uncertain about the possibility of parasites in seafood need to understand that if fish is properly frozen or cooked, the risk is of no concern. Furthermore, the risk of parasites exists in other types of food. For example, over the years consumers have become accustomed to cooking pork until it is well done to reduce the risk of infection by the trichinae worm.

Molluscan Shellfish

Mollusks -- clams, oysters, mussels and scallops -- are filter feeders which process large quantities of water in their quest for food and oxygen. As a result, these bivalves, as they are also known, can pick up and harbor illness-causing bacteria and viruses which are present when the shellfish are harvested (illegally) from polluted waters closed to commercial fishing. Adequately cooking

molluscan shellfish renders any present bacteria and viruses harmless.

One way to increase the likelihood that oysters and clams are safe for raw consumption is to make certain that they were harvested from

clean waters approved by state authorities. "That way, raw oysters and clams are quite safe products for healthy people," asserts Dr. Gary Rodrick, a shellfish microbiologist at the University of Florida.

High Risk Individuals

Individuals with chronic liver disease or compromised immune systems should avoid consuming raw or partially cooked molluscan shellfish. The FDA has advised that a common saltwater microorganism, *Vibrio vulnificus*, carried at times by oysters, especially in summer months from the warm waters of the South Atlantic and Gulf of Mexico, can be the cause of severe illness and possible death for individuals with such medical conditions as:

* AIDS
* Liver disease, including cirrhosis and hemochromatosis;
* Chronic alcohol abuse;
* Cancer (especially if taking anti-cancer drugs or radiation treatment)
* Diabetes mellitus;
* Chronic kidney disease;
* Inflammatory bowel disease (or any person receiving immunosuppressive drugs);
* Steroid dependency (for conditions such as chronic obstructive pulmonary disease);
* Achlorhydria (a condition in which the normal acidity of the stomach is reduced or absent).

Similarly, small children, pregnant women, elderly consumers and transplant recipients should eat molluscan shellfish that has been fully cooked.

Adequate cooking means heating the shellfish until it is piping hot, ideally when it reaches an internal temperature of 145 degrees F. Dr. Herbert DuPont, an expert on infectious diseases at the University of Texas Health Science Center recommends steaming clams and oysters for four to six minutes (after the water returns to a boil) to inactivate harmful microorganisms.

Educational efforts to teach "at risk" populations and the medical community about the potential health hazards of *V. vulnificus* are underway. The Molluscan Shellfish Education Task Force, a coalition consisting of the Interstate Shellfish Sanitation Conference, Florida Department of Natural Resources, Louisiana Seafood Promotions & Marketing Board, Pacific Coast Oyster Growers Association, New England Fisheries Development Association, Virginia Marine Products Board, the National Fisheries Institute, American Seafood Institute, the National Marine Fisheries Service, Bon Secour Fisheries, W.F. Morgan & Sons, and the University of Florida Institute of Food and Agricultural Sciences, formed last April to alert the public about potentially dangerous exposures to *V. vulnificus*.

For more information write: Molluscan Shellfish Education Task Force, c/o NFI Communications, 1525 Wilson Blvd., Ste 500, Arlington, VA 22209.

Using Pictures Big

Running an illustration very large as the visual focus of the page makes the illustration serve as a second headline. Three questions above the illustration, set similar to pull quotes, pull readers into the story and tell them exactly what to expect from the article. The heavy rule above the headline and the doctor's bag are printed in blue, while the headline is printed from overlapping screens of blue and black.

Name *Planning for Health*

Publisher *Kaiser Permanente, Washington, D.C.*

Purpose/audience *Service to members*

Production *By hand*

Printing *Black and blue on white offset paper*

Format *8¹/₂-by-11 inches, sixteen pages*

Design *Harry Knox*

Awards *Communication Concepts, Healthcare Marketing Report*

Recruiting Quality Physicians

by William J. McAveney, M.D.

Only one out of every eight physicians who apply are invited to join the Capital Area Permanente Medical Group (CAPMG), the group of physicians who provide your medical care at Kaiser Permanente.

Every year, our office receives hundreds of applications from physicians interested in joining our practice. These physicians are attracted to the Medical Group for many reasons including our reputation for quality, the ability to work directly with specialists, and our location in the Washington-Baltimore area.

Maintaining the high standards of our medical group is vitally important to us. All physician applicants are interviewed and their credentials are carefully evaluated by physician managers knowledgeable about their medical specialties, training and related medical activities.

In order to be considered for a full-time position with the Capital Area Permanente Medical Group (CAPMG), a physician must at least meet the following criteria:
* graduate of an accredited medical school

How much do you know about the physicians who care for you?
•
What are their credentials?
•
Why do they join us?

* either board certified in their specialty or eligible to take the board examination (e.g. physicians who have just finished residency training)
* technical proficiency and knowledge, ethical values, and the ability to work well in a group practice

All applicants' credentials are reviewed through the American Medical Association master file. There is also a detailed inquiry into past training and experience, at least three letters of references, as well as telephone reference checks. We may also speak to chiefs of service, former or present partners, and/or peers. We will also check with our other Regions if an applicant indicates prior experience with Kaiser Permanente. In addition we use the states' licensing processes which provides a further review of credentials.

As soon as data is available, we will routinely inquire into the National Practitioner Data Bank for physicians, which is expected to be available this year. The Bank was developed to reduce the number of physicians who move from state to state to escape previous histories of malpractice and licensure sanctions.

Each applicant's final acceptance by the medical group is contingent upon successful credentialling. This process includes licensing by the state's board of medical examiners and obtaining privileges at the community hospitals we use. During the hospital credentialling process, the applicant's training and previous work experience is once again meticulously and thoroughly examined.

After the physicians are hired, they then go through an intensive orientation. Physicians must meet all requirements before seeing their first patients. We are proud of our highly committed physicians and the excellent care they provide to you, members of Kaiser Permanente.

William J. McAveney, M.D., is an associate medical director of the Capital Area Permanente Medical Group. He is a board certified pediatrician.

3

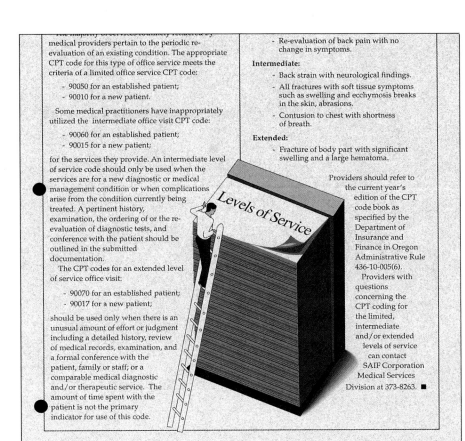

The majority of services routinely rendered by medical providers pertain to the periodic re-evaluation of an existing condition. The appropriate CPT code for this type of office service meets the criteria of a limited office service CPT code:

- 90050 for an established patient;
- 90010 for a new patient.

Some medical practitioners have inappropriately utilized the intermediate office visit CPT code:

- 90060 for an established patient;
- 90015 for a new patient;

for the services they provide. An intermediate level of service code should only be used when the services are for a new diagnostic or medical management condition or when complications arise from the condition currently being treated. A pertinent history, examination, the ordering of or the re-evaluation of diagnostic tests, and conference with the patient should be outlined in the submitted documentation.

The CPT codes for an extended level of service office visit:

- 90070 for an established patient;
- 90017 for a new patient;

should be used only when there is an unusual amount of effort or judgment including a detailed history, review of medical records, examination, and a formal conference with the patient, family or staff; or a comparable medical diagnostic and/or therapeutic service. The amount of time spent with the patient is not the primary indicator for use of this code.

- Re-evaluation of back pain with no change in symptoms.

Intermediate:
- Back strain with neurological findings.
- All fractures with soft tissue symptoms such as swelling and ecchymosis breaks in the skin, abrasions.
- Contusion to chest with shortness of breath.

Extended:
- Fracture of body part with significant swelling and a large hematoma.

Providers should refer to the current year's edition of the CPT code book as specified by the Department of Insurance and Finance in Oregon Administrative Rule 436-10-005(6).

Providers with questions concerning the CPT coding for the limited, intermediate and/or extended levels of service can contact SAIF Corporation Medical Services Division at 373-8263. ∎

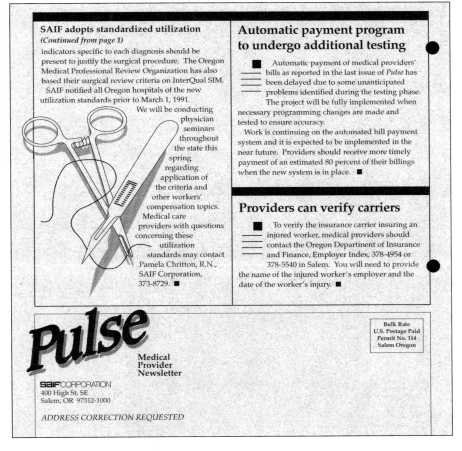

SAIF adopts standardized utilization
(Continued from page 1)

indicators specific to each diagnosis should be present to justify the surgical procedure. The Oregon Medical Professional Review Organization has also based their surgical review criteria on InterQual SIM. SAIF notified all Oregon hospitals of the new utilization standards prior to March 1, 1991.

We will be conducting physician seminars throughout the state this spring regarding application of the criteria and other workers' compensation topics. Medical care providers with questions concerning these utilization standards may contact Pamela Chritton, R.N., SAIF Corporation, 373-8729. ∎

Automatic payment program to undergo additional testing

∎ Automatic payment of medical providers' bills as reported in the last issue of *Pulse* has been delayed due to some unanticipated problems identified during the testing phase. The project will be fully implemented when necessary programming changes are made and tested to ensure accuracy.

Work is continuing on the automated bill payment system and it is expected to be implemented in the near future. Providers should receive more timely payment of an estimated 80 percent of their billings when the new system is in place. ∎

Providers can verify carriers

∎ To verify the insurance carrier insuring an injured worker, medical providers should contact the Oregon Department of Insurance and Finance, Employer Index, 378-4954 or 378-5540 in Salem. You will need to provide the name of the injured worker's employer and the date of the worker's injury. ∎

Pulse

Medical Provider Newsletter

SAIF CORPORATION
400 High St. SE
Salem, OR 97312-1000

Bulk Rate
U.S. Postage Paid
Permit No. 114
Salem Oregon

ADDRESS CORRECTION REQUESTED

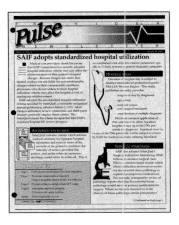

Using Infographics

Illustrations built directly into text may become infographics. The designer keeps these drawings tightly associated with the copy by running them in the same ink color as that used for type — dark jade ink on light green paper. The dark ink works beautifully and inexpensively!

Name *Pulse*

Publisher *SAIF Corporation, Salem, OR*

Purpose/audience *Service to customers*

Production *QuarkXPress and Illustrator on Macintosh IIcx*

Printing *Dark jade on light green offset paper*

Format *8½-by-11 inches, four pages*

Design *Lisa A. Taaffe and Ann Grim*

Award *International Association of Business Communicators*

Better Charts, Graphs and Diagrams

When possible, readers expect data to be presented as charts, graphs or diagrams. These pages show two styles and placements. Infographics with type running around them, as shown here, link to their supporting articles. The drop shadow behind the chart on page one makes the box protrude into the article.

Name *Wine Institute News*

Publisher *Wine Institute, San Francisco, CA*

Purpose/audience *Service to members*

Production *PageMaker on IBM*

Printing *Black and burgundy on white offset paper*

Format *8¹/₂-by-11 inches, twelve pages*

Design *Jim Ales and Mark Stuertz*

Award *American Society of Association Executives*

Grape Crop Forecast: Whites up, Reds Below Normal

California Agricultural Statistics Service forecasts place the California wine grape crop at 2.15 million tons this year, about the same level as the average annual crop of 2.11 million tons during the 1986-1989 period.

From 1940 to 1970, the California wine grape crop averaged 590,000 tons per year. But during the past two decades, the crop has increased dramatically, topping the one-million-ton mark in 1973, the 1.5-million-ton mark in 1977, and the two-million-ton mark in 1980.

Early field reports show heavy sets for white varieties, which suggests that, given favorable weather during the remainder of the year, Colombard, Chenin Blanc, and Chardonnay crops will be relatively heavy. It is unlikely that the Chardonnay crop will approach the incredible 5.03-ton-per-acre average of 1989, but with

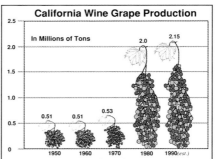

new acreage coming on line, a four-ton-per-acre performance would result in a Chardonnay crush of about 150,000 tons.

Preliminary reports indicate key red varieties have relatively light sets this year. Zinfandel yields are expected to be down, and North Coast Cabernet Sauvignon and Merlot bunches are on the light side. Nevertheless, the increase in bearing acreage of the three red varieties (+ 10,000 acres since 1985) will partially compensate for the predicted below-normal yields.

Correction
In the July Economic Report (page 3), first quarter wine sale import figures for 1989 and 1990 are reversed in the graph. Imports for 1990 should read 14 million gallons and imports for 1989 should read 15 million gallons.

Application Process for 1991 TEA Program Concluding

The Foreign Agricultural Service (FAS) has announced the 1991 TEA program and is accepting proposals with the understanding that program

commodities to help offset the adverse effects of unfair trade practices such as quotas and subsidies.

advertising, participation fees for non-government sponsored trade shows and in-store promotions.
Applications for the TEA

1990 Crush Totals Register Slips in Tonnage, Value

California's 1990 grape crush totalled 2.6 million tons, a 5 percent drop from 1989 figures, according to final data from the California Department of Food and Agriculture. The value of the crush also took a dip, slipping 12 percent: from $809 million in 1989 to last year's $708 million, as prices for almost all varieties declined. However, compared to just a few years ago, the crush value remained relatively high topping 1985's $452 million total by 57 percent.

The complexion of the crush total reflects the surging varietal growth that has characterized the California wine market over the past decade. Chardon-

Last year, the combined crush value of Chardonnay and Cabernet Sauvignon grapes reached $283 million, or 40 percent of the value of all varieties crushed. In 1980, the combined value of these two varieties represented just 10 percent of the total value.

While the market for grape varieties such as Char-

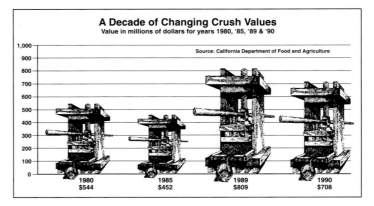

donnay and Cabernet Sauvignon has been strong over the past decade, the demand for other varieties has declined significantly.

In 1980, 185,000 tons of Carignane grapes were crushed compared to only 83,000 in 1990. During the same years, the crush of Rubired fell from 108,000 to

SAM STATS

A look at statistics that shape our industry.

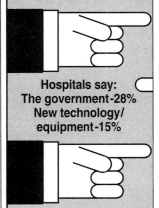

POINTING THE FINGER

Who is the most responsible for
the high cost of health care?

Hospitals say:
The government-28%
New technology/
equipment-15%

Source: National Research Corp. su...

SAM STATS

A look at statistics that shape quality patient care.

KEEP IT CLEAN

DSMC's Mater-
ials Manage-
ment dept.
sterilized more
than **9,937**
instrument
sets, single
instruments &
other sterile
items in

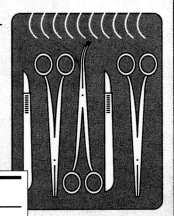

...gement

SAM STATS

A look at statistics that shape giving.

TREE OF LIFE
KEEPS ON GROWING
& GIV...

Since it's dedication
Good Samaritan's 75th
bration, the medical ce
has raised **$45,072**
the sale of gold and sil
to fund community edu
programs, hospital p
Samaritan Safe Sitte
Poison Prevention for
& continuing educ

Source: GSRMC Gift Development

SAM STATS

A look at statistics that shape aquatic therapy.

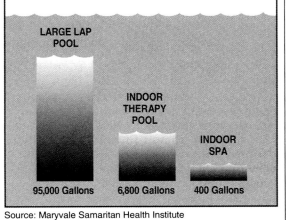

AQUATIC THERAPY POOLS & SPA

Maryvale Samaritan's Health Institute's indoor therapy pool,
spa and outdoor lap pool provide unique therapy programs
and community exercise classes to West Valley residents.

**LARGE LAP
POOL**

**INDOOR
THERAPY
POOL**

**INDOOR
SPA**

95,000 Gallons   6,800 Gallons   400 Gallons

Source: Maryvale Samaritan Health Institute

Featuring Bite-Size Data

The Sam Stats infographics that
appear throughout the publication
present morsels of data that readers
might not otherwise ingest. Giving
each a subhead helps introduce the
data and invites readers to inspect
the visual. Using only black ink with
screen tints is economical as well as
effective.

Name *Samaritan Today*

Publisher *Samaritan Health Services, Phoenix, AZ*

Purpose/audience *Service to members*

Production *PageMaker and FreeHand on Macintosh*

Printing *Black on white offset paper*

Format *11-by-17 inches, eight pages*

Design *Dona Shaver*

President's Christmas Message

Special holiday greetings to each of you and your families.

The thought occurs to me this Christmas season...wouldn't Mr. J.J. and Mr. Clarence Haverty be pleased to see what has grown from a humble start 104 years ago. They would be very proud to know the fine group of

friends and associates who are working together to carry on their endeavors.

Our Christmas wish for all of you is that we remain close and strong in our affections for one another and that we always remember the importance of each individual toward making our company great.

We hope that all of you spend a

happy and pleasant Christmas with your families and friends and use this great holiday enthusiasm to create many happy memories.

Christmas is a festival, so let's celebrate the birth of Christ and the love that he taught us all.

From all of us here, to all of you, a Merry Christmas and a Happy Holiday.

Frank S. McGaughey

Bigger Can Be Better

When the image tells the story or creates the mood, run it big. This bold approach captures the feeling of the season and leaves just the right amount of room for a holiday greeting.

Name *Half Hour*

Publisher *Haverty Furniture Companies, Inc., Atlanta, GA*

Purpose/audience *Service to employees*

Production *PageMaker on Macintosh*

Printing *Black and red on white matte-coated paper*

Format *8 1/2-by-11 inches, sixteen pages*

Design *Phil Knox*

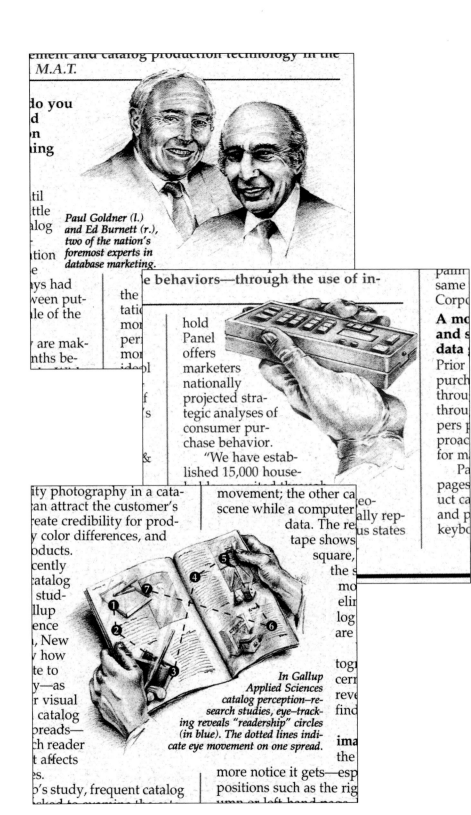

Paul Goldner (l.) and Ed Burnett (r.), two of the nation's foremost experts in database marketing.

In Gallup Applied Sciences catalog perception–research studies, eye–tracking reveals "readership" circles (in blue). The dotted lines indicate eye movement on one spread.

Matching Art and Paper

Aiming at executives in the graphic arts, the designer used a high budget for top quality paper instead of four-color printing. The design takes full advantage of the lavish surface and color of the felt text paper by substituting drawings for photos, letting the surface of the paper add dimension to the images. Dark blue ink in the nameplate, headlines and drop caps contribute to a corporate look and are balanced by the pencil drawings that make the feel of the newsletter informal.

Name *Merchandising Advertising Technology*
Publisher *Bestinfo, Inc., Media, PA*
Purpose/audience *Service to customers*
Production *Bestinfo software on IBM*
Printing *Black and dark blue on light gray felt text paper*
Format *8½-by-11 inches, eight pages*
Design *Steve Smith and Jim Morris-Lee*

Tattered Cover

2955 EAST FIRST AVENUE • DENVER, COLORADO 80206 • 303-322-7727

The books pile up. . . . In the first ones, there were full moons, jasmine from the islands; the last ones are only solitudes: snow kingdoms, stirrings of reindeer.

Pablo Neruda
Fall 1990

The Tattered Cover Scary Story Contest

Children from kindergarten through tenth grade are invited to enter our Seventh Annual Scary Story Contest. The deadline for entries is Friday, October 5. First and Second Prizes will be awarded in six different grade categories. Each first prize consists of a $25 gift certificate. Each second prize consists of a $15 gift certificate. Complete contest rules are available in the children's section. Winners will be invited to read their stories at a special Halloween storytime on Saturday, October 27, at 10:30 a.m.

Books by Phone

Due to space restrictions, we are unable to include an order form in this issue of our

"Enemies of the Book," by Gustave Dore

Banned Books Week

Autographings and Events

Bach Among the Books

An ensemble from the Denver Chamber Orchestra will play for Tattered Cover browsers on the third floor at 7:30 p.m., Friday, November 9.

Colorado Cookie Tasting and Autographing Saturday, November 17

On Saturday, November 17, from 11:00 a.m. to 1:00 p.m., Cyndi Duncan and Georgie Patrick, authors of **Colorado Cookie Collection**, will offer a tasting of sweet treats from their superb new cookie book while signing copies for readers. Please join us for this delicious event.

Meet Miss Manners Tuesday, November 20

Judith Martin, a.k.a Miss Manners, is a syndicated newspaper columnist and a regular contributor to *Morning Edition* on National Public Radio. She is the author of **Miss Manners' Guide to Excruciatingly Correct Behavior** and **Miss Manners' Guide to Rearing Perfect Children**, among other books. We are pleased to welcome her to the Tattered Cover for an autographing of **Miss Manners' Guide for the Turn of the Millennium**, on Tuesday, November 20, at 5:30 p.m. If you are one of a multitude of Judith Martin fans, we encourage you to attend this more-than-polite affair.

All autographings and events are subject to unexpected changes beyond our control. Please feel free to call the Tattered Cover to confirm the date and time of the event that you plan to attend. We will be happy to update you.

The *Tattered Cover* newsletter is written and published by the Tattered Cover Book Store, Inc., Denver, CO. ©Copyright 1990. All rights reserved.
Editor-Illustrator: Patty Miller
Production Artist: Ann Martin

Coming Attractions

The Tattered Cover Book Club meets quarterly and is open to the public. The next gathering will be held on Monday, November 19, at 7 p.m. We will discuss the book, **From Beirut to Jerusalem**, by Thomas L. Friedman, available in paperback for $12.95. Join us on the third floor of our store in the autographings and events area. We look forward to seeing you.

The Third Annual Children's Bookmark Contest will take place after the holidays. Look for information and contest rules in our children's section beginning on January 15.

1990 Jewish Book Festival

The 1990 Jewish Book Festival, sponsored by the Tattered Cover and the Central Agency for Jewish Education, will begin on Sunday, November 11, and continue through Sunday, November 18, at the Jewish Community Center, 4800 East Alameda Avenue, in Denver. There will be an extensive bookstore, featuring a large selection of adult and children's Judaica as well as secular children's books. There will also be author lectures, autographings, and a cafe offering light snacks. Scheduled to appear are Eileen Bluestone Sherman, Ida Nudel, Martin Mayer, Ronit Lentin, Jerry Lande, Tom Teicholz, Marsha Kunstel, Peri Klass, Rabbi David Wolpe, Sharon Niederman and a number of local authors. For more information, please call 399-2660 or 871-3020.

Special Holiday Hours

Between December 1 and December 25, the Tattered Cover will observe the following holiday business hours:

Monday-Saturday	9:30-9:00
Sundays	noon-6:00
Christmas Eve	9:30-6:00
New Year's Eve	9:30-6:00

Mailing List Corrections

The quickest and most efficient way for us to record corrections on our mailing list is to use the address label from the newsletter(s) you received. The label contains a code number in the upper left corner which enables us to locate and eliminate any problems quickly.

If an error has been made regarding your mailing information, please send us the mailing label(s) you received, along with a notation indicating the required changes; or call and make your request by reading the code number to us over the phone. We will make every effort to adjust your file promptly. Thank you for your patience.

The next *Tattered Cover* newsletter will coincide with the spring publishing season, arriving in your mailbox by April 15, 1991. At that time, in an effort to do our part for the environment, the paper on which it is printed will be changed to a recycled stock.

Over fifty thousand new titles are published each year in this country alone, continually increasing the enormous wealth of ideas, information, and entertainment to which books give us ready access. While no bookstore in the world is large enough to house all manner of printed material, the Tattered Cover continues optimistically to push back its walls and make room for the ever-expanding universe of ideas. Thus we are pleased to announce our latest outgrowth: the lower level of our store is now open to provide more space for books and readers, strengthening the number of titles available throughout our four floors.

Being the "largest" bookstore is not our objective. We believe that every bookshop, large or small, is a place of supreme importance, where wisdom lives, history thrives and free-thinking flourishes. Each in its own way serves society and begs the patronage of all booklovers. Within that context, our aim is simply to be the best that we can be, doing more of what makes all good bookstores better: placing books in the hands of people, providing a broad selection, a helpful staff, room to browse, lamplight and comfortable chairs in which to linger over favorite volumes.

Since the Tattered Cover opened its doors in 1971, we have been fortunate in receiving the support of a vibrant reading community. It is your loyalty, high standards and hungry minds that have made it possible for us to grow and evolve from modest circumstances to an inventory of more than 136,000 titles and over 400,000 books. Our progress over the years speaks volumes to your generous support, and with renewed commitment to the Denver reading community, we express our heartfelt thanks.

Enclosed is a map of the Tattered Cover, reflecting the section changes that have taken place over the last few months, floor by floor. It also shows the newly expanded Bargain Books and Children's sections now residing on the lower level. Enlarged copies of this map are located at the registers for your convenience. We cordially invite you to visit our store this holiday season.

3

Using Standout Illustrations

Standout illustrations are wonderfully woven throughout the text columns, adding visual interest, and never overdone. Seasonal issues use a nature theme in the main heads. For more calendars, see pages 25-27 and 130-131.

Name *Tattered Cover*

Publisher *Tattered Cover Bookstore, Denver, CO*

Purpose/audience *Service to customers*

Production *PageMaker and CorelDRAW on IBM*

Printing *Black on cream offset paper*

Format *8¹/₂-by-11 inches, varies from eight to thirty-two pages*

Design *Patty Miller*

Mixing Illustration Styles

Using more than one style of illustration requires flexible design skills. Illustrations on the calendar for *Bank Notes* signal the eclectic range of events that appeal to an equally diverse audience. The contrast in styles is heightened by printing the masks and mortarboard in black and the jester in green.

Name *Bank Notes*

Publisher *Bank Street School for Children, New York, NY*

Purpose/audience *Service to parents and friends*

Production *PageMaker on Macintosh II*

Printing *Black and green on ivory laid text paper*

Format *11-by-17 inches, four pages*

Design *Joan Auclair*

Awards *Council for Advancement and Support of Education, Newsletter Clearinghouse*

4

WHEN PATIENTS TURN VIOLENT

I N HER 23 YEARS ON THE JOB, NEW YORK rehabilitation assistant Marla Chilson has been involved in many violent confrontations with patients —managing always to avoid personal injury. But two years ago Chilson, an AFT-affiliated Public Employees Federation member who cares for mentally retarded and physically handicapped patients, became a victim. Unlucky enough to get in the way of an angry female patient, Chilson sustained a deep bite to the breast.

Then last year, Chilson was on the receiving end of yet another act of violence when she came to the aid of a female co-worker who was the intended target of a male patient. Chilson managed, as she's been trained, to secure the patient in a physical restraint known as a "standing wrap." The profoundly retarded man tried to get away, sinking his teeth into Chilson's right index finger. "There was no doubt in my mind that he was going to bite it right off," she says. He didn't, but the bite did sever the tendons and ligaments. After lengthy treatments, including orthopedic surgery, Chilton is left with a permanently immobilized finger.

Although many incidents of patient violence are never documented, they happen an average of once a month,

says Linda Kelly, R.N. Kelly is the associate chief for nursing service in education and clinical affairs at the Samuel S. Stratton Department of Veterans' Affairs Medical Center in Albany, N.Y. A former psychiatric nurse, Kelly is a frequent consultant to the state on psychiatric nursing, conflict resolution and the art of working with difficult people.

Patient violence can be generated by factors ranging from an adverse response to a medication to frustration at serving time in the emergency waiting room, says Kelly. Health care workers see more violent behavior on wards with demented or Alzheimer's patients and elderly people. "In environments that are restraint free to preserve dignity, violent incidents can happen once a week," Kelly says.

BY ALEXANDRA ROCKEY

Recycling Art

The art director chose this unusual trim size to allow ample room for large illustrations while avoiding the oversized feel of a tabloid. In this issue, the illustrator takes full advantage of the size by repeating the theme of the cover art for a story inside. The size allows for cost-effective bleeds off top and bottom.

Name *Healthwire*
Publisher *Federation of Nurses and Health Professionals/AFT, AFL-CIO, Washington, D.C.*
Purpose/audience *Service to members*
Production *By hand*
Printing *Black and red on white offset paper*
Format *10³/₄-by-14¹/₂ inches, six pages*
Design *Charles Glendinning*
Award *International Labor Communications*

KLEINFELD & ZABLUDOWSKI
Attorneys & Counselors At Law

Trends

Fall 1990

The State of Florida: A 'Haven for Debtors' who seek to shelter their wealth

Passing on the family business

KLEINFELD & ZABLUDOWSKI
Attorneys & Counselors At Law

Trends

Winter 1989-90

How real estate developers and business owners can protect their assets from creditor and tort liability

Lawsuits are replacing baseball as the national pastime and governmental regulation is becoming the nation's religion.

In particular, developers and owners of real estate have undergone a tremendous increase in areas of possible liability. In addition to financing liability, new statutory or legal theories of personal and corporate liability, such as environmental or toxic wastes laws, have emerged while possible defenses to liability are being reduced.

You are at risk and you must use strategic asset protection planning to provide for the economic well-being of yourself, your company and to protect the financial future of your family. The asset protection specialist is a legal advisor who can develop an individual plan, taking into account such diverse areas as real estate law, creditor-debtor rights, bankruptcy law, investment and financial planning, securities law and, often overlooked, estate planning.

An overall plan or blueprint, such as using the Global Protective Trust™ plan, is required to take into account each person's unique planning requirements by blending traditional planning techniques and modern, sophisticated strategies.

Standard asset protection planning generally involves the use of irrevocable trusts, converting cash assets into an "exempt" form (generally by the purchase of insurance or funding pension plans), and opening wage accounts. Transferring property completely to a spouse or putting property in tenants by the entirety is not usually a good idea as a practical matter. A divorce or premature death of the spouse would be disastrous. In any event, co-ownership may just be poor estate planning. For new projects, family limited partnerships or the limited liability company may be acceptable wealth transferring devices.

Global Protective Trust™

As of January 1, 1988, the rights of creditors have increased as a result of Florida's adoption of the Uniform Fraudulent Transfer Act. In substance, the Act has given creditors new and improved causes of action. Transfers can be voided by creditors if they are constructively fraudulent. Intent is no longer a consideration. Future creditors can now have a right to remedies as well as present creditors. Furthermore, the creditor can now obtain prejudgment relief. This new act dramatically affects all traditional planning techniques.
Continued on Back Page

The move to Southeast Financial Center...

To accommodate the growth of its practice and to better serve the needs of its clients, Kleinfeld & Zabludowski recently moved its offices to the 36th floor of the Southeast Financial Center in the heart of Miami's financial district.

With a commanding view of the city, Biscayne Bay and Miami Beach, the atmosphere of the new offices is one of comfort and relaxation where clients may interact with professionals. The firm was also anxious to maintain an ambiance of "family," which characterizes the relationship among the partners and support staff, regardless of growth and expansion.

The partners believe that from their new headquarters in downtown Miami, and from corresponding offices in Boca Raton, Florida and London, England, the firm will serve its clients even better in the United States and overseas.

KLEINFELD & ZABLUDOWSKI
Attorneys & Counselors At Law
Southeast Financial Center, 36th Floor,
200 South Biscayne Boulevard, Miami, Florida 33131-2394
Telephone: (305) 358-0600 / Facsimile: (305) 358-6541

KLEINFELD & ZABLUDOWSKI
Attorneys & Counselors At Law

Trends

Fall 1990

The State of Florida: A 'Haven for Debtors' who seek to shelter their wealth

Florida is known nationwide as an important center for local and international commerce and it's a relatively stable real estate market. It is also acquiring the reputation as a haven for individuals who seek to protect and preserve their wealth from creditors.

Individual exposure to risk, liabilities and creditor's claims in other states are streaming into Florida, attracted by Florida laws that shield certain personal assets. Additionally, Florida has no personal income tax and, effectively, no inheritance tax. In the past few years it has enjoyed a dynamic economy and its growth is among the highest in the United States.

Many individuals are beginning to understand that, while the federal Bankruptcy Code applies everywhere, each state can write its own rules about which assets are exempt from creditors. In Florida the major exemptions are for "homestead" (your principal home of unlimited value), wages of head of household, insurance and annuities, qualified pension and profit sharing plans, and IRAs.

Attempts by frustrated bill collection and collectors lawyers to stem the exploitation of Florida's exemptions have received a chilly reception in Tallahassee, the state capital. Florida law makers are currently disinclined to revise the exemption laws which would, in the words of one legislature, "put widows and orphans out on the street." The effect of the law is to achieve some balance between the rights of creditors to enforce judgments and the ability of debtors to maintain some independent means of support so as not be place on the public dole.

While long considered the state for "sun and fun," Florida has developed into a major international economic center. By keeping the tax burden low, requiring fiscal responsibility of its state government, being a "right to work state," benefiting from a relatively stable economy, as well as debtor-oriented exemption laws, Florida is becoming the haven many individuals are seeking for a wide range of reasons, including those who want to shelter their wealth.

Passing on the family business

The good news for some is that the baby boom generation is potentially just beginning to receive the largest transfer of wealth in the history of the world. A substantial part of this wealth is contained in privately-held and family-held businesses. The bad news is that planning for the transfer of these privately held and family businesses is fraught with dangers and presents opportunities for disasters.

The list of famous family businesses ruined by family feuds or catastrophic estate taxes is catalogued every day in the daily newspapers around the country. However, the transition of the privately held or family business from one generation to the next can be achieved without families abandoning their business because of inter-family rancor or inability to pay estate taxes.

We can advise you to follow three basic rules in dealing with this problem. *First*, realize the problem and plan early with great diligence; *second*, choose your successor early and ease him or her into the job; and *third*, recognize that there will be estate taxes and develop a practical plan to pay for them.

The transferring of a privately-held family business to the next generation is serious business these days and tougher than it used to be. It must be approached responsibly and pragmatically.

KLEINFELD & ZABLUDOWSKI
Attorneys & Counselors At Law
Southeast Financial Center, Suite 3650
200 South Biscayne Boulevard, Miami, Florida 33131-2394
Telephone: (305) 358-0600 / Facsimile: (305) 358-6541

Duotones That Bleed

Blue hand lettering in the nameplate creates an informal contrast with the black type and balances the formal illustration of the headquarters building that bleeds off the bottom of the page. The illustration of the building, a blue-black duotone, adds the authority of a strong vertical element. The illustration repeats from issue to issue, serving as a logo.

Name *Trends*

Publisher *Kleinfeld & Zabludowski, Miami, FL*

Purpose/audience *Service to clients*

Production *QuarkXPress on Macintosh SE/30*

Printing *Black and gray-blue on white matte-coated paper*

Format *8½-by-11 inches, four pages*

Design *Neil D. Littauer*

Award *Newsletter Clearinghouse*

All About Mastheads

Each issue of your newsletter needs a masthead, the element designed to provide business information. The masthead tells the name and address of your sponsoring organization, your name as editor, and how readers can reach you. You should also list the names of graphic designers, photographers and other professionals who have contributed to your newsletter.

Depending on the wishes of your organization, your masthead could also tell frequency of publication and subscription costs, if any, and give names of key officers and contributors. Potential contributors look in your masthead to learn if you solicit articles and photographs and what you pay for them.

Your masthead should have the same content and stay in the same location from one issue to the next. If you pasteup by hand, make PMT copies to use for each issue. If you assemble pages using a computer, establish the masthead as a macro or as part of your format file.

If your newsletter is copyrighted, this notice also belongs in your masthead. You can include an International Standard Serial Number (ISSN). You should have an ISSN if you want librarians to catalog your publication. Newsletters that are mailed second class must display either an ISSN or a post office identification number in their nameplate, masthead or return address. The National Serials Data Program of the Library of Congress, Washington, D.C. 20540, assigns ISSNs at no fee.

Notes

The health newsletter of The Medical Center of Central Massachusetts provides up-to-date medical information to the local community. The Med Center comprises the Hahnemann, Holden and Memorial campuses and is a major teaching affiliate of the University of Massachusetts Medical School.

The Med Center offers a wide range of medical/surgical and psychiatric services, inpatient and outpatient clinics, rehabilitation and visiting nurse services.

It is the regional referral center for women with high-risk pregnancies and the regional intensive care nursery for seriously-ill and small newborns. The Med Center is also the site of the regional kidney dialysis center, the New England Area Hemophilia Center and is a major teaching and research facility.

President & CEO, MCCM, Inc.
   David A. Barrett
Physician-in-Chief
   Peter H. Levine, M.D.
Vice President, Public Relations
   Robert J. Ristino
Editors
   Cathleen LaCroix and Cynthia Prunier

KLEINFELD & ZABLUDOWSKI
A Partnership of Professional Associations
ATTORNEYS & COUNSELORS AT LAW

Southeast Financial Center
36th Floor
200 South Biscayne Blvd.
Miami, Florida
33131-2394
(305) 358-0600

Corresponding offices in Boca Raton, Florida and London, England

Trends is published to provide our clients and friends with information concerning recent legal developments. These developments are discussed in general terms and should not be acted upon without first seeking professional advice. ©1989, Kleinfeld & Zabludowski. All rights reserved.

Motivation is like a fire: Unless you continue to add fuel, it goes out.

THINK & GROW RICH
NEWSLETTER

THE PRACTICAL GUIDE FOR HIGH ACHIEVEMENT AND PERSONAL FULFILLMENT.
208 Keowee Trail
Clemson, South Carolina 29631

A Napoleon Hill™ Publication

PURPOSE
To strengthen you with a monthly infusion of positive ideas. To reinforce you in motivating yourself and others to high achievement, self-fulfillment, peace of mind and wealth in every endeavor—financial, professional, personal.

The newsletter explores the ideas and principles in Dr. Napoleon Hill's classic best-seller of the same name . . .the book that inspired the Positive Mental Attitude (PMA) movement that over the past 50 years has fueled achievements of America's most successful men and women.

THINK & GROW RICH NEWSLETTER
Editor, Ross Cornwell.
Contributing Editors, Paul Friedman, Dot Yandle, Myrle Swicegood, Greg Wilson.
Publisher, Rives Cheney.
Associate Publisher, Margaret Blair.
Editorial Services Manager, Patsy Melsheimer.
Subscription Services, Penny Klein.
Editorial Production, David Bill.

Napoleon Hill Foundation
President, W. Clement Stone; Executive Vice President, Dr. Charles Johnson; Vice Presidents, Senator Jennings Randolph, Dr. Horace W. Fleming Jr. and Delford M. Smith; Secretary and Treasurer, Michael J. Ritt Jr.; Trustees, Wally Amos, Dr. Bill Atchley and James Oleson; Honorary Trustee, Lt. Col. (Ret.) David Hill.

SUBSCRIPTION ORDER FORM
THINK & GROW RICH NEWSLETTER is an excellent gift for business associates or members of your family.

To subscribe or give a gift, call 1-800-237-7967 or complete the coupon and mail us a copy.
Please enter a subscription for $39:

From: (if a gift)

NAME   TITLE
COMPANY/ORGANIZATION
ADDRESS
CITY   STATE   ZIP
☐ Check attached ☐ Bill me
☐ Charge my credit card: ___ MasterCard ___ VISA ___ American Express
Card No.
Signature

Subscription Services, THINK & GROW RICH NEWSLETTER P.O. Box 1746, Clemson, SC 29633
Rates: $39/year (12 issues). Canadian and Foreign: $68. Single Copy: $5. For multiple subscription rates, call us at 1-800-237-7967. FAX No. 803-654-7275.

For:

NAME   TITLE
COMPANY/ORGANIZATION
ADDRESS
CITY   STATE   ZIP
Expiration Date

WINE INSTITUTE

Wine Institute News is a monthly newsletter for members of the Wine Institute. For inquiries contact: Wine Institute, 425 Market Street, Suite 1000, San Francisco, CA 94105. Phone: (415) 512-0151. FAX: (415) 442-0742.

Editor: Mark Stuertz, *Publications Manager*
Editorial Board: Elisabeth Holmgren, *Director, Health and Social Issues*
   Linda Lawry, *Director, New York Office*
   Wendell Lee, *San Francisco Counsel*
   Nancy Light, *Director, Communications*
   Joe Rollo, *Director, International*
   Wade Stevenson, *Director, Economic Research*
   Jerry Vorpahl, *Vice President, Industry Affairs*

A digest of advancements in wholesale and retail

Tattered Cover

2955 EAST FIRST AVENUE • DENVER, COLORADO 80206 • 303-322-7727

APRIL 19, 1991

A BEST WESTERN EMPLOYEE PUBLICATION

All About Nameplates

Your nameplate belongs at the top of the front page, the area that readers see first and most often. The nameplate sets the tone for your entire publication.

A nameplate should stay the same issue after issue, telling the name and subtitle of your newsletter and its publication date. It might also show a logo, illustration, photo or issue number. With a marketing newsletter, include the address and phone number of your organization.

There are five guidelines to effective nameplate design. Nameplates such as those on this spread do not have to be in color to meet these guidelines.

• *Full information.* Certify accuracy of all data such as subtitle, date, logo and publisher's name.

• *Impact.* Examine the design for balance, contrast and unity.

• *Simplicity.* Verify uncluttered design that readers can understand at a glance.

• *Harmony.* Ensure that the design suits the format for the text.

• *Practicality.* Check for cost-efficient printing that will meet deadlines.

EUGENE/SPRINGFIELD, OREGON: Fit for Business, Fit for Living

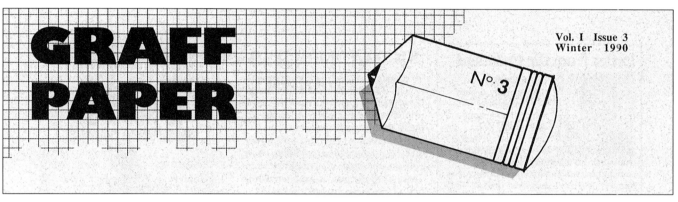

GRAFF PAPER

Vol. I   Issue 3
Winter   1990

N°. 3

The Service Edge®

For Creating and Maintaining Distinctive Service

August 1991 — Vol. 4, No. 8

SCENE

B R A I L L E   I N S T I T U T E

Spring   1990

Chapter 5

Color

Color makes some elements of design more vivid, therefore more dramatic and interesting. And newsletters, appealing to the full range of human interests, invite the full range of color possibilities. The newsletters shown on the following pages include pastels, metallics, primaries and many more.

While adding emphasis, color may detract from legibility. Type—even headlines—printed in color slows reading and reduces reader understanding. Printing each issue in two or more colors increases costs for little gain in appeal or readability. Very few newsletters are printed using four-color process. Most use only one ink color, in addition to black, to achieve their colorful effects. Many achieve the effect of several colors by using both black and a second ink as screen tints as well as printing them at 100 percent.

Paper influences color as much as ink. Bright colors work best on coated stock, soft colors on uncoated sheets. Unfortunately, photographic reproductions of colors, such as the illustrations used in this book, cannot fully convey the impact of paper.

To achieve soft colors and earth tones, many designers select recycled paper. Recycled paper is not bleached as heavily as virgin stock and absorbs ink more readily, producing more muted hues.

Food Insight ®

International Food Information Council   July/August 1990

*The Inside Report
on America's New Competitiveness*

June 1991 • Volume 2 • Number 6 ®

N E W S L E T T E R

BBB

A PUBLICATION OF THE ALTERNATIVE DISPUTE RESOLUTION DIVISION · COUNCIL OF BETTER BUSINESS BUREAUS

All About Preprinting Color

Cost-conscious designers use preprinting to add a second color to newsletters. Preprinting calls for printing the second color for many monthly issues at once, then printing individual monthly issues using black ink only. For example, a newsletter needing 1,000 copies per month would preprint 12,000 copies—a supply for one year—then produce the monthly press run in black.

Preprinting Nameplates

These examples show the use of preprinting in nameplates. The technique is also used to produce colorful rules, screen tints, standing headlines and other elements that remain the same issue after issue. Careful planning with preprinting can also yield simulated third and fourth colors by overlapping screen tints. For examples of overlapping tints, see pages 78-81.

Maximizing Two-Color Printing

Two-color illustrations seem to be printed in many colors because they are produced by overlapping screen tints. The illustrator and designer for the art reproduced on this page are the same as for the *Free Spirit* newsletter reproduced on pages 80-81.

Name *In House Graphics*

Publisher *United Communications Group, Rockville, MD*

Purpose/audience *Service to subscribers*

Production *PageMaker on Macintosh*

Printing *Black and red on natural offset paper*

Format *8 1/2-by-11 inches, eight pages*

Design *Ronnie Lipton*

Award *Newsletter Clearinghouse*

Overprinting Colors

Because screen tints of red blend so well with tints of black, red is the most popular color when overlapping screens. *Food Insight* prints in Pantone 32; *In House Graphics*, at left, uses the slightly more orange Pantone 185. The difference between the two reds is very subtle, especially when they are screened and overlapped with black. To ensure vibrant color, *Food Insight* is printed on 80-pound matte-coated paper.

Name *Food Insight*

Publisher *International Food Information Council, Washington, D.C.*

Purpose/audience *Service to members and friends of the council*

Production *QuarkXPress on Macintosh*

Printing *Black and red on white matte-coated paper*

Format *8 1/2-by-11 inches, eight pages*

Design *Dick Rabil*

Award *American Society of Association Executives*

Food Insight.

Current Topics in Food Safety and Nutrition

International Food Information Council   July/August 1990

Upbeat on Fiber

This Oldie-But-Goodie Is Back on the Dietary Hit Parade

In the 1800s, Sylvester W. Graham gained fame espousing the benefits of roughage in the diet. His cracker is still with us, but surprisingly, dietary fiber has had a harder time staying in favor. Since the turn of the century, the fiber intake of Americans has steadily declined.

But today dietary fiber is making a comeback, as studies have multiplied linking it to a lower risk for some of the leading causes of death in America. Just what is this food component, and why do the experts tell us to eat more of it?

What is Fiber?

Dietary fiber generally refers to parts of fruits, vegetables, grains, nuts and legumes that can't be digested by humans. Meats and dairy products do not contain fiber.

There are two basic types of fiber—insoluble and soluble. Most fiber-containing foods feature both, but one or the other type often predominates in specific parts of a food and determines the characteristic texture of that portion of the food.

For example, insoluble fibers produce the tough, chewy feel of wheat kernels, popcorn, apple skin and nuts. Essential to the cellular structure of plants, insoluble fibers include cellulose, hemicelluloses and

Continued on page 4

Matching Color and Audience

A bubble gum tinted illustration layout that would seem overdone for an adult audience is just right for *Free Spirit* readers ages ten to fourteen. This newsletter's large format and sturdy paper make it easy to find in the incoming mail, and also says to others in the household that the recipient is special for getting such a big package.

Name *Free Spirit*

Publisher *Free Spirit Publishing Inc., Minneapolis, MN*

Purpose/audience *Subscribers, youths ages ten to fourteen*

Production *QuarkXPress and Illustrator on Macintosh IIci*

Printing *Two colors on white offset paper*

Format *11-by-17 inches, eight pages*

Design *Punch Design—Rick Korab*

Awards *Magazine Design and Production, Educational Press Association of America, Newsletter Clearinghouse*

Science Fun from the Backyard Scientist
By Jane Hoffman

Jane Hoffman, the Backyard Scientist, is the author of many books of hands-on experiments for ages 4–14. All of the experiments she describes use materials commonly found in most homes. Her books are used by home schoolers and educators around the world. For more information, write to: Jane Hoffman, P.O. Box 16966, Irvine, CA 92713.

Gather the following supplies:
1 bottle of lemon-lime soda (7-Up or Sprite)
1 balloon

Start experimenting:
1. Being very careful not to shake the soda, place it into the refrigerator overnight until it is cold.

2. After the soda is cold, remove it from the refrigerator and carefully, without shaking the soda, remove the cap.
3. Take the balloon and carefully place it over the mouth of the bottle.
4. Run hot water over the outside of the bottle. Careful—don't burn yourself.
5. Hold the balloon on the bottle and shake the bottle carefully.

Can you answer these questions from your observations?
1. What took place inside the bottle?
2. What happened to the balloon?
3. What is inside the bottle, making the balloon expand?

Turn to page 8 for the solution.

FREE SPIRIT REVIEWS

By Jerry Simmons

Jerry Simmons graduated high school a year early and attends West Valley Community College in California. He lives in San Jose and is a frequent contributor to Free Spirit.

Speaking for Ourselves, compiled and edited by Donald R. Gallo (Urbana, IL: National Council of Teachers of English, 1990). ISBN 0-8141-4625-2, paperback, 231 pages, $12.95.

This is a collection of autobiographical sketches of famous authors of books for young adults. It's one of the most interesting books I've read in a long time. I found it fascinating to read about the people who are behind the books young people read today. Some are shy people who like isolation, others are very outgoing. Some turn out books by the dozens, others put out a single book every few years.

The storylines of many books I've read by profiled authors fit perfectly with the author's personality. But some authors write books that seem to be completely removed from their own backgrounds.

The authors profiled are truthful and express deep feelings, so readers will get a glimpse of the "real" person behind the books they've read. ★ ★ ★ ★

Market Guide for Young Artists and Photographers by Kathy Henderson (Crozet, VA: Betterway Publications, 1990). ISBN 1-55870-176-1, paperback, 174 pages, $10.95.

This is an excellent resource guide for any young person interested in art or photography as a hobby or career. It includes an extensive listing of contests and events for young people's work, a section on how to prepare work for submission, biographies of successful young artists, and words of encouragement from the author.

Although this book is impressive in that the author managed to pull together an extensive listing of worthwhile contests to answer, I did find some flaws. First, the author didn't seem to write the book as if she was an expert in this subject area. There is also little or no logical transition between sections, and there wasn't enough substance in the "getting started" section.

Despite these flaws, *The Market Guide for Young Artists and Photographers* is still valuable as a reference book for young people interested in art and photography. There isn't any other single book targeted toward young artists and photographers that pulls together quite so much information on markets for their work. ★ ★ ★ ½

How to Cope with Feeling Worried, Afraid, and Confused about the War: A Special Message from *Free Spirit*

If the war with Iraq has made you feel worried, afraid, and confused, you're not alone. Millions of people share your feelings. We share your feelings. We hope that the war will be over soon, and that the men and women serving in the Gulf will come home safely.

In talking about the war, kids have told us, "We feel powerless. It's true that you're powerless to stop the war. But you have a great deal of personal power, even in times like these.

1. **You have the power to talk** about your feelings. Talk to your friends. Talk to your parents and teachers. Talk to your school counselor. Don't keep your feelings locked inside.

At Westridge Middle School in Orlando, Florida, students in teacher Kathleen Oleland's social studies class wrote short journal entries and poems about the war and their feelings. They discussed the issues, then printed on symbols of peace to wear. You may want to write about the war in your journal. If you don't already keep a journal, why not start one now?

2. **You have the power to learn** about the war. Read the newspaper and news magazines. Study maps. Watch the news on television. Read books about the Mideast, or ask your parents and teachers to read them and tell you what they learn.

If you enjoy challenges, try to see both sides of the conflict. Things are seldom all right or all wrong. If world leaders could see both sides, we might not be at war.

3. **You have the power to form** your own opinions about the war. You may decide that you support the war. You may decide that you oppose the war. But support the people who are serving so it. (This isn't as mixed-up as it sounds. Many people feel this way.)

4. **You have the power to get on with** your life. You can still go to school, do your homework, feed the cat, set the dinner table, play with your friends, laugh with your family, and dream happy dreams about your future.

5. **You have the power to ask** your parents and other adults for reassurance. It's their job to keep you safe, no matter what. It's okay to say, "I need a hug," or, "I'm feeling scared right now—can you help?"

6. **You have the power to make your** own life more peaceful. Start at home, with your parents and brothers and sisters. Instead of arguing, try talking and listening. Be more peaceful at school. Be more peaceful in your neighborhood.

And be more peaceful inside yourself. Thinking can help. Meditating can help. Praying can help. Listening to quiet music can help.

You are right to be concerned about the world. But don't forget to take care of you.

Peace,

Jody, Pamela, Liz, Nancy, Rick, Douglas, and Harry for Free Spirit

ARE YOU MOVING? HAVE YOU MOVED?

Help us to deliver your *Free Spirit* on time. Let us know as soon as you can to month before your move is back. Send us both your old AND new address. That way we won't miss each other.

Joint Assignments, Shared Successes

By Claudine Wirths and Mary Bowman-Kruhm

Claudine Wirths and Mary Bowman-Kruhm have written four books together. Two of them are Where's My Other Sock?—How to Get Organized & Drive Your Parents & Teachers Crazy and I Hate School—How to Hang In & When to Drop Out (both HarperCollins). Mary did most of the work on this article. But Claudine gets her name as senior author because it was her idea.

When was the last time you saw a sculpture by Ralph Beeswax and Frank Sandstone? Or a painting by Eloise Hairbrush and Joanna Camelspit? Yet every day, teachers expect students to work together on a project or assignment. Or sometimes students ask teachers if they can join forces. Educators call this cooperative learning, but it can be a cooperative disaster for students.

Oh, sure, the idea of sharing the job and work with a classmate or classmates starts off okay. One minute, you're sitting in English or social studies or science. The teacher has just given you details about the assignment and the due date. Your mind is blank. Then one of you gets an idea and suddenly you're laughing and finishing each others' sentences and so excited that the teacher glares in your direction.

Remember that moment! It may be the best one you have until you receive your joint grade. Cooperation can be a real belly-flopper.

What can you do to save your sanity, get the grade you deserve, keep from having to do all the work, and actually enjoy learning? How can you make sure that you and your partner will still speak to each other when it's all over?

These guidelines can help you turn cooperative learning into shared success. Depending on your assignment, you can probably add a few guidelines of your own. Most of ours are for groups of two, but they can be modified for larger groups as well.

1. **If you can choose your partner, pick someone with the same temperament type as you.** Your best friend may be loads of fun because of an impulsive nature, jolly sense of humor, and playful attitude toward life. But if you work best by being organized and planning ahead, don't pick this person for a partner. The same principle holds if you're the carefree one who stays up to complete a project the night before it's due.

2. **Decide who will be "Senior Author."** To keep the assignment on track and running smoothly, one of you must have the power to say "Whoa!" or "The best way to handle that is..." You may want to pick as Senior Author the person who first thought of the topic (if it wasn't assigned, of course).

Since the Senior Author makes final decisions, the other person is free to toss out all kinds of creative, way-out ideas. The Senior Author is responsible for sorting them out in return for the honor of holding that position.

3. **Schedule joint work sessions.** These are required! Joint work sessions keep you feeling guilty. Telling your partner you haven't done anything in two weeks is a lot harder than looking in the mirror and telling yourself.

You can begin a session with school gossip—limited to the first fifteen minutes. Then you also want to bring in some food. Enjoying a pizza together may remind you of the fun you were supposed to have when you decided to do this project together.

4. **Each person must stick to the agreed-upon work schedule.** If not, tack yourself for not following guideline #1 above. If you had no choice about your working partner, confer with your teacher early on. Don't complain and whine. Just state the facts about the problem you're having and try to understand the teacher's reasons for making the choice.

5. **Assume that a catastrophe will happen before your assignment is finished.** Agreeing to work with someone else for a major grade practically guarantees sickness, family disaster, or an upset love life for one of you. The partner who is in the hospital, in a plane flying to grandma's, or in tears must give full emotional support to the one who isn't.

The partner who keeps working on the assignment has the right to this support. Even if it sounds something like this: "Do whatever you think is best—anything is fine with me. But don't forget to SAVE on the computer. And remember to use a semi-colon somewhere; teachers think a report with one of those looks real professional. And also... But as I said, anything is fine with me."

6. **The one who is best at using a computer gets to pick the software and make the final hard copy.** The other person graciously agrees to make 20 trips to the library in freezing weather and trace detailed drawings on onion skin paper.

If neither of you has a computer or typewriter, brainstorm how to access one, since research shows that professional-looking papers get better grades than those that are handwritten. This may involve doing yard work for a neighbor in return for typing, learning the basics of using a computer at the library, or finding some other creative solution.

7. **Each partner must listen to comments and criticisms from the other. Neither partner may seek revenge.** Not even when your partner lists eight big problems in what you thought was a perfectly written, obviously dynamite piece of work.

8. **And finally: Whatever your final grade, neither of you will blame the other.** Each of you will smile and say, "We did our best." If the assignment gets an A, celebrate with your partner. If the grade is lower than you both expected, commiserate with each other and jointly share the responsibility.

A few last words: If, in the end, you feel totally frustrated with your partner, chalk your feelings up to learning experience. Resolve not to work with that person again, but you can still be friends.

Don't bad-mouth your partner to the teacher, your family, or other classmates. Work off your frustration by listing the reasons why you never again want to share an assignment with that person. Save the list. Then, if you find yourself in a similar situation in the future, you're lucky to schedule a conference with your teacher.

Would you like to be a *Free Spirit* Pen Pal? Send your full name, your age, your COMPLETE home or school address, and a brief description of your interests to: Free Spirit/PEN PALS, 400 First Avenue North, Suite 616, Minneapolis, MN 55401. Meanwhile, you can write to any of these kids who want to be your pen pal:

Nicole Barnabee, 10 1/2
PO Box 4047
Waynesville, MO 65583
"I like Nintendo, books, and especially Teenage Mutant Ninja Turtles."

Stormi Nicks, 10 1/2
21 Collier St.
Ft. Leonard Wood, MO 65473
"I like the New Kids, books, and love to talk."

Tabitha Ann Wimmer, 9 3/4
407 Center Circle
Clyman, WI 53016
"I have short blonde hair and blue eyes. I'm in 4th grade. I like horses, books, school, and Paula Abdul. My birthday is February 5, 1981."

Jonah Klevesahl, 11 3/4
5153 Chowen Ave. So.
Minneapolis, MN 55410
"I'm in 6th grade and I like talking on the phone, writing notes, Nintendo, airplanes, and the United States military."

Coming Up in *Free Spirit*

* **May/June 1991:** LOOKING TOWARD THE FUTURE (With the winners of our Third Annual *Free Spirit* Writing Contest). Article submission deadline extended to MARCH 15, 1991.
* **September/October 1991:** BACK-TO-SCHOOL (stress-free). Article submission deadline JULY 1, 1991.
* **November/December 1991:** DIVERSITY AND MULTICULTURAL LEARNING. Article submission deadline SEPTEMBER 15, 1991.
* **January/February 1992:** ARTS ISSUE (With the winners of our Fourth Annual *Free Spirit* Cartoon Contests. Article submission deadline NOVEMBER 1, 1991.
* **March/April 1992:** SPORTS & FITNESS (including mental). Article submission deadline JANUARY 1, 1992.
* **May/June 1992:** SAVE THE EARTH (With the winners of our Fourth Annual *Free Spirit* Writing Contest). Article submission deadline MARCH 1, 1992.

BE A FREE SPIRIT AND SUBSCRIBE NOW!

To order your subscription, or to give a gift of *Free Spirit*, call us toll-free at 1 (800) 735-7323 or complete this order form and send it to us at:
FREE SPIRIT, 400 First Avenue North, Suite 616, Minneapolis, MN 55401.

☐ **YES!** Please enter a one year subscription (5 issues) of *Free Spirit* for just $10.00 per year.

☐ Better yet, send two years of *Free Spirit* (10 issues) at the special rate of $16.00. (A savings of 20%)

Canadian rates: $13.00 per one-year subscription. Orders in Canada should be sent in Candian Currency Funds (use U.S. currency for other countries). Overseas rates: Please add $5.00 per year to each subscription price for overseas postage. Payment must accompany order and be paid in U.S. funds.

☐ I've enclosed my check for $ _____
☐ Bill me
☐ VISA ☐ MasterCard

Signature _____ Exp. Date _____

☐ Please send me discount information for classroom subscriptions. (Teachers who order 10 or more subscriptions receive a free teacher's supplement with each issue.)

NAME _____
ADDRESS _____
CITY/STATE/ZIP _____
TELEPHONE _____

Send subscriptions to (if different from above):

NAME _____
ADDRESS _____
CITY/STATE/ZIP _____

Creating the Illusion of Many Colors

Each issue is printed in only two ink colors. Skillful use of screen tints in the illustrations, many of which overlap to become color builds, produces the illusion of many colors. Black and the second color can each print in 10 percent, 20 percent and 30 percent tints as well as running solid. Each of these tints can combine with any other tint, resulting in a palette of nine color builds.

To ensure uniform dot patterns and correct screen angles, the tints in *Free Spirit* are stripped in by the printer, as are the tints on the publications on pages 82-83.

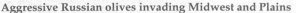

Aggressive Russian olives invading Midwest and Plains

The Russians are here!

The Russians I'm referring to are Russian olives (*Eleagnus angustifolia*) and they are fast becoming an enemy in the Midwest and Plains.

When I moved to Minnesota in 1969, I saw my first Russian olive in Hastings Park. I still remember its attractive silvery foliage, dark bark, and almost sculpture-like form.

As a landscape designer in the 1970s, I installed many Russian olives in my landscape plans, although we worried then about the verticillium wilt that besieged the plant, rendering it wilted, brown, and partially dead. (Wisconsin nurseries actually stopped producing and selling it for awhile.) But the wilt passed and we continued planting the Russian olive, which is a native of Europe. After all, besides its aesthetic strengths, the plant also tolerates a wide range of soils, droughty conditions and a cold climate. We all planted a large number of the plants for screens and windbreaks.

But the Russian olive's broad range of tolerance is making it an enemy! When birds carry the tasty berries across the landscape, the dropped seeds have no problem establishing anywhere, and the plants quickly take advantage of each new opportunity.

On a recent cross-country trip through Iowa, Nebraska, Colorado, and New Mexico, I saw Russian olives

E. angustifolia

Aggressive Russian olives are a menace to the Midwest region of the United States.

growing in pastures and river valleys, displacing prized grazing land and replacing valuable lowland wildlife habitat. The trees can be as much of a problem as red cedar in the Midwest and mesquite in the Southwest. Because all these plants are easier to establish than to eliminate, severe vegetation management techniques are used, further disrupting and degrading the land.

For example, in Texas, native juniper and mesquite trees are "chained off" by bulldozers dragging chains to uproot the trees. But that method further degrades the pastures, allowing pioneer weeds to quickly take advantage of the disruption.

I have no easy solution for stopping any of these aggressive plants.

But, based on my observations during my driving trip, I will no longer plant or recommend planting Russian olives. If you need to see for yourself, you also can take a driving trip — not cross-country — but simply along T.H. 169 south of Shakopee, Minn. You will see pasture land dotted with Russian olives spreading across the landscape.

Birds aid the Russian olive's movement, and its broad range of tolerance allows its easy establishment. Believe what you see — we have a problem with this Russian!

Bonnie Harper-Lore
Midwest Office
Program Coordinator

Bonnie Harper-Lore, program coordinator of the Wildflower Center's Midwest Regional Office, spoke this spring at the University of Wisconsin Arboretum in Madison and at the Michigan Wildflower Association's annual conference in Detroit.

Midwest Office information officer Maria Urice and Bonnie presented a number of talks at local workshops, conferences, and garden club meetings this spring. The staff also appeared on a call-in talk show on radio station KUOM in Minneapolis to discuss "Native Plants for Residential Use."

Bonnie has met with Bloomington,

MIDWEST UPDATE

Minn., city officials to discuss changes in the city's lawn ordinance. The city is interested in making changes that will allow the use of native vegetation in planned landscapes.

This spring, the Minnesota-based environmental group "Kids for Saving Earth" distributed packets of wildflower seeds through Target stores to kids across the United States. The regional office was part of

the initial planning stages of the project, defining species lists, locating seed sources, and advising the project coordinators about the importance of using native plants.

A traveling display for the regional office is now available.

The book *Vascular Plants of Minnesota: A Checklist and Atlas*, by University of Minnesota emeritus professors Gerald Ownbey and Thomas Morley, is now available. The regional office is co-sponsoring a book-signing with the Minnesota Native Plant Society to honor the authors.

May/June 1991 3

Membership Department makes sure you belong

The thousands of National Wildflower Research Center members have one thing in common: their interest in wildflowers and native plants.

When Wildflower Center staffers meet members, they're always impressed with the members' knowledge of native flora.

"We're always amazed and delighted to learn how knowledgeable and enthusiastic members are about native plants. It's always a treat to discover," says Mae Daniller, director of development.

The Center's membership program started in 1984 with 1,700 members at year's end. Now, more than 15,000 people are members of the Wildflower Center.

Mae says the staff is always eager to serve Wildflower Center members better. "We want you to tell us what you like and don't like."

Besides Mae, two other Wildflower Center staff deal directly with members' concerns. Tony Martinez processes and maintains the Center's membership records, and Marianne Pfeil deals personally with member correspondence.

Wildflower Center members receive the newsletter and the journal as part of their membership benefits package. Both award-winning publications were developed to respond to members' requests for native plant information.

Other membership benefits in

the Center include free, priority handling of information requests from the Clearinghouse, a 10-percent discount on purchases through the gift shop and catalog, plus invitations to seminars, tours, and a special membership open house each year.

Sometimes members forget that the Clearinghouse can provide free native plant information; Mae wants to encourage you to take advantage of the service.

"Even if you live in Oregon, or North Carolina, or New York, or anywhere else, members can write to us and get free information on wildflowers and native plants," she says.

The seminars, tours, and open house allow Wildflower Center staff members to meet their "constituents."

"We know we can't meet each and every one of our members, but we want to meet as many of them as we can," Mae says.

Mae says the Center's goal is to grow to 35,000 members by 1994. Even when membership becomes that large, she says, the Membership Department will still be eager to serve members with the same prompt and caring attitude.

"The greatest compliment a current member can give us is to give a gift of Center membership to a friend! Then we know that you appreciate our programs and benefits so much that you wish to share them with others," Mae says. "It makes us all feel good!"

Membership Growth 1984 to 1990

Year	Members
1984	1700
1985	4229
1986	7631
1987	7112
1988	14398
1989	15802
1990	15356

New book offers "wildflowers all year long"

Wildflower Center trustee Bette W. Castro has published a book of poetry celebrating the beauty of American wildflowers.

The hard-bound 5-inch by 7-1/2 inch book, with 48 pages and illustrated with watercolors by Marjorie Stodgell, features an introduction by Lady Bird Johnson and a foreword by Helen Hayes — co-chairs of the Wildflower Center.

Miss Hayes says the book has given her "spring on the coldest, darkest, winter days and wildflowers all year long."

A portion of the book's proceeds benefits the Wildflower Center.

Mrs. Johnson says the book "speaks to the heart. [Bette Castro] has captured the essence of wildflowers, giving us a heightened sense of community with the natural world."

Copies of *The Wildflower* are available from the Wildflower Center for $9.95, plus $3 shipping for each book. Please use the order form in the enclosed catalog, or write to "Books," at the address listed on the newsletter's back page.

May/June 1991 4

Type That Enhances Color

Elegant, willowy type reinforces the pastel graphics and botanical illustrations. Dark green is the theme color, used for type as well as tint blocks and drawings. Tints of burgundy create a lilac hue. The total effect is delicate color that unites readers in their affection for wildflowers—a fine example of matching technique to message.

Name *Wildflower*

Publisher *National Wildflower Research Center, Austin, TX*

Purpose/audience *Service to members and friends of the center*

Production *PageMaker on Macintosh IIe*

Printing *Green, yellow and burgundy on light green offset paper*

Format *8 1/2-by-11 inches, six pages (six-panel foldout)*

Design *Patty Alvey and Elaine Walker*

Awards *Newsletter Clearinghouse, Society for Technical Communications*

INSTRUCTIONAL
LEADER
Volume IV, No. 2 — April 1991

THE SCHOOL AS A HOME
FOR THE MIND

Arthur L. Costa

"Since the goal in cognitive coaching is self-coaching, coaches help teachers develop the ability to recall accurately and in detail what happened in a lesson by questions…"

The Cognitive Coaching Postconference

by
Dr. Robert Garmston
Professor of Educational Administration
California State University, Sacramento

EDITOR'S NOTE: Dr. Robert J. Garmston, Co-Director of the Institute For Intelligent Behavior and Professor, teaches management, counseling, supervision and organizational development in the Dept. of Ed. Admn. at California State University, Sacramento. The author of numerous books and articles on education, management and training, he is a former principal, superintendent, and has served as a consultant to such diverse groups as the Arabian American Oil Company and the Danforth Foundation.

Additional articles, "How Administrators Support Peer Coaching," appear in the February 1987 Educational Leadership, and "Is Peer Coaching Changing Supervisory Relationships: Some Reflections," in the Winter '90 CASCD's Journal for Supervision and Curriculum Improvement.

In the February, 1991 Instructional Leader, Cognitive Coaching was described as a set of nonjudgmental supervisory practices built around a preconference, lesson observation and postconference in which teacher autonomy and self-renewing growth is the goal. In fact, the purpose of coaching could be said to modify teachers' capacity to modify themselves.

This article continues with a description of the postconference and comments briefly on school cultures that foster ongoing faculty learning and self-renewal. This will complete our discussion of three maneuvers principals take to leverage the small amount of discretionary time available to them by:
• communicating a comprehensive vision
• emphasizing coaching over appraisal and
• creating collegial environments.

The Postconference

The postconference frequently begins with an open-ended statement such as "How do you feel the lesson went?" Such an open-ended beginning allows the teacher to decide how he or she will enter the conversation. The second question may be something like, "What are you recalling in the lesson that's leading you to those inferences?" We're now focusing on one of the many cognitive functions that's important to good teaching—recalling what happened during a lesson. This is different from some supervision systems in which the coach reads back what was observed. Notice in the following example how the coach begins open endedly and then asks the teacher to recall specific indicators of student behavior the teacher is using to support his impressions.

Marilyn: Well, how do you think it went, Lloyd?

Lloyd: I'm not sure yet. I think I have to talk it through a little bit. I think it went well. During the first three minutes of interaction, I got back from the students what I expected to get back from this group—that they wouldn't have any specific gross misconceptions about the two concepts. When we started to do the exemplars however, I felt as though, at least at one point, that I was losing them. I had the feeling I was talking with or working with only about five or six students.

Marilyn: What did they do that made you feel that way?

Since the goal in cognitive coaching is self-coaching, coaches help teachers develop the ability to recall accurately and in detail what happened in a lesson by questions

like the last one above. The self-generation of specific data is fundamental to their self-analysis and their ability to modify themselves.

Next, the teacher is asked to do some comparative thinking: "How did what happened in the lesson compare with what you wanted?" The teacher might then be asked to explain what he or she observed happening in the lesson in terms of cause-effect relationships. The teacher may be asked, if it's appropriate, about some things that in hindsight he or she might have done differently that could have led to different results. Interestingly, the greater trust principal and teacher have, and the greater knowledge both have of the goals and procedures of Cognitive Coaching, the fewer questions of this type the coach actually asks. Note in the following excerpt from a postconference, how the teacher volunteers an evaluation and self-prescription in response to the coach's first open-ended question.

Diane: That was fun watching you in action today.

Ellie: It was a lot more fun for me than I thought it would be. I thought I was going to be real aware of what I was doing, what the kids were doing. And actually it was just like teaching a regular lesson. The kids acted like they always do.

Diane: So you didn't feel that having me there really got in the way.

Ellie: I guess I'm getting used to you.

Diane: That's good. How did you feel about the lesson in general?

Ellie: Well, if I had it to do over, I would leave out the part about multiplying and having it be eight times bigger because that just seemed like one extra thing for

Continued on page 12

"…the purpose of coaching could be said to modify teachers' capacity to modify themselves."

REFERENCES

Costa, Art, Garmston, Robert and Lambert, Linda. "Evaluation of Teaching: The Cognitive Development View" in Teacher Evaluation: Six Prescriptions for Success, Alexandria, VA: Association for Supervision and Curriculum Development, 1988.

Costa, Art, Garmston, Robert, Zimmerman, Diane and D'Arcangelo, Marcia. Another Set of Eyes: Conferencing Skills Teacher Manual, ASCD, 1988.

Foster, N. The Impact of Cognitive Coaching on Teacher's Thought Processes as

Perceived by Cognitively Coached Teachers in the Plymouth-Canton Community School District. Doctoral dissertation, 1989. Michigan State University, Detroit.

Garmston, Robert. "Cognitive Coaching and Professor's Instructional Thought." Human Intelligence Newsletter, Volume 10, No. 2, pp. 3-4, Spring-Summer 1989.

Rosenholtz, Susan. Teachers' Workplace-The Social Organization of Schools. Longman, Inc. White Plains, NY, 1989.

Color in Running Heads

The green and white chalkboard above the black rule appears as a running head that bleeds off each page. The strong illustration and headline for the story make good use of the second color already on press for the chalkboard. The quote next to the illustration serves as a caption. Other pull quotes help the designer spread or shrink a story to fit.

Name Instructional Leader

Publisher Texas Elementary Principals and Supervisors Association, Austin, TX

Purpose/audience Service to members of the association

Production PageMaker and Illustrator on Macintosh SE/30

Printing Red and blue preprinted; black and green on light gray offset paper

Format 8½-by-11 inches, twelve pages

Design Design II and Sarah Hubert

Awards Magazine Design and Production, International Association of Business Communicators, American Society of Association Executives

Getting Color Fancy

The designers of *Ligature*, published by a service bureau, have fun with colors in the vertical nameplate as it changes from issue to issue. The huge letter L always forms a background for fanciful images that test the limits of artistic vision and showcase the company's production skills.

Name *Ligature*

Publisher *L. grafix, Portland, OR*

Purpose/audience *Service and marketing to customers*

Production *QuarkXPress on Macintosh*

Printing *Four-color process on coated or uncoated paper, depending on the style of illustrations*

Format *8 1/2-by-11 inches, four pages*

Design *Rich Sanders, Judith Quinn and Terri Thompson*

ear. It looks somewhat like a traditional hearing aid.

From here, sounds travel by cable to a **speech processor.** Important elements in speech are taken from the incoming signal and converted to electrical code. You can wear the speech processor on your belt or in a shirt pocket.

The code is sent back up the cable from the speech processor to a **transmitter** attached to the side of your head. The code is transmitted through your skin to a **receiver-stimulator** implanted in bone behind your ear. (Magnets on the transmitter and receiver-stimulator secure the transmitter.)

The receiver sends the signal to the stimulator. The stimulator sends the code down a tiny bundle of wires threaded directly into your cochlea. Here, nerve fibers are activated by the electrodes. The signal is sent via your auditory nerve to your brain, which interprets it as a form of hearing.

Single-channel vs. multichannel

Cochlear implants were developed in the early 1960's. When first approved by the Food and Drug Administration in 1984, the only type available was a single-channel implant.

The multichannel implant has 22 electrodes that are threaded directly into the cochlea. This greatly increases the amount of sound information received by your auditory nerve.

The multichannel implant compounds its effectiveness by taking advantage of how the cochlea works. The cochlea processes high frequencies in the outer part of the spiral, and lower pitches toward the center of the spiral.

By breaking sounds into varying frequencies and stimulating the

electrode in the appropriate part of the cochlea, the multichannel implant supplies more extensive sound information to your brain.

Who can have one?

A cochlear implant is not a fancy hearing aid. To be a candidate for one, you'll first undergo a careful auditory and medical evaluation. If you are accepted, surgery follows. As with any surgery, risk is involved.

To receive an implant, you must have a severe-to-profound inner ear (sensorineural) hearing loss in both ears and obtain no measurable benefit from a hearing aid. The following criteria also play a role in selection of candidates:

■ *Language acquisition* — If you learned language before becoming deaf, this increases the possible benefit of a cochlear implant.

■ *Duration of deafness* — The shorter the time you've been deaf, the greater your potential for a successful implant.

■ *Age* — Implants are done on persons two years of age and

Cochlear implants aren't obtrusive. Arrow points to cable carrying signal from microphone, hidden behind ear, to a speech processor you wear in a pocket or on a belt (see illustration, adjacent page).

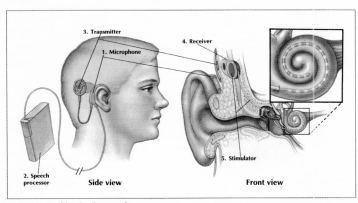

3. Transmitter
4. Receiver
1. Microphone
5. Stimulator
2. Speech processor
Side view   Front view

Here's how cochlear implants work: A microphone (1) picks up sounds. The sounds travel through a thin cable to a speech processor (2). You can wear the processor on a belt or in a pocket. The processor converts the signal into an electrical code and sends the code back up the cable to a transmitter (3) fastened to your head. The transmitter sends the code through your skin to a receiver-stimulator (4 and 5) implanted in bone directly beneath the transmitter. The stimulator sends the code down a tiny bundle of wires threaded directly into your cochlea (snail-shaped primary hearing organ). Nerve fibers are activated by electrode bands on this bundle of wires. Your auditory nerve carries the signal to your brain, which interprets the signal as a form of hearing.

older. (See "Implants for children.")

■ *Positive mental attitude* — A strong desire to hear will maximize your benefit.

Evaluation, surgery and rehabilitation

First, an extensive hearing assessment is done to measure your degree of deafness. Also, your doctor will examine you for boney growths that could complicate implantation surgery.

The surgery is done under general anesthesia and usually takes two or three hours. During surgery, a portion of the mastoid bone is removed and a tiny hole is drilled in the cochlea for the electrode wire. You can expect to leave the hospital in one or two days, but the

healing process takes about six weeks.

Once healing is complete, you are "hooked up" to your speech processor, which is programmed to send comfortable levels of sound to each electrode. Rehabilitation follows to help you "relearn" how to hear.

What can you "hear"?

Cochlear implants offer a wide spectrum of hearing benefit. Before implantation, it's impossible to predict where you will land on that spectrum. The degree of success can vary greatly from person to person.

Some implant recipients report hearing only sounds such as sirens or slamming doors. Others say

voices they knew before they became deaf sound much the same after having a multichannel implant.

Hearing is a highly subjective experience, but phrases recipients use to describe their newfound hearing are revealing: "It's computer-like," "the way I remember sound," "full and round," "tinny," "mechanical," or even "almost normal."

A recent study found the most striking difference between single-channel and multichannel users was in their ability to understand words with no visual cues such as lipreading.

Multichannel users understood words in a sentence over 30 percent of the time, while single-channel users scored below 1 percent

Instructional Four-Color Art

Printing in four-color process allows Mayo designers flexibility for both photos and illustrations. They use both to help readers understand their health and lifestyle choices. Medical illustrators prepare the drawings by hand, giving them the professional look familiar to generations of medical students. Notice that the type in the captions is consistent with other type throughout the publication. Another example of this newsletter appears on page 28.

Name *Mayo Clinic Health Letter*

Publisher *Mayo Foundation, Rochester, MN*

Purpose/audience *Service to subscribers*

Production *PageMaker for Windows on IBM*

Printing *Four-color process on natural offset paper*

Format *8½-by-11 inches, eight pages*

Design *George E. DeVinny and David E. Swanson*

Awards *National Coalition for Consumer Education,*
Newsletter Clearinghouse

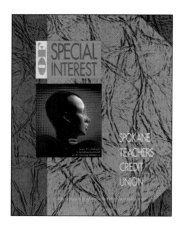

Vibrant Art for Vibrant Impact

Few newsletters change formats in mid issue. Although the front and back pages of *Of Special Interest* present the familiar 8½-by-11-inch image, the inside opens to two pages of 11-by-17 inches. And the interior of this broadside holds nothing back, using its larger canvas to present vibrant color. Lavish four-color illustrations and clever photo silhouettes demand that we read the headlines nearby.

Name *Of Special Interest*

Publisher *Spokane Teachers Credit Union, Spokane, WA*

Purpose/audience *Service and marketing to members*

Production *PageMaker and FreeHand on Macintosh*

Printing *Four-color process on white gloss-coated paper*

Format *11-by-17 inches folded to 8½-by-11 inches, four pages*

Design *Brad Hunter and Dale Davaz*

Spring 1991

The human mind. For the better part of fifty years psychologists have been poking, prodding, and probing its inner reaches to discover the roots of human behavior. Freud took a long, controversial look at mental disorders. Jung explored our secret "peak experiences." B. F. Skinner exposed the importance of "learned" patterns. And Dr. Ruth–well–little needs to be said about her role in popular psychology.

Their findings have often been startling–not so much in the bizarre stories of extreme cases, but more so in those behaviors we all seem to share. Who isn't relieved to hear that everyone, to one degree or another, experiences the same fear of falling, fear of loud noises, and fear of public speaking? And who isn't comforted in finding out that the personality "quirks" we think are ours alone are really shared by many?

Following in this long, honored tradition, "Special Interest" moves the clinic couch into the loan department lobby for a light-hearted glimpse at some of the more notable personality "types" for borrowers. It's a strictly non-scientific survey–and though you probably won't fit the profiles perfectly, in each you may find a hint of your own borrowing tendencies, as well as ways that Spokane Teachers Credit Union helps to accommodate your own personal style.

"Rachel the Researcher." Remember Marion the Librarian from "The Music Man"? If so, you can spot Rachel the Researcher. Prim, conservative, and never without a stack of books in her arms. Half of the fun of buying a car for Rachel is snooping through old copies of "Consumer Reports" for the best values. The other half comes with finding the best financing rate in town. With a dogged diligence she shops till she drops, going from one financial institution to the next, reading the fine print as she goes. For Rachel, a visit to the loan department becomes a virtual "credit crusade."

Purdue University's Credit Research Center reports that nationwide, about one-third of all borrowers fall broadly into Rachel's "shop around" category. They are likely to be college graduates, earn in excess of $40,000 a year, and have household debt burdens consuming at least 40 percent of their gross pretax income. And they *love* a good deal. With their upscale, educated profile, it's not surprising that many STCU members find

Loan Psychology: What Kind of Borrower Are You?

themselves cast from this "Rachel Researcher" mold–and who wouldn't be proud to say so!

For Rachel, then, Spokane Teachers Credit Union offers friendly, efficient service on two fronts: finding the best car, and finding the best financing. With her STCU membership Rachel gets free access to our NADA blue book listings and AIS new car cost guides–indispensable resources in her quest for value. And with free, no-obligation loan rates quoted right over the phone, she has STCU's low A.P.R. figures to use as the standard to judge all others.

"Timid Tammy". If you haven't seen her slinking up the Main Office stairs under cover of darkness, you've seen her hiding somewhere out behind the Valley's drive-through lane. Long trenchcoat, dark glasses–Timid Tammy has been thinking about getting a new boat loan since 1985, has a good credit history, but for all these years she hasn't been able to muster up the courage for a face-to-face encounter with a loan officer. For Tammy, a trip to the loan department is like a trip to the dentist chair. Confused, often embarrassed–she bases her fears on any number of the following reasons.

"The forms will be way too hard to fill out." The myth remains that a credit application is the financial institution's equivalent of a Rubic's cube–pages on pages of complicated financial questions, in language surely drafted by tax attorneys. Turn it, twist it, and you still can't figure out a loan application. But not at STCU–the sidebar story below walks you through our single four-page form, used for almost all personal consumer loans. Questions? Call us, and we're more than glad to answer any questions.

"I'm just sure I'll get turned down." Fear of failure affects us all, and there's perhaps no greater blow to our egos as failing a test of our financial worthiness. Still, as a financial institution we're bound to carefully scrutinize borrowers to assure our own financial integrity. If you're nervous about your own credit worthiness, try switching roles with a loan officer. Look at your occupation, income, and the length of time you've been on the job. Look at your credit history by contacting any number of credit reporting agencies in your area. For a small fee, you can get a detailed printout of the same information we use. How well have you managed your credit? If you were a lender, how would someone with your personal credit record fair? Try not to be too hard on yourself–you don't always need a perfect record for approval. But even if you do have credit problems, talk to us–we're glad to suggest ways to work through them for your next loan application. Most of all, try not to feel threatened by the process itself–and find comfort in the fact that nearly four of every five credit applications at STCU are approved.

"I don't know the first thing about loans, and I'll be so embarrassed." Many borrowers are paralyzed by an awareness of their own "lending naivete." Fearing a fierce interrogation by lenders, Timid Tammy's feel helpless. Yet this insensitivity to people's uncertainties points to problems with the

Anatomy of a Loan Application

Most of us remember high school biology lab and the infamous frog disection project. Remember how squeamish you were at the thought of making that first incision, but then how anticlimactic it was when he was all opened up? A Spokane Teachers loan application is much the same: spend just one minute inspecting it part by part and those haunting fears about "long, complicated loan forms" will, in an instant, be set at ease.

It's four pages long, made up of 12 sections. 10 of those sections ask the following simple questions:

Section 1 ....What kind of loan would you like?
Section 2 ....Are you applying with a co-signer?
Section 3 ....What's your name, address, etc.?
Section 4 ....What's your job? Where do you work?
Section 5 ....How much income do you receive?
Section 6 ....Who can we call as references?
Section 7 ....Do you own assets, like a home or car?
Section 8 ....Do you have current debts?
Section 9 ....Have you had past credit problems?
Section 12 ....Do you want credit insurance?

Pretty basic, right? In section 10 it's our turn, and we provide a description of the terms of your loan. Section 11 is where you sign on the line, agreeing to those terms.

So where's the hard stuff? It's not there! No "what's and wherefors", and certainly no blood and guts. Proof again that at STCU, we make the business of borrowing simple.

Next, build a reserve fund to provide for the unexpected. A reasonable target amount might be $5000–all uncommitted money. The absence of this reserve is likely to pose a greater risk than any investment risk you're apt to deal with. How do you put that much aside? Pay yourself first– take a part of your income right off the top, and put it into savings. Think of this savings commitment like any other bill you pay, and put it at the top of the list.

Third, set your goals. Decide what you'd like to save for, when the funds are needed, and the cost. Then when the goals are set, prioritize them. Finally, make sure that funds dedicated to an investment portfolio are truly affordable. Use common sense here–if cash set aside for retirement leaves you with mammoth credit costs, it's money that's probably better used in the present. Let the "first things first" principle be your guide. And by all means, feel free to call and set up an appointment for a personal review your needs. Dial 326-1954 and ask for Tom at extension 119.

Board of Directors Election Results

In the recent election held to decide four seats on the Spokane Teachers Board of Directors, Gilbert Brooks, Keith E. Rostvold, Georgia Miller, and Jack Mathews were chosen by STCU members to lead their credit union into the years ahead. Brooks, Rostvold, and Miller have been long-time veterans of the Board; Mathews steps in as a new Director.

Those four will join John Young, Jasper Johnson, Edith Manildi, C. William Anderson, Geraldine Carlson, Robert Howard, Robert Richards, John Rodkey, and Eugene Sivertson in fulfilling the Board's volunteer policy-making responsiblities.

Following the March 18 Annual Meeting, John Young was retained as Chairman of the Board of Directors. Successful in his re-election bid for a Supervisory Committee post was John W. Parrott, Manager of EWU's Administrative Support Unit. He rejoins Ed Feldheusen and Dave Sackville-West in a continuation of the service he has offered for the past 12 years.

Employee Merit Award Winner: Sue Katz

That path you seem to notice worn in the Main Office carpet– it leads right to the desk of Sue Katz. Sue is the bright spot in the day for many STCU members, and they certainly know the way to her station! One would certainly get the same message from the bright, floral bouquets and boxes of candy gracing her desk–given by our members in their appreciation for her excellent service.

> "I REALLY ENJOY MY JOB– AND I'M SO LUCKY TO BE ABLE TO SAY THAT!"
>
> SUE KATZ

A native of California, Sue has lived in Spokane for 11 years. STCU has been lucky to have her as an employee for nine of those years, two of them were spent as a teller. She's been in Member Services for seven years, and she says with a sparkle, "I really enjoy my job–and I'm so lucky to be able to say that!"

Sue and her husband, Bernie, have four children ranging in ages from 5 to 23 years old. She loves participating in activities with them, which include boating and camping. She also likes to bowl–but at the absolute top of her list, she loves to SHOP!

"My job is ever-changing, and it is always an on-going challenge– especially with the phenomenal growth we've experienced these last several years," Sue comments. In nominating Sue for this quarter's Merit Award, one co-worker claimed that "if I had to go to war, I'd want Sue by my side– she's that kind of friend." What greater compliment can be paid than that! A hearty congratulations, then, to Sue Katz, the latest recipient of the Spokane Teachers Employee Merit Award.

Catt Tales: Back to the Basics

Pop quiz! We know the shortest distance between two points is a straight line, but for STCU members, what is the shortest distance between them and their money? Not a teller line, but a phone line. All thanks to CATT, our all-day, all-night Computer Aided Telephone Teller, which performs many common transactions from any touch-tone phone. How much time and energy will CATT save you? Read on.

How often do you make a special trip to one of our offices just to find out your current or available balance? How about to see if a check you've written has cleared? How many times are you inquiring about a due date, payment amount, or payoff balance on an STCU loan?

Wouldn't it be nice to just pick up a phone and have CATT answer the questions, anytime and from anywhere?

CATT can transfer funds from savings to checking or vice versa. From savings or checking to your loan. Or transfer a minimum of $300 from a Silver Eagle account to any other account. It even issues cashiers checks–to you, or to a third party.

All quickly and easily. And if you haven't yet signed up for CATT, it's just as simple. Return the FYI coupon in this newsletter, stop by any STCU office, or call us at 326-1954 or 1-800-858-5750.

Safe Deposit Boxes Available at Valley Branch

STCU to Sponsor Junior Bloomsday Patch Program

National Car Sale Scheduled for April 27

National RX Joins the STCU Family

STCU Members Visiting Canada Urged to Use Visa Cards

Using Color to Get Attention

Color focuses attention on the sidebar that seems to have been torn off a notepad. A regular feature of the newsletter, the "Noteworthy" panel was part of a click art series purchased on disk. Bleeding its shadow off the left margin gives it an extra lively dimension.

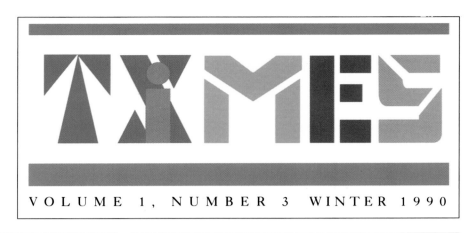

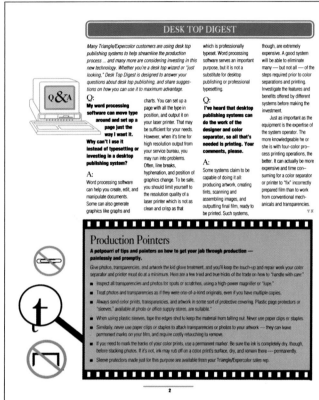

Simulating Metallic Ink

TX Times uses a flexible five-column grid to accommodate the photos and graphics demanded by its audience of printing buyers and graphic designers. The nameplate and inside rules use color builds to simulate use of metallic ink, an effect enhanced by printing on premium 100-pound gloss-coated paper. The blue, however, is true metallic ink run as a fifth color. Note: Due to the process used to print this book, metallic inks will not reproduce.

Name *TX Times*

Publisher *Triangle/Expercolor, Skokie, IL*

Purpose/audience *Service and marketing to customers*

Production *PageMaker on Macintosh SE/30*

Printing *Four-color process plus metallic blue on premium white gloss-coated paper*

Format *8 1/2-by-11 inches, four pages*

Design *The Newsletter Group, Inc.*

Award *Newsletter Clearinghouse*

Using Metallic Ink to Communicate

This is a perfect example of newsletter design that complements its subject matter. Using silver metallic as the second color, the designer brings to life the publisher's message of control over metals. The metallic ink seems to change from silver to cool blue almost to bronze, depending on how light strikes it. As the ultimate professional touch, the paper is premium dull coated (slightly better than matte). The dull surface contrasts with the silver and reduces the gloss of the black, making the silver seem even more like genuine metal. Note that the silver of the gloss-coated reply card matches that of the newsletter itself. (Note: Due to the process used to print this book, metallic inks will not reproduce.) For another example of color matching in a reply card, see page 101.

Name *Inside Extrusion Processing*

Publisher *Conair Gatto, Hauppauge, NY*

Purpose/audience *Service and marketing to customers*

Production *PageMaker and FreeHand on Macintosh IIcx*

Printing *Black and metallic silver on white matte-coated paper*

Format *8¹/₂-by-11 inches, twelve pages*

Design *The Morris-Lee Group—James Morris-Lee and Steven Smith*

Award *Newsletter Clearinghouse*

A quarterly update on extrusion technology for pipe, profile and tubing processors from Conair Gatto

Special Cutting Issue

Inside Extrusion Processing

VOLUME I, NUMBER 1

ENHANCING PRODUCTIVITY

Increased productivity, profitability for profile and tubing processors through better in-line cutting

HEAVY quality-control responsibility falls to the "lowly" cutter downstream on the line.

We can carefully blend polymer to exact customer specification.

We can fine tune the extruder and line to pull product exactly.

But if the cutter's substandard—if it shatters product, collapses tubing, interrupts the line or simply cuts poorly—your final product won't meet the specs your customer's expecting.

To improve product quality,

production flexibility and system reliability, you need a good cutter.

At best, an inaccurate cutter will increase operating costs by forcing you to order extra material to accommodate waste or by forcing you to add a secondary cutting or finishing operation.

At worst, it can cause rejection of a shipment, loss of a customer or the inability to get new customers.

A cutter's flexibility can also determine whether an extrusion line *Please see* **Productivity,** *page 8*

Cutting complex shapes—Even small or asymmetric shapes process more easily when the cutter carefully matches its extrusion line.

NEW EQUIPMENT

New Conair Gatto on-demand cutters now have U.S.-built vacuum clutch/brake

SINCE 1985, processors who wanted a U.S.-made cutter with the Forêt vacuum clutch/brake had one option: buy from a single manufacturer near Philadelphia.

Some fore... into the U.S... clutch/brake... problems. If... out, it must... for repair—... had a new u... But a ne... October 198

Gatto to offer the U.S.-built Forêt vacuum clutch/brake in its new line of on-demand cutters. Now, processors who need the vacuum unit can take advantage of Conair's full-line

THE INSIDE VIEW

Control the process, increase the profits

by Ernie Preiato, Vice President–Sales
Conair Gatto

THE difference between a profitable and an unprofitable extruder line usually comes down to a question of process measurement and control.

In a profitable extruder line, the raw material mix, feed rate and moisture content are controlled correctly. Then, the extruder speed and temperature profile is controlled accurately and correctly for each product, keeping product quality high and protecting the extruder itself from damage.

Downstream equipment, such as pullers, water baths and cutters, operate at the right speed, temperature and cut length.

And all this process information is recorded and filed to meet customer SQC requirements.

That's a tough task, and it's getting more difficult all the time.

High-performance resins and complex extrusion shapes require close control of process conditions, and customers are demanding better product quality as well as more process documentation.

That's why microprocessor-based controls are being applied to the ...essors, or ...do ...l electro-...ls can, ...e relia-

...at would ... of the *...rol, page 2*

Inside Extrusion Processing

For a free subscription, complete and mail card

Name: _____

Title: _____

Company: _____

Number of extrusion lines: _____

Street address: _____

City: _____ St.: ____ Zip: _____

Process (check all that apply): ☐ Tubing ☐ Profile ☐ Pipe ☐ Other: _____

Phone: (_____) _____

Please send information on these products/processes covered in this issue:

Please check reader service number	Product	Use now	Bought in last year	Plan to buy this year	Please check reader service number	Product	Use now	Bought in last year	Plan to buy this year
#1 ☐	Vacuum clutch/brake	☐	☐	☐	#8 ☐	Pullers	☐	☐	☐
#2 ☐	Fast-ship program	☐	☐	☐	— ☐	New extrusion line	☐	☐	☐
#3 ☐	On-demand cutters	☐	☐	☐	— ☐	Saws	☐	☐	☐
#4 ☐	Granulators	☐	☐	☐	— ☐	Coilers	☐	☐	☐
#5 ☐	Conair Gatto dies	☐	☐	☐	— ☐	Tanks	☐	☐	☐
#6 ☐	Convertible screenchangers	☐	☐	☐	— ☐	Chillers	☐	☐	☐
					— ☐	Conair leasing	☐	☐	☐
#7 ☐	Other Conair products	☐	☐	☐	— ☐	Blenders	☐	☐	☐

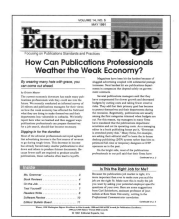

VOLUME 14, NO. 5
MAY 1991

The Editorial Eye

Focusing on Publications Standards and Practices

How Can Publications Professionals Weather the Weak Economy?

By wearing many hats with grace, you can come out ahead.

Magazines have been hit the hardest because of sluggish advertising coupled with substantial postage increases. Next hardest hit are publications departments in companies that depend solely on government contracts.

Several publications managers said that they have compensated for slower growth and decreased budgets by cutting costs and taking fewer creative

---

THE EDITOR

Weak Economy *(Continued from p. 1)*

implemented few, if any, layoffs so far, and what cuts have been made appear to have been executed equitably across department lines.

But almost everyone indicated that some type of hiring freeze had been implemented. Fewer new publications positions are being created, many vacant positions are not being filled, and some positions have been eliminated. One proofreading manager at a national circulation magazine said, "Those employees who leave are not replaced, and those who don't produce perish."

Not surprisingly, staffers are less likely to leave

MAY 1991

Right Job? *(Continued from p. 1)*

● "How much feedback will I get on the job?" Without feedback, you don't learn and improve.

● "How thoroughly will the editorial supervisor review my work?" The answer you want is "Very thoroughly." If a supervising editor doesn't read behind

---

THE EDITORIAL EYE

Ms. Grammar *(Continued from p. 3)*

to find continual use of the third person burdensome, and so they revert to the first person for relief. Ms. Grammar can only speculate on their state of mind when they commit this breach.

Whatever the cause, the result is on paper. Enter now Ms. Grammar wearing her copyeditor's eyeshade. Does she change every instance of the first person to third person? Not invariably. Does she permit the mixed-person sentences to stand? Surely you jest. She recasts some sentences to permit the company name and the first person to coexist. Thus,

Quick and Dirty Corp. places *our* facilities at your service

✔ Change to a less-expensive paper stock.
✔ Rely on industry consultants rather than freelancers to write columns and standing departments. Consultants will often accept honoraria instead of the higher freelancer fees.
✔ Write more material in-house.
✔ Use less color.
✔ Limit the number of industry publications to which you subscribe, and maintain memberships only in those professional organizations that give you information and contacts you can get nowhere else. ∎

Ms. Grammar

who's in third?

This column on grammar is concocted by a veteran EEI editor whose identity will remain cloaked in mystery. The Eye claims no responsibility for Ms. Grammar's musings—unless they are well received.

A letter has poured in asking *The Eye* to pass judgment on a particular aspect of a pronoun-antecedent problem—that of changing person from third to first in midstream. The writer cites such examples as the following:

In addition to *our* important moves in Florida and New York, *Short-Hop Airlines* made a number of...

Color That Adds Flair

Huge red folios contrast with lots of white space in the drop sinks to make a lively combination. With a relatively large proportion of text, using plenty of subheads, bullets (also in red) and generous leading lets readers move easily through the pages. The overall effect is just the right blend of conservative image with imaginative flair.

Name *The Editorial Eye*

Publisher *Editorial Experts, Inc., Alexandria, VA*

Purpose/audience *Service to subscribers*

Production *Ventura Publisher on IBM*

Printing *Black and red on natural offset paper*

Format *8 1/2-by-11 inches, twelve pages*

Design *Ann Molpus and Dana Mitchell*

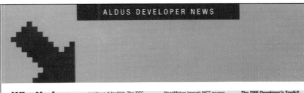

ALDUS DEVELOPER NEWS

What's in a Toolkit?

Throughout this newsletter you'll find frequent references to our Developer's Toolkits. For those of you who have not yet used one, here's a brief review of the purpose, contents, and availability of the two Aldus products we currently offer to third-party developers.

TIFF Developer's Toolkit

If you produce digital-image hardware or software that supports the TIFF standard, you need the the TIFF Developer's Toolkit. The kit includes TIFF utilities, sample files, and the latest version of the TIFF specification. The documentation explains both how to use the toolkit and how TIFF is supported and administered. It also supplies answers to questions frequently asked by TIFF developers.

The toolkit disks contain a TIFFRead, a utility for dumping a TIFF header, and the C libraries that make up the TIFF reader. You'll also find six black-and-white images, 10 grayscale images, three palette-color images, and three 24-bit full-color images for both the Macintosh and PC platforms.

Aldus Developers Association (ADA) members can order the TIFF Developer's Toolkit free of charge; nonmembers can

purchase it for $50. The TIFF Developer's Toolkit may also be downloaded from the Aldus bulletin boards on CompuServe and AppleLink.

Filter Developer's Toolkit

The Filter Developer's Toolkit provides the technical documentation and utilities necessary to write import and export filters for PageMaker 4.0 (Macintosh and Windows platforms).

Documentation on text filters explains filter basics, the import/export mechanism, the Aldus file and memory-manager interfaces, Microsoft Windows text filters, and other vital facts.

You'll also find documentation on graphic filters and import basics

PageMaker import; PICT screen image (for Macintosh), TIFF, or metafile; screen image for Windows; and more.

The Filter Developer's Toolkit disks contain sample files for text import and export, C include files for filter routines, and testbench debugging tools and source code.

ADA Developers Association members can order the Filter Developer's Toolkit free of charge; nonmembers can purchase it for $100.

designs and templates. Contact: Glen Cruzen, Image Express, 1915 Orangewood Avenue, Second Floor, Orange, CA 92668; phone (714) 633-6291.

DesignWorks has announced Professional Portfolio, a collection of 1,000 designs organized into 50 business and informal identity systems. Targeted for the quick-print industry, Professional Portfolio includes templates, a counter book for customer design

The TIFF Developer's Toolkit and the Filter Developer's Toolkit can be ordered by contacting the Aldus Developers Desk.

ALDUS DEVELOPER NEWS

ElseWare C... shipped Che... Macintosh. D... bureaus, gra... the desktop... CheckList's ... inside PageN... conflicts that... printing proc... the documen... files, allows ... change print... all the data i... file. Page co... shown for de... electronic no... attach speci... CheckList al... print-to-disk ... in Aldus Fre... Illustrator, Q...

Aldus News

Page-imposition program acquired

Aldus recently acquired exclusive worldwide marketing rights to a forthcoming Macintosh-based page-imposition software program. The yet-to-be-named product is currently under development by Emulation Technologies Inc. of Cleveland, Ohio, in coordination with the San Francisco-based Professional Prepress Alliance.

Imposition is the arrangement of pages from a document

Aldus introduces License Pack

Aldus has responded to customer requests for a convenient and economical way to purchase multiple copies of Aldus products for use in the small workgroup or department environment. The Aldus License Pack gives the owner of a full retail version of an Aldus software product the right to make one copy of that product for use on another computer. Individual License Packs are now available

Aldus to host International Developers Workshop

On November 12-13, 1991, Aldus will host a Developers Workshop in London. The event will be held at the Edwardian International Hotel, at Heathrow, with developers from England, Scotland, Germany, France, Sweden, Italy, The Netherlands, Spain, and a number of Pacific Rim countries expected to attend.

Technical sessions include desktop color issues, OPI (Open ...

all meals, and one night's hotel accommodation. For information on the workshop or to register, contact Sally Broomfield, Aldus Europe, West One Business Park, 5 Mid New Cultins, Edinburgh, Scotland EH11 4DU; phone 44-31-453-2211; fax 44-31-453-4422.

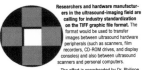

ALDUS DEVELOPER NEWS

Medical Imaging Community Urged to Standardize on TIFF

Researchers and hardware manufacturers in the ultrasound-imaging field are calling for industry standardization on the TIFF graphic file format. The format would be used to transfer images between ultrasound hardware peripherals (such as scanners, film recorders, CD-ROM drives, and display consoles) and also between ultrasound scanners and personal computers.

The effort is spearheaded by Dr. Philippe Jeanty of Vanderbilt University's radiology department. Jeanty predicts benefits such as more efficient image publishing and archiving, increased flexibility as the hardware evolves, and speedier professional consultation with distant experts.

At the June meeting of the American Institute of Ultrasound in Medicine (AIUM) in Washington, DC, Jeanty organized a discussion with a number of ultrasound-related equipment manufacturers. In the July issue of the medical journal *The Fetus*, he published a set of articles responding to his proposal for TIFF standardization.

Mark Magrane, staff engineer at Quantum Medical Systems in Issaquah, Washington, supports Dr. Jeanty's proposal. His company chose to standardize on TIFF for their ultrasound system, which combines a frame grabber and a desktop viewing station. Magrane envisions several future applications that could be made possible by uniform use of TIFF. One example is the storage of sound as audio Doppler to accompany the visual image, accompanied by voice annotation. Another possibility is the display of short sequences of images for real-time display, offline calculations, and patient report generation.

"Proprietary standards, i.e., not adapting a common standard, can have some short-term benefits for the manufacturer, but is a hindrance to third-party developers and a disservice to the customer," according to

another proponent of the standard, Dave Thomas, engineering product support manager for Acoustic Imaging in Phoenix, Arizona. His company currently provides its customers with a conversion utility for TIFF so that Acoustic Imaging's images can be used with existing software packages on the PC, Macintosh, and Sun platforms.

Len Grenier, vice president of engineering at A.L.I. Technologies, a vendor of Image Management Systems, is also "committed to supporting standards that facilitate the interchange of data between ultrasound systems, image management systems, and peripherals such as hardcopy devices." Grenier believes that broad adoption of consensus-based standards will benefit the entire ultrasound community.

Aldus supports the efforts by the medical imaging industry to standardize on TIFF. We have invited Dr. Jeanty to lead a new TIFF medical-imaging subgroup and will refer others in this industry to him and help publicize the subgroup.

MCI Mail

A Hotline for ADA Members

As an Aldus Developers Association member, you'll receive a double benefit when you use MCI Mail—special pricing on your MCI Mail account and direct access to our Third Party Marketing department.

First, the savings: MCI will waive the first year's registration fee for any individual or multiple-user (REMS) account that is registered through the ADA. You'll also receive a 10 percent discount on all electronic mail messages (Instant Letters) you send. MCI Mail charges only for outgoing messages, not for messages received.

Your extra benefit is priority access. Using MCI Mail and a modem, ADA members can send text messages (and binary files) directly to Aldus via a toll-free telephone number. Your message will arrive in the personal E-mail box of the Third Party Marketing employee who has been designated to answer your questions. (ADA members receive a Contacts List for our department staff.)

This double benefit through MCI Mail is designed to provide ADA members the best service possible. Messages appearing in Aldus E-mail boxes are easy for employees to receive, respond to, or forward to others. And that means you can get answers to your questions as quickly as possible.

Place
Boston
San Diego
Las Vegas (Hilton Exhibit Hall)
New York City (Javitz Center)

Join the Aldus Developers Association!

We invite you to join the Aldus Developers Association (ADA). Membership offers many benefits—free Aldus software, direct access to the Aldus Developers Desk, and discounts on MCI electronic mail, to name just a few. The annual dues of $300 entitles you, for example, to one free copy each of Aldus FreeHand, PrePrint, PageMaker, and Persuasion. ADA members can also order Developer's Toolkits free of charge.

To join the Aldus Developers Association, please mail or fax us a brief description of your business and product on your company letterhead. Membership is open to all who are currently developing products compatible with the Aldus product line.

Specing Tints for Drama

Only two ink colors produce this stunning combination of color and type. The cinnamon runs at 100 percent and as tints of 20 percent and 40 percent. Other issues use colors such as dark green or burgundy in place of cinnamon. To maintain the dramatic contrast, the black runs only at 100 percent. Printing on thick, absorbent offset paper makes the colors rich but not glossy.

Name *Aldus Developer News*

Publisher *Aldus Corporation, Seattle, WA*

Purpose/audience *Service to third-party developers*

Production *PageMaker and FreeHand on Macintosh IIcx*

Printing *Black plus a different second color from issue to issue on white offset paper*

Format *8 1/2-by-11 inches, four pages*

Design *Don Bergh and Colleen Burnham*

EASY ACCESS: SKIDATA TICKETING

WATCH FOR OUR WATCH

With the new season, Mt. Bachelor will inaugurate its European-style Skidata automated ticketing system. To put it in perspective, Skidata is to ticketing what quad chairs were to surface lifts. A revolution.

Access to lifts will become easier and more flexible than ever before. The liftline process will be streamlined and short-ened. And doing will be available by days or points. You choose.

Here's how it works.

When you buy a lift ticket, you can buy a single-day, multi-day or point ticket. (Season and mini passes are also available.)

Whatever your choice, all the details of your purchase will be encoded right onto your ticket, which can then use somewhat like a debit card throughout the ski experience.

At each lift base, Mt. Bachelor has installed a sensing device. Instead of waiting to have your ticket manually verified, you'll just insert the electronically encoded end of your ticket into the device, and you're on your way.

Mt. Bachelor is one of the first U.S. ski areas to install this system, and the very first to offer the lineup of flexible ticketing options, including the "flex-time" point ticket.

Flextime skiers can purchase a 200-point or 400-point ticket. With every lift ride, the appropriate number of points will be debited from the ticket value. The sensing devices will even display your "point balance," so you'll always know how many points

Introducing the most multi-clock feature of the new SkiData system: The Mt. Bachelor Keywatch. The Keywatch combines the speed and convenience of the Skidata system with the modern technology of interprocessors and indie-terror.

you have left.

Each lift has been assigned a point value, calculated by lift type (fixed grip or express), length, vertical rise, and mountain area served.

So with over 200-point ticket, ride the super express chars 10 times, or ride the Orange, Sunrise and Yellow chairs 13 times, or some combination of the above. Over a day or over a season. It's all up to you.

Even the ticket look is all-new, as you see here. "Ski Zips," which attach to garments and hold a Velcro ticket, are sold at ticket accessories on-mountain, as are "key-watches," which replace the ticket altogether (see adjacent article).

Of course, Mt. Bachelor will continue to offer all its traditional ticket categories in addition to the new point tickets.

THE TOP 1%

To put 1991 ski publication ratings in context, Subscribers and readers have had their say, and the nation's ski areas have been ranked accordingly.

The results? Both Ski and Snow Country magazines rated Mt. Bachelor in the Top Ten.

Ski readers, for example, put us at Number Eight, with a push that included Vail, Deer Valley, Snowmass, Wheeler/Blackcomb, Aspen, Steamboat and Beaver Creek.

Then they put us at Number Three, nationally for our network of lifts, and Number Six among all U.S. resorts for snow quality and family programs.

So there you are, more than 600 ski areas nationwide. And Mt. Bachelor ranks in the Top Ten. That's the top 1%. Let it snow or we can all celebrate the bottom.

Color That Suits the Subject

The Summit Express nameplate introduces color used throughout the publication, inviting readers to join the colorful world of skiing. Using vibrant colors that are more familiar in formal presentations than in newsletters, the designer captures the freedom and energy that skiers feel on the slopes. Printed on sturdy offset paper, the piece can take abuse in the mail or as an insert without the images scratching or fading.

Name Summit Express

Publisher Mt. Bachelor Ski Area, Bend, OR

Purpose/audience Service and marketing to customers and the media

Production PageMaker and SuperPaint on Macintosh

Printing Four-color process on white offset paper

Format 11-by-17 inches, four pages

Design Mandala Communications

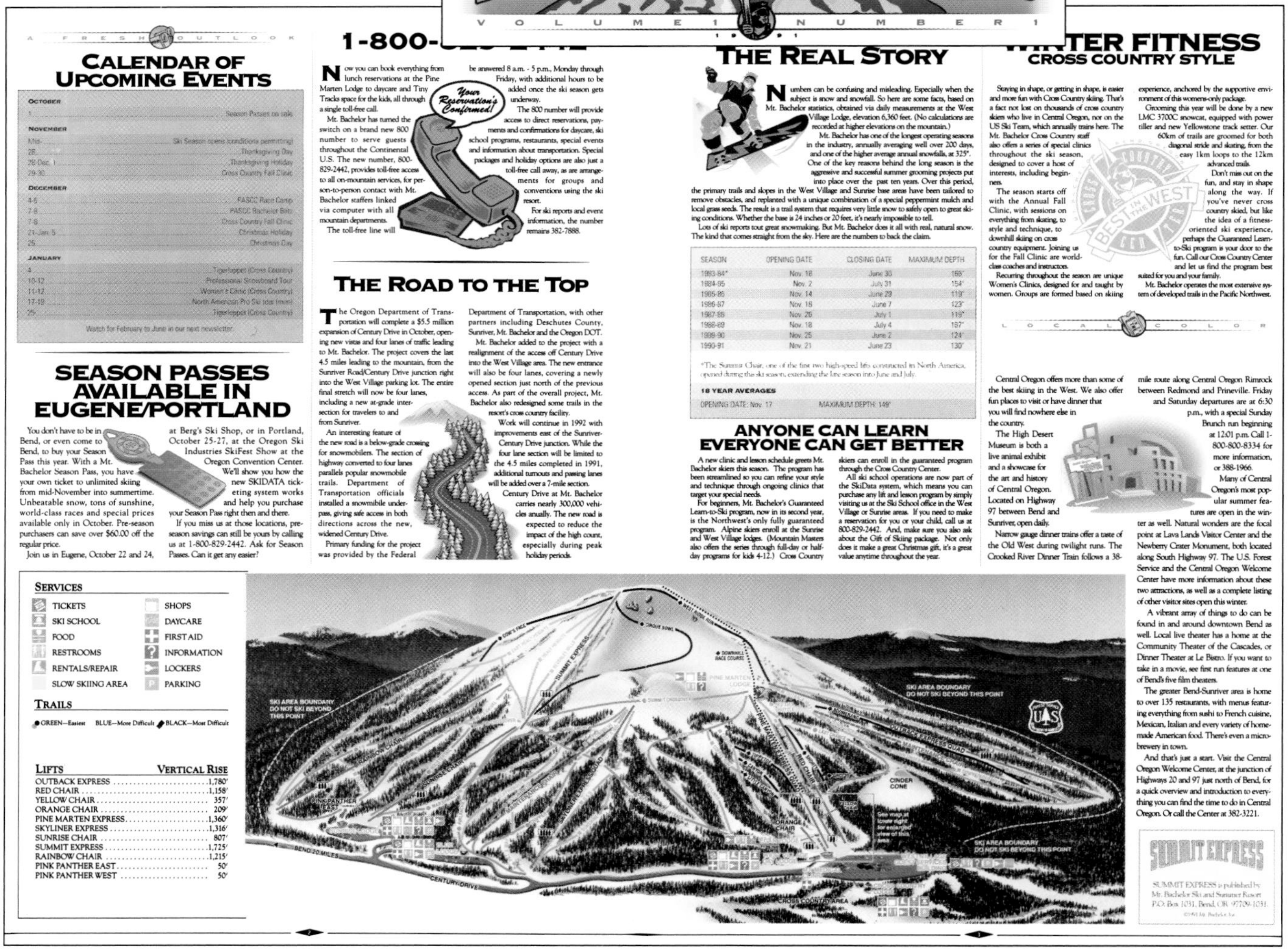

CALENDAR OF UPCOMING EVENTS

OCTOBER
Season Passes on sale

NOVEMBER
Mid- .... Ski Season opens (conditions permitting)
28 .... Thanksgiving Day
28-Dec 1 .... Thanksgiving Holiday
29-30 .... Cross Country Fall Clinic

DECEMBER
4-6 .... PASCC Race Camp
7-8 .... PASCC Bachelor Blitz
7-8 .... Cross Country Fall Clinic
25 .... Christmas Holiday
25 .... Christmas Day

JANUARY
4 .... Tigertopper (Cross Country)
10-12 .... Professional Snowboard Tour
11-12 .... Women's (Cross Country)
17-19 .... North American Pro Ski tour (event)
25 .... Tigertopper (Cross Country)

Watch for February to June in our next newsletter.

SEASON PASSES AVAILABLE IN EUGENE/PORTLAND

You don't have to be in Bend, or even come to Bend, to buy your Season Pass this year. With a Mt. Bachelor Season Pass, you have your own ticket to unlimited skiing from mid-November into summertime. Unbeatable snow, tons of sunshine, world-class races and special prices available only in October. Pre-season purchasers can save over $60.00 off the regular price.

Join us in Eugene, October 22 and 24,

at Berg's Ski Shop, or in Portland, October 25-27, at the Oregon Ski Industries SkiFest Show at the Oregon Convention Center. We'll show you how the new SKIDATA ticketing system works and help you purchase your Season Pass right then and there.

If you miss us at those locations, pre-season savings can still be yours by calling us at 1-800-829-2442. Ask for Season Passes. Can it get any easier?

SERVICES

TICKETS	SHOPS
SKI SCHOOL	DAYCARE
FOOD	FIRST AID
RESTROOMS	INFORMATION
RENTALS/REPAIR	LOCKERS
SLOW SKIING AREA	PARKING

TRAILS

GREEN—Easiest   BLUE—More Difficult   BLACK—Most Difficult

LIFTS	VERTICAL RISE
OUTBACK EXPRESS	1,780'
RED CHAIR	1,158'
YELLOW CHAIR	357'
ORANGE CHAIR	209'
PINE MARTEN EXPRESS	1,360'
SKYLINER EXPRESS	1,316'
SUNRISE CHAIR	807'
SUMMIT EXPRESS	1,725'
RAINBOW CHAIR	1,215'
PINK PANTHER EAST	50'
PINK PANTHER WEST	50'

1-800-

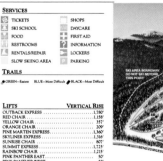

Now you can book everything from lunch reservations at the Pine Marten Lodge to daycare and Tiny Tracks space for the kids, all through a single toll-free call.

Mt. Bachelor has named the switch on a brand new 800 number to serve guests throughout the Continental U.S. The new number, 800-829-2442, provides toll-free access to all on-mountain services, for person-to-person contact with Mt. Bachelor staffers linked via computer with all mountain departments.

The toll-free line will

be answered 8 a.m. - 5 p.m., Monday through Friday, with additional hours to be added once the ski season gets underway.

Your Reservation's Confirmed

The 800 number will provide access to direct reservations, payments and confirmations for daycare, ski school programs, restaurants, special events and information about transportation, Special packages and holiday options are also just a toll-free call away, as are arrangements for groups and conventions using the ski resort.

For ski reports and event information, the number remains 382-7888.

THE ROAD TO THE TOP

The Oregon Department of Transportation will complete a $5.5 million expansion of Century Drive in October, opening new vistas and four lanes of traffic leading to Mt. Bachelor. The project covers the last 4.5 miles leading to the mountain, from the Sunriver Road/Century Drive junction right into the West Village area. The entire final stretch will now be four lanes, including a new at-grade intersection for travelers to and from Sunriver.

An interesting feature of the new road is a below-grade crossing for snowmobiles. The section of highway converted to four lanes parallels popular snowmobile trails. Department of Transportation officials installed a snowmobile underpass, giving safe access in both directions across the new, widened Century Drive.

Primary funding for the project was provided by the Federal

Department of Transportation, with other partners including Deschutes County, Sunriver, Mt. Bachelor and the Oregon DOT.

Mt. Bachelor added to the project with a realignment of the access off Century Drive into the West Village area. The new entrance will also be four lanes, covering a newly opened section just north of the previous access. As part of the overall project, Mt. Bachelor also redesigned some trails in the resort's cross country facility.

Work will continue in 1992 with improvements east of the Sunriver-Century Drive junction. While the four lane section will be limited to the 4.5 miles completed in 1991, additional turnouts and passing lanes will be added over a 7-mile stretch.

Century Drive at Mt. Bachelor carries nearly 300,000 vehicles annually. The new road is expected to reduce the impact of the high count, especially during peak holiday periods.

THE REAL STORY

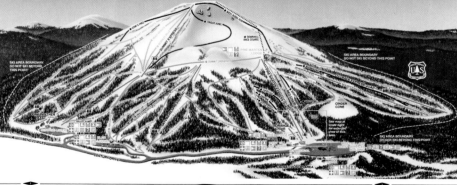

Numbers can be confusing and misleading. Especially when the subject is snow and snowfall. So here are some facts, based on Mt. Bachelor statistics, obtained via daily measurements at the West Village Lodge, elevation 6,360 feet. (No calculations are recorded at higher elevations on the mountains.)

Mt. Bachelor has one of the longest operating seasons in the industry, annually averaging well over 200 days, and one of the higher average annual snowfalls, at 325". One of the key reasons behind the long season is the aggressive and successful summer grooming projects put into place over the past ten years. Over this period, the primary trails and slopes in the West Village and Sunrise base areas have been tailored to remove obstacles, and replanted with a unique combination of a special peppermint mulch and local grass seeds. The result is a trail system that requires very little snow to safely open to great skiing conditions. Whether the base is 24 inches or 20 feet, it's nearly impossible to tell.

Lots of ski reports tout great snowmaking. But Mt. Bachelor does it all with real, natural snow. The kind that comes straight from the sky. Here are the numbers to back the claim.

SEASON	OPENING DATE	CLOSING DATE	MAXIMUM DEPTH
1983-84*	Nov. 18	June 30	168"
1984-85	Nov. 7	July 31	154"
1985-86	Nov. 14	June 29	119"
1986-87	Nov. 18	June 7	123"
1987-88	Nov. 25	July 1	110"
1988-89	Nov. 18	July 4	197"
1989-90	Nov. 25	June 2	124"
1990-91	Nov. 21	June 23	130"

*The Summit Chair, one of the first two high-speed lifts constructed in North America, opened during the ski season, extending the late season from June until July.

18 YEAR AVERAGES

OPENING DATE: Nov. 17	MAXIMUM DEPTH: 148"

ANYONE CAN LEARN EVERYONE CAN GET BETTER

A new clinic and lesson schedule greets Mt. Bachelor skiers this season. The program has been streamlined so you can refine your style and technique through ongoing clinics that target your special needs.

For beginners, Mt. Bachelor's Guaranteed Learn-to-Ski program, now in its second year, is the Northwest's only fully guaranteed program. Alpine skiers enroll at the Sunrise and West Village lodges. (Mountain Masters also offers the series through full-day or half-day programs for kids 4-12.) Cross country

skiers can enroll in the guaranteed program through the Cross Country Center.

All ski school operations are now part of the SkiData system, which means you can purchase any lift and lesson program by simply visiting us at the Ski School office in the West Village or Sunrise areas. If you need to make a reservation for you or your child, call us at 800-829-2442. And, make sure you ask about the Gift of Skiing package. They really does it make a great Christmas gift, it's a great value anytime throughout the year.

WINTER FITNESS
CROSS COUNTRY STYLE

Staying in shape, or getting in shape, is easier and more fun with Cross Country skiing. That's a fact not lost on thousands of cross country skiers who live in Central Oregon, nor on the US Ski Team, which annually trains here. The Mt. Bachelor Cross Country staff also offers a series of special clinics throughout the ski season, designed to cover a host of interests, including beginners.

The season starts off with the Annual Fall Clinic, with sessions on everything from skating, to style and technique, to downhill skiing on cross country equipment. Joining us for the Fall Clinic are world-class coaches and instructors.

Recurring throughout the season are unique Women's Clinics, designed for and taught by women. Groups are formed based on skiing

experience, anchored by the supportive environment of this women-only package.

Grooming this year will be done by a new LMC 3700C snowcat, equipped with power and new Yellowstone track setter. Our 60km of trails are groomed for both diagonal stride and skating, from the easy 1km loops to the 12km advanced trails.

Don't miss out on the fun, and stay in shape along the way. If you've never cross country skied, but like the idea of a fitness-oriented ski experience, perhaps the Guaranteed Learn-to-Ski program is your door to the fun. Call our Cross Country Center and let us find the program best suited for you and your family.

Mt. Bachelor operates the most extensive system of developed trails in the Pacific Northwest.

LOCAL COLOR

Central Oregon offers more than some of the best skiing in the West. We also offer fun places to visit or have dinner that you will find nowhere else in the country.

The High Desert Museum is both a live animal exhibit and a showcase for the art and history of Central Oregon. Located on Highway 97 between Bend and Sunriver, open daily.

Narrow gauge dinner trains offer a taste of the Old West during twilight runs. The Crooked River Dinner Train follows a 38-

mile route along Central Oregon Rimrock between Redmond and Prineville. Friday and Saturday departures are at 6:30 p.m., with a special Sunday Brunch run beginning at 1201 p.m. Call 1-800-820-8334 for more information, or 388-1966.

Many of Central Oregon's most popular summer features are open in the winter as well. Natural wonders are the focal point at Lava Lands Visitor Center and the Newberry Crater Monument, both located along South Highway 97. The U.S. Forest Service and the Central Oregon Welcome Center have more information about these two attractions, as well as a complete listing of other visitor sites open this winter.

A vibrant array of things to do can be found in and around downtown Bend as well. Local live theater has a home at the Community Theater of the Cascades, or Dinner Theater at Le Bistro. If you want to take in a movie, we host fun features at one of Bend's five film theaters.

The greater Bend-Sunriver area is home to over 135 restaurants, with menus featuring everything from sushi to French cuisine, Mexican, Italian and every variety of homemade American food. There's even a microbrewery in town.

And that's just a start. Visit the Central Oregon Welcome Center, at the junction of Highways 20 and 97 just north of Bend, for a quick overview and introduction to everything you can find the time to do in Central Oregon. Or call the Center at 382-3221.

SUMMIT EXPRESS is published by Mt. Bachelor Ski and Summer Resort. P.O. Box 1031, Bend, OR 97709-1031

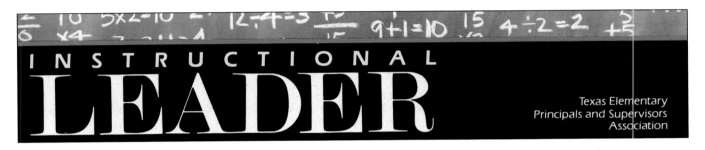

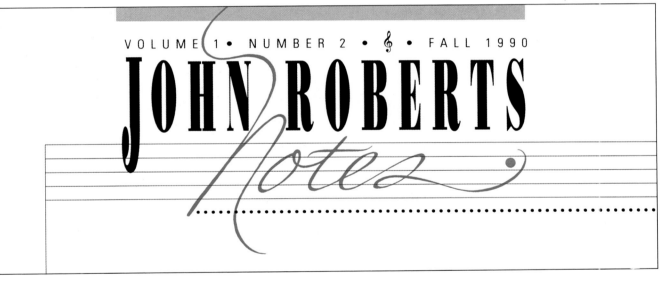

Texas Elementary
Principals and Supervisors
Association

VOLUME 1 • NUMBER 2 • ♪ • FALL 1990

Effective Nameplates

The nameplates reproduced on the following pages meet the guidelines described on page 72. In addition, their designers use type, art and color to create many of the following specific results. Most of these outcomes may be found in more than one of the nameplates that follow.

- Dark inks on off-white paper convey competence and authority.

- Type reverses out of an ink color that is also used for a screen tint.

- Good design looks clean and simple, not cluttered.

- Black outlining and drop shadows make the design seem conservative and dependable.

- Script type and letters set at an angle create an upbeat, friendly impression.

- Off-center design yields lively, dramatic feeling; centered design feels steady, dependable.

- Primary colors seem playful and safe.

- Pastel colors seem contemporary and nonthreatening.

- Earth colors seem caring and responsible.

Where to turn for design ideas & techniques...
on a desktop or not

The Newsletter of the National Wildflower Research Center   *Volume 8, Number 3   May/June 1991*

WILDFLOWER

A nonprofit organization dedicated to researching and promoting wildflowers to further their economic, environmental, and aesthetic use.

Perspectives on Political and Economic Trends in the Americas

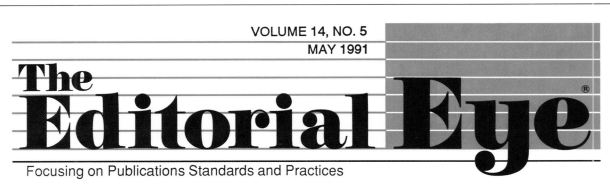

VOLUME 14, NO. 5
MAY 1991

The Editorial Eye®

Focusing on Publications Standards and Practices

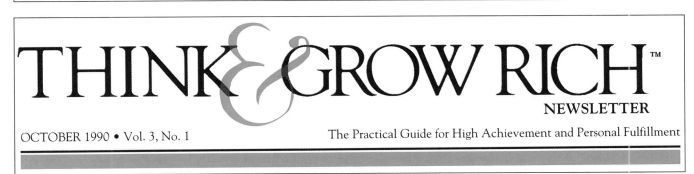

THINK & GROW RICH™

NEWSLETTER

OCTOBER 1990 • Vol. 3, No. 1

The Practical Guide for High Achievement and Personal Fulfillment

Aldus Developer News

September/October 1991

Volume 1, Number 2

Using Graduated Screens

To create the unique step index, the designers of *Hemisfile* used graduated screen tints of the second color. Printing is on 25-by-38-inch sheets, the basic size for text paper. Each parent sheet yields four newsletter sheets. When trimmed to 11³/₄-by-17⁵/₈ inches, all sheets bleed along the index edge. The six visible edges are created by folding each sheet in a different place. Collated sheets shingle to form the step index.

Name *Hemisfile*

Publisher *Institute of the Americas, La Jolla, CA*

Purpose/audience *Service to members of the institute*

Production *PageMaker and Illustrator on Macintosh*

Printing *Two colors on 70-pound, chalk-white text paper*

Format *9¹/₂-by-11³/₄ inches, twelve pages*

Design *Benelli Design, Jeffrey Carmel and Karen Abrams*

Award *Women in Communications*

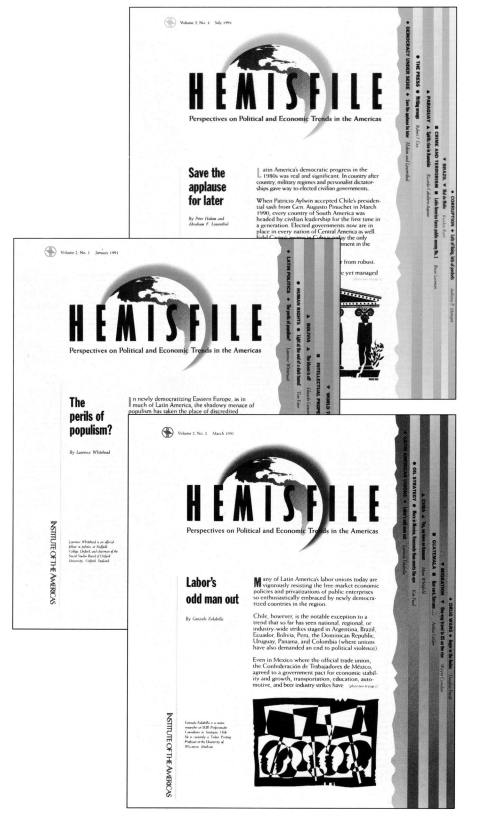

One-way travel to US on the rise

By Wayne Cornelius

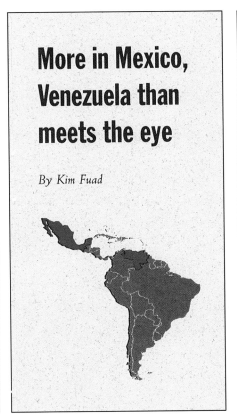

More in Mexico, Venezuela than meets the eye

By Kim Fuad

A jump start — at long last?

By Carlos A. Primo Braga

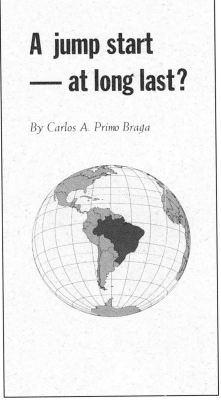

A new player in the oil and gas field

By Kim Fuad

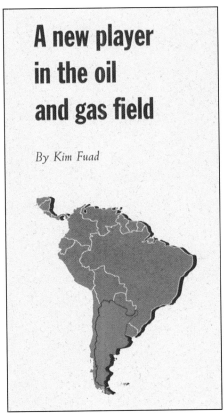

Using Color in Infographics

Hemisfile tells readers what country a story features by showing it on a map in a second color. Used consistently throughout every issue, the maps form a series of visual standing headlines. Each gets instant recognition.

Instead of using photos, *Hemisfile* uses illustrations by David Dias to create the mood for key stories. The distinctive style of the drawings, run from issue to issue, asserts the publication as authoritative and in tune with the geographic region on which it reports.

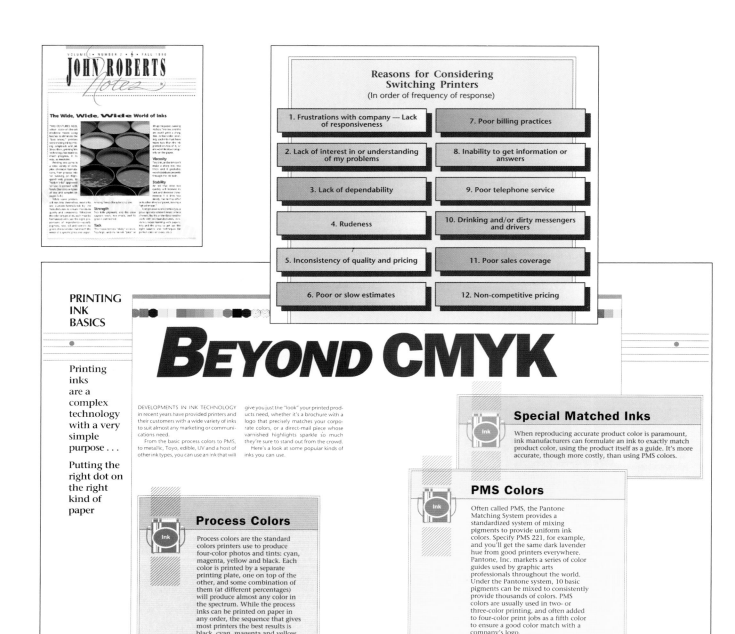

Using Four-Color for Drama

Four-color process printing yields dramatic photo images, vivid illustrations or effective infographics, all on the same press sheet. *John Roberts Notes* showcases all three results in every issue. To create a musical theme, articles on other pages end with a small upper clef sign as a dingbat and the top of each page has the subtle marketing graphic "Orchestrating Printing" in gold ink.

Name *John Roberts Notes*

Publisher *The John Roberts Company, Minneapolis, MN*

Purpose/audience *Service and marketing to customers*

Production *By hand*

Printing *Four-color process plus gold metallic on premium white gloss-coated paper*

Format *8 1/2-by-11 inches, twelve pages*

Design *Don Picard*

Award *Printing Impressions*

Pigments for the Paper Industry

During Autumn, 1990, CIBA-GEIGY will introduce a new product range to the paper industry. This range will contain thirteen pigments - all of which are suitable for paper application and of which nine are suitable for use in the decorative laminates industry. The new range will be composed of the following products:

Irgalite Yellow G-L	Pigment Yellow 1	Workhorse bright gre... paper and lami... Pre-1958 l...
Irgalite Yellow GF-L	Pigment Yellow 13	Hi...
Irgalite Yellow 2R-L	Pigment Yellow 83	
Irgalite Orange G-L	Pigment Yellow...	
Irgalite Red B	Pigment Re...	
Irgalite Red 3B	Pigmen...	
Irgalite Red G-L	Pigm...	
Irgalite Violet B-L	Pigm...	
Irgalite Violet M	Pigme...	
Irgalite Blue R-L	Pigment B...	
Irgalite Green 2G	Pigment Green...	
Irgalite Green G-L	Pigment Green 8	
Irgalite Black 2B-L	Pigment Black 7	Workm... rative lam... 1958 listing.

All products in the new pigment range are available in a paste dispersion form only. If you are in... in evaluating these pigments for use in your paper or decorative laminates system, please contact your sales representative or call 1-800-334-9481, extension 7042.

– Joey McNeill

5

Creating Contrast With Color

The large "responsible care" logo run in graduated tints of blue makes an elegant contrast to the rainbow colors in the nameplate. The logo is the work of two designers, both using FreeHand. It was output from QuarkXPress as part of the separations for page one. The color patches, on the other hand, were gang scanned from actual swatches. While the designer could have used tint builds to create the patches, scanning yielded quicker and more dependable results.

Name *Hues & Views*

Publisher *CIBA-GEIGY Dyestuffs & Chemical Division, Greensboro, NC*

Purpose/audience *Service and marketing to customers*

Production *QuarkXPress, FreeHand and Photoshop on Macintosh IIfx*

Printing *Four-color process plus two flat colors on white gloss-coated paper*

Format *8 1/2-by-11 inches, six pages (six-panel foldout)*

Design *Ling Lee*

Fall 1989

Kennestone Gives
Birth Back to the Family

The most significant change seen over the years at Kennestone's Maternity Center has little to do with technological advances. It goes beyond high-tech equipment and new birthing techniques. The *biggest* change is seen in the family and in the way each member benefits from taking part in the birth experience.

The Maternity Center at Kennestone promotes *Family Centered Maternity Care*, based on the philosophy that families — not just mothers — have babies. Throughout the pregnancy — from classes, to labor, to visitation — the family is encouraged to get involved and share in the process.

Through a wide range of class selections, involvement extends well past mom and dad. Siblings can learn to prepare for the new family member, and grandparents can better understand the changing family roles when they attend classes that address their specific concerns.

"Couples are *very* well educated now," says Lucinda Epps, clinical coordinator of The Maternity Center. Prospective parents are encouraged to talk with their physicians, learn the available options, evaluate them and then develop their preferred birth plan.

As the first all LDR facility in metro Atlanta, The Maternity Center is a very flexible birthing environment. Whether the mother wants to walk, sit, stand, or even be in a warm

In This Issue:

Kennestone at Windy Hill
Caters to Outpatients   2

Independence, Companionship
Go Hand-in-Hand at
Atherton Place   4

KennMed: The Caring
Professionals in
Your Neighborhood   4

New Sports Medicine Center
Can Put You
Back in the Game   7

What's Your Risk?
We'll Help You Find Out   8

bath during labor, couples are encouraged to express what they want, and also what they don't want. Kennestone's LDR (Labor, Delivery, Recovery) room concept promotes family involvement and flexibility, while still providing exceptional medical care.

The primary benefit of the LDR room is that the family labors, delivers and recovers together — and all in one place.

Teri Woodard of Kennesaw describes her

recent delivery: "It was a *wonderful* experience! My husband and I were together throughout the entire event. The staff was great, very helpful and supportive. They stayed with me the whole time, too. They thought of so many little details that made it a lot easier."

The Maternity Center's LDR rooms are a warm, home-like environment, but with the medical technology to ensure everyone's well-being. Each room has a comfortable birthing bed, rocker, recliner, TV, telephone, big birthing mirror, a huge wall-clock and a private bath — complete with tub. Each LDR room

also has a fully equipped nursery area, so that your newborn needn't be whisked away to some place down the hall.

LDR rooms can accommodate any type of birth except a cesarean-section, says Epps, "from unmedicated — with the mother up and walking around, to sitting in the tub, to a premature delivery, to epidural anesthesia."

Within The Maternity Center there are two C-section (cesarean-section) rooms and a high-risk labor room. Having these facilities

Continued on page 3

Battling Allergies? Arm Yourself
With Information

Atlanta sometimes seems like the allergy capital of the world to the many who are plagued by runny noses, itchy eyes and the generalized misery of hay fever. The *Kennestone Scene* talked to allergists Dr. J. Michael Halwig and Dr. Robert Bennett Berkowitz about allergies and methods of coping.

Question: What causes allergies?
Berkowitz: Allergies are the result of people reacting against substances that naturally occur in the environment. Often it's pollen, since we have pollens present 10 to 11 months out of the year in the Atlanta area. Another problem we see frequently is reaction to the dust mite, a microscopic insect that feeds off the skin cells in house dust.

Question: How many people have allergies?
Halwig: Probably 15 to 20 percent of the population, with the biggest group suffering from allergic rhinitis, more commonly known as hay fever. Approximately 5 to 7 percent have asthma, and a smaller number develop hives or gastrointestinal symptoms.

Question: What is the worst time of year for allergy sufferers?
Berkowitz: If you're allergic to inside allergens, your symptoms will appear during the winter months when the house is closed up, and you spend a lot of time indoors. If pollen is the problem, Atlanta pollen counts are the highest in March and April and September and October.

Question: How do people develop allergies?
Halwig: Allergies are inherited. You are born with the tendency, and, at some point in your life, you start making a protein against a material that we are all exposed to. Your body then starts to recognize that substance as being foreign, and this results in an allergic reaction.

Question: Do allergies ever just go away?
Halwig: As children with asthma go through puberty, a significant percentage get better, but in adulthood, problems pretty much stay the same or get worse. If you move to a different area of the country where your allergen is not present, you may improve initially, but even-

Continued on page 2

Colors That Add a Personal Touch

Although packed with medical information, *Kennestone Scene* reaches readers in a personal way. Illustrations of people helping people reflect the muted pastels of the rules and other graphic elements. Even the type prints in dark gray, not black.

Name *Kennestone Scene*

Publisher *Kennestone Healthcare Systems, Marietta, GA*

Purpose/audience *Service to members*

Production *By hand*

Printing *Four-color process on gloss-coated paper*

Format *11-by-17 inches, eight pages*

Design *Carrie Owen*

Awards *Newsletter Clearinghouse, Publishing and Production Executive, Healthcare Marketing Report*

Creative Color in Calendars

Standing heads and illustrations for the calendar use colors kept consistent throughout the publication. For more calendars, see pages 26-27. For another example of color matching in a reply card, see page 89.

❧ KENNESTONE CALENDAR

FALL AND WINTER CLASS SELECTIONS

Each season, Kennestone offers a wide selection of classes to help you achieve a healthy lifestyle. Save this listing as a reminder of the opportunities you have to be well on the way to the very best you! Call the class location to register, or for more information. For classes without an introductory session, pre-payment is necessary to guarantee reservation. Payment can be charged by phone. VISA and Master-Card are welcome! Due to limited class size, payment is non-refundable. (See map on page 4 for class locations. Classes held at Health Place or at the Community Services Building are located on the Kennestone Hospital campus at Church Street.) Discounts available for KRHCS employees, Health Place members and for more than one participant from the same family.

AQUATICS

Arthritis Aquatic Program
Sponsored by the Arthritis Foundation and Health Place. Offers gentle exercise for anyone suffering from pain and/or impairment from arthritis. Warm water provides an excellent medium for relaxing arthritic joints. Cost: $26 (per month)
- Ongoing — Monday, Wednesday and Friday
  12:05–12:50 p.m.
  Health Place Pool
  Call 426-2600 for more information

Scuba
Learn the marvels of the underwater diving world with PADI (Professional Association of Diving Instructors). Certification granted upon completion of open water dive. Course covers all classroom and pool work. A check-out-dive trip is required. Students will need a mask, fins, snorkel, an empty weight belt and a scuba manual. Cost: $125
- November 4 and 11 (Saturdays)
  9:00 a.m.–4:00 p.m.
  Call 426-2600 to register

CPR

CPR (Cardiopulmonary Resuscitation)
Instruction in one-rescuer CPR and obstructed-airway (conscious, unconscious) for adult, child and infant lifesaving. Cost: $20

All classes 9:00 a.m.–4:00 p.m.
- November 4 or December 2
  KennMed Shallowford
  Call 587-0454 to register
- November 18
  KennMed Kennesaw
  Call 426-5665 to register
- November 9 or December 14
  Kennestone Hospital at Windy Hill
  Call 951-3381 to register
- November 24 or December 15
  Health Place
  Call 426-2600 to register

CPR (Basic Life Support) Instructor Course
This two-day comprehensive course is designed to prepare an individual to teach Basic Life Support. Cost: $35
- December 7 & 8
  9:00 a.m.–4:00 p.m.
  Community Services Building,
  Kennestone Hospital,
  Classroom 3
  Call 426-3226 to register

CPR–Recertification
For professionals needing to update basic life-support skills. (CPR card expired for less than 60 days.) Cost: $20
- November 10 or December 8
  9:00 a.m.–12:30 p.m.
  Kennestone Hospital at Windy Hill
  Call 951-3381 to register

FITNESS

The Barbell Connection
Whether you are a bodybuilder or a beginner at free weights, learn how to incorporate strength training into your complete workout. Cost: $7
- December 7 (Thursday)
  6:30–8:00 p.m.
  Health Place
  Call 426-2600 to register

NUTRITION

Seasons Eatings
'Tis the season to be jolly...and healthy. Don't let holiday meals and party snacks sneak up on you. Learn which are the most nutritious and low-to-moderate calorie items to eat during this holiday season. Class taught by a registered dietician. Concludes with sampling of holiday food fare. Cost: $15
- December 4 (Monday)
  6:00 p.m.–7:30 p.m.
  Health Place Classroom
  Call 426-2600 to register

HEALTH PROMOTION SERVICES

- **LIFT (Low Impact Fitness Training)** — LIFT, an exercise video produced at Kennestone, and developed by exercise physiologists and other health professionals, is a safe, effective, low-impact workout tape. LIFT includes a five minute warm-up and cool-down plus 25 minutes each of low-impact aerobics and conditioning exercises. Real people (not models!) are the "stars" of the program, which is suitable for men and women of all ages. Clear instructions help adapt the exercises to all fitness levels, as well as to the special needs of pregnant women. Now available at the special price of $19.95. Call 426-3226 or 426-2600.

- **Do you know your cholesterol level?** Blood Lipid Screenings (Total Cholesterol, H.D.L., Health Risk Ratio and Glucose test available) every Tuesday, 7:00–8:30 a.m. Call 426-2600 to make an appointment.

- **Free classes in Breast/Self Examination.** Call 429-7518.

5

Chapter 6

Photos

Effective photos for publication are made, not taken. Whether the photographer is an amateur, such as a newsletter editor using a point-and-shoot camera, or a professional using studio equipment, the photo image must serve a clear editorial goal. The photo must fit the format of the newsletter as well as complementing the article it accompanies.

Photos often work better than words to capture emotions. A good photographer can see the feelings behind the words and capture those in a dynamic photo. It is important to work with the best photos you can get, because even a master designer or printer can do little to turn a drab photo into a dynamic image.

Good design controls photos technically as well as editorially. The examples on the following pages show how to plan and combine well-exposed photos with specifications for screens and paper surface to yield the best possible results. In addition to controlling contrast, designers crop photos for drama and frame them to ensure that the message is highlighted. Frames are most often devised by printing keylines, but may be enhanced by reversing the halftone out of a light screen tint. The following pages include several examples of this technique.

SHAREHOLDER

Just Say "No" — And Walk

Chris Scheurich, Kelso, Washington, got a lot of dealer double-talk when she bought her 1986 Nissan 300ZX. "It was atrocious," she says.

The problem was the finance and insurance (F&I) man. "The salesman who sold me the car was wonderful," says Chris, a registered nurse and nursing instructor for many years. "There was no pressure, and he was courteous."

For the paperwork, Chris had to deal with the F&I man. "Until he found out I was paying cash, he was nice," she says. "After that, he was terrible."

He began by telling Chris she could make between $3,000 and $4,000 by financing the car and investing her $10,000 cash outlay. His pitch: Because Chris could finance at 12 percent and earn 8 percent on the cash, she'd only be paying off a 4 percent loan. Chris kept insisting on cash, admitting she didn't understand his point.

The more the F&I man tried to get her to finance, the more Chris insisted on cash. "He'd get this 'you've got to be kidding' look," says Chris. But the badgering continued, with the F&I man eventually insulting Chris for not being smart enough to finance. "He also kept saying he wished he had my money to throw away," she says.

Chris demanded to see the owner. When he didn't show up, she left — with the car paid for in cash. "I was near tears," she says.

Chris knows she made a mistake by telling the F&I man she wasn't good at math. "Once he knew that, he kept flashing numbers on his computer screen," she says.

Although horrified by her experience, Chris learned a valuable car-buying lesson: Hold your ground — and walk if necessary. It helped Chris get what she wanted: a sporty car — for cash.

> **When buying a car, know what you want and "hold your ground."**
> — Chris Scheurich

Dealing With The Doublespeak

Much of the fast-talk at dealers today is not with the car purchase but the financing. Because of heavy competition, dealers aren't making as much on cars as previously. Instead, they must rely for profits on financing and insurance — and sometimes unnecessary extras like rustproofing.

Beware: F&I men routinely mix sense with nonsense. Consider the four-year, $10,000 dealer loan Chris was offered.

four-year, $10,000 dealer loan four years, she could earn $3,000 to $4,000 in interest on $10,000 — but only by ignoring the effect of taxes. An 8 percent yield then is reduced to $2,584 (assuming a 28 percent tax rate).

Borrowing from someone else almost always costs money. If possible, it's cheaper to "borrow" from yourself. Example: A 12 percent, would cost Chris $263 a month, or $12,640 for four years. But if she paid cash for the car and "repaid" herself $263 a month (invested at 8 percent), she'd be $1,593 ahead after four years!

If an F&I man confuses you with numbers, have him write them down. Then contact your credit union. We'll explain what's what.

Weyerhaeuser Credit Union
Longview, Washington

Silhouetting Photos

Silhouettes are often difficult to build into a design, but when done cleanly they can jump right off the page. These images rely on the motif of bright, primary colors used throughout. The seven-panel cartoon strip succeeds especially well because of the broadside format.

Name *Shareholder*

Publisher *Weyerhaeuser Credit Union, Longview, WA*

Purpose/audience *Service and marketing to members*

Production *PageMaker and Illustrator on Macintosh*

Printing *Four-color process on white gloss-coated paper*

Format *11-by-17 inches, four pages*

Design *Brad Hunter and Tom Sentori*

Awards *Credit Union Executive Society, International Association of Business Communicators*

Advice From A Retired Dealer

Whether you're buying a new or used car, Ivan Thornley has some advice: Talk financing first and then make your deal with the dealer (taking the rebate if available). "By talking money before you visit the dealers," says Ivan, "you get the numbers you need to compare financing options."

Ivan, who owned Thornley Oldsmobile Cadillac, in Longview, Washington, for 36 years, says the best way to avoid getting trapped — and get the deal you want — is to plan ahead. This includes deciding in advance what kind of car you want, how much you can spend and where to finance. A good dealer, along with the folks at Weyerhaeuser Credit Union, will help.

"Tell the dealer what you want," says Ivan. "You might specify GM, approximate age, if a used car, and price you can afford," he says. "Then wait until the dealer finds the car for you." This tactic, he says, is especially important when buying a used car. "Top used cars rarely stay on the lots, or even get there, so ask for the dealer's help," says Ivan. "There's no obligation."

Is now a good time to buy? "Yes," says Ivan, a Weyerhaeuser Credit Union member since the late '30s. "I expect plenty of rebates this January and February. The dealers will be using them to move inventory." However, even with rebates, there's room to negotiate price.

AUTO FACT #1

Refinance an existing car loan at the credit union. Since the rate probably is lower than elsewhere, you save money. You might even be able to shorten the term and still keep the same monthly payments.

Ivan Thornley

To get the best possible deal, Ivan shares three other tips:

- **Manufacturer's warranty.** Dealers may not mention these warranties are transferable. Yet, they add great value to used cars.

- **Front-end accidents.** Even though late-model cars don't have frames, they do have small subframes where the engines sit. In acci-

dents, these frames bend[?] dions, weakening the ca[?] ing future alignment prob[?] some dealers may not div[?] formation, have frames [?] used cars you might buy[?]

- **Odometer readings** ican cars, the odometer [?] at 100,000 miles. Once [?] pens, some dealers den[?] mileage and "sell" only [?] pears on the odometer.

Before buying a car, Iv[?] talking with neighbors, [?] co-workers. "You won't [?] the good guys, but you [?] about the bad guys," he[?]

If you're pressured by [?] says, be prepared to w[?] cars are on the market ev[?] there are lots of other ch[?] Ivan. He also advises c[?] to dealer management [?] exist. Generally, you'll[?] faction.

Cut Car Insurance Costs

Insurance companies consider all sorts of factors when determining rates. Among them: age, sex, marital status, type of car you drive, use of vehicle, previous driving record — even smoking.

Yet, there's plenty you can do to cut costs. Driving a Toyota Camry rather than a Toyota Supra will lower premiums. So will no speeding tickets or accidents. Discounts also are available for anti-lock brakes and air bags.

To save even more, says Stan Stieben, Pacific Pioneer Insurance, Longview, Washington, you can raise deductibles on collision and comprehensive. "Rather than a $100 deductible consider $250 or $500," he says. "The more expensive the car, the more you'll save."

Or, drop collision coverage if your car has lost more than half its initial value — which can happen within five years. At this point, the coverage may not be worth the cost.

Driving fewer than 7,500 miles a year also may reduce costs. "You'll save about 5 percent on liability," says Stan, whose company writes various group and individual coverages for many Weyerhaeuser Credit Union members. Another cost savings: Get auto and homeowners insurance from the same insurer; many offer discounts.

Periodic cost comparisons also can cut insurance costs. However, Stan advises caution when considering purchases over the phone or through mail solicitations. Switching agents or dealing with an 800 number may not be worth it.

An additional caution: Lack of coverage can be far more costly than paying for what you need. "If you own any property at all," says Stan, "you should have minimum liability coverage of $100,000 for a single injury, $300,000 for all injuries, and $100,000 property damage." For those in car pools, he recommends additional bodily injury coverage. A personal umbrella policy also might be a good idea.

Know what you're buying, says Stan. People often realize too late they don't have the right coverage. Ask questions of your agent. Don't assume you are getting the coverage you need.

Lower miles ma[?]
lower in[?]
rat[?]
Stan S[?]

---

7 Plays To Win The Car Buyin[g]

The best defense is a good offense. It's as true for car buying as spc[?] When you're in charge, you win — not the dealer. Here's how to score your best deal ever:

1

Know What You Want

Do you want a Pontiac Grand Prix? Or a Plymouth Voyager? Think about what you need — and can afford. Worry less about what you think you want. Narrow your choices to two or three models before you start to shop.

2

Get The True Cost

This is the base invoice price, or what the dealer paid for the car (on average about 15 percent off the sticker). The result: You can save from $1,500 to $2,000 on an intermediate-sized car. Your best source for dealer costs is WCU. You can access the information yourself through a computer terminal in the Longview lobby. Or, call for information.

3

Line Up Credit

Ask your credit union for a pre-approved loan. Having cash in hand: (1) allows you more opportunity to negotiate price with dealers, and (2) helps control what you spend. With cash in hand, you can ignore dealer financing plans and concentrate on car prices.

4

Shop Arou[nd]

Since prices vary greatl[y] available at several diffe[rent] Record sticker prices a[nd] them with the invoice p[rice] tracked down. The diffe[rence] amount you can bargain[?] quotes that spell out wha[t] and what isn't.

Make Borrowing Smart

9.9 percent new car rate," ...nn Waters, Weyerhaeuser ...nion loan officer, "is really ...tive both locally and na-" In the Longview area, a ...ank rate is 11.25 percent. ...percent rate attracts new ...embers from all over the ..., she says.

...haeuser Credit Union mem-...alize other savings, too: ...re no hidden charges on ...ncing. "We don't charge for ...check or for early loan pay-...d for loan balances up to ..., our credit life insurance

AUTO FACT #2

...ure the contract spells out ...price, dealer prep charge, ...payment, trade-in value (if ...rading), destination charge, ...es tax, and total cost.

doesn't cost extra," Joann says.

Payroll deduction also makes credit union borrowing smart. "A lot of our members like this service," Joann says. "It's convenient. And if members have several loans, they can have all payments made the same day or, say, on the first of the month and the 15th."

Another smart tactic: Use the equity in your car to consolidate all your bills at used-car rates. "Because our rates are only 10.5 to 11.5 percent APR, they are a less expensive way to finance than a signature loan," says Joann.

Costs also can be cut with short terms and large down payments. "You pay a lot less interest," Joann says. For people with a lot of debt, she recommends five years and 20 percent down. Otherwise, the finance charges become too stiff.

As for longer-term loans, Joann is leery. "You pay so much more in-

We have no hidden charges with our auto financing.
— Joann Waters

terest than with a short-term loan," she says. "Unless you make a large down payment, you might not accumulate any equity the first two years." In addition, you may need to replace parts like battery, tires and muffler while you're still making payments. Can you afford replacement *and* financing costs?

Borrow smart. Call Joann or any other Weyerhaeuser Credit Union loan officer. We're here to help.

AUTO FACT #3

Take the sales contract home and read it at your leisure — without pressure from the dealer. If the dealer refuses, get a written purchase agreement that spells out all the details. Once you're satisfied, have the agreement written into the contract.

...hat The Ads Don't Tell You

...ills the pages of your local ...er? Car ads. What's often ...however, is the information ...y need. Here's what the ads ... you:

...a can't have it all. If you ...count financing, you can't ...rebate, too. It's one or the

...e fine print speaketh ..., Oftentimes, the most ...t information is buried in ...st print, for example, how ...ify for the attention-getting ...e.

... good to be true probably ...nicky phrases like *no one* ...*redit* might force you into a ...ed deal you can't afford. *Dis-...from manufacturer's sug-*

gested retail prices (MSRPs) still leaves hidden profit since MSRPs often are highly inflated.

• **Numbers can trick you.** Car dealers use all sorts of fancy figuring to make bad deals sound good. The folks at your credit union can help you understand the facts.

• **Haste makes waste.** Ads often are designed to trigger impulsive buying. Do your homework and take your time.

1991 — A Great Time To Buy

If you're in the market for a new car — or have postponed a decision to buy — now's the time to act. According to *Consumer Guide*, this is a buyer's market.

Here's why:

• **Sluggish economy.** Demand is low. To sell off inventory, dealers need to offer lots of deals.

Be careful. Some deals, particularly those for gas guzzlers, could end up being costly. Even though the price is low, the cost to fill up the tank won't be low. Five years from now, the car isn't likely to be a good trade-in, either.

• **Strong competition.** With lots of cars to sell, dealers should be willing to deal. There's also a growing number of directly competitive models.

• **Stable prices.** A strong dollar — and fierce competition — has kept price increases modest.

• **Traditional incentives.** Cash-back rebates, primarily ranging from $500 to $1,500, are common. Even popular models now have them. Some manufacturers may eliminate rebates and roll back prices.

Avoid other incentives. Low-rate financing, for example, applies only to very short-term loans and the least popular models. It also takes away your ability to negotiate. You're almost always better off with a price reduction and a higher-interest-rate loan at your credit union.

• **New incentives.** Some auto-makers now offer long warranties, roadside assistance plans, and exchange policies. With the latter, you can return the car within 30 days or 1,500 miles and receive credit toward the purchase of another car from the same dealer.

Let Others Haggle For You

Another way to win with dealers is through auto brokers and buying clubs. You eliminate the hassle of negotiating with a dealer — and save money.

Brokers locate the car you want and arrange a firm price with the dealer. Discounts range from $100 to $500 over dealer cost. More difficult to obtain are discounts on hot-selling cars.

With buying clubs, you do the shopping — at designated dealers. The sponsor (often a membership organization) guarantees a rock-bottom price and no hassle.

If these services are available to you, compare prices offered. Make sure any broker you use is legitimate (by asking for and calling recent customers). Some brokers have collected deposits and left town without delivering their cars.

Gives Her Car-Buying Confidence

...ruck demolished her ...knew she'd have to ..."I was terrified," she ...ng about car buying." ...mer '90 issue of the ...arned what happened ...edit Union members. ...nfidence," says Lisa, ...nician, Weyerhaeuser ...mbus, Mississippi. "I ...nes."

...ht a car ...ow she's ...on my ...wsletter ...le to say

...nost im-...g about ...nanced ...aved ...e for my ...it union ...he interest

...r, worked ...what I ...ent and ...came up ...ord," says ...now than

...er who got ...also influenced ...ore me up," she ...e thing happening to ...n people at work, I ...n deal for a new car." ... Protegé.

Although Lisa remembered reading an article in an earlier *Shareholder* about car negotiations, she hadn't kept it. (A similar article appears in this issue.) "From now on, I'm saving the *Shareholder*," she says. "Other members should, too."

Good advice, Lisa.

Moore gets lots of good consumer advice by ...ting and saving the credit union newsletter

5
...ake A Deal

...e salesperson your figures ...an offer. Suggest a price ...er than what you can rea-...xpect to pay. Once a coun-...s made, you can start ... If you get resistance, be ...to walk. A willingness not ...y be the best strategy of all.

6
Ignore Trade-in Price

Without it, you can dicker better. A trade-in also can disguise a bad deal on the new car. Use prices from the *N.A.D.A. Official Used Car Guide* to determine what your old car is worth (available by phone from your credit union). Unless the dealer's willing to give you that price, consider selling outright and using the money as a down payment on the new car.

7
Take Your Time

If you don't get the price you want, go elsewhere. Neither should you hesitate taking up the dealer's time. You're the one spending the money.

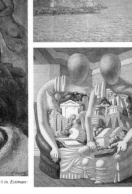

The Power of Five Colors

Designer Linda Stillman loves her freedom to run large photos on the cover and the budget that allows a fifth color. She uses a different flat color each issue, carefully selecting a hue that picks up colors in the art featured on the cover. Technically perfect photographs feature the finest *objets d'art*. What reader could possibly set this aside to read at a more convenient time?

Name *Auction News*

Publisher *Christie, Manson and Woods International, Inc., New York, NY*

Purpose/audience *Service and marketing to customers*

Production *QuarkXPress on Macintosh IIcx*

Printing *Four-color process plus fifth color on white gloss-coated paper*

Format *9-by-12 inches, twelve pages*

Design *Stillman Designs—Linda Stillman and Connie Circosta*

Highlights of Future Sales

Josef Sudek, Still Life in the Style of Caravaggio (first variation), 1956, gelatin silver print, 9¼ x 11⅜ in. To be sold April 16. Estimate: $3,000-4,000.

above: Michael Cohn, Space Cup #51, *1981, blown and fabricated glass, 6 x 14½ x 9 in. To be sold March 18 at Christie's East. Estimate: $4,000-5,000.*

Irving Penn, Three Women of Rissani, Morocco, 1971, multiple printed and hand-coated platinum-palladium print on Rives paper with aluminum backing, printed in 1978, 21⅝ x 19½ in. To be sold April 16. Estimate: $18,000-22,000.

Erté, L'Ivoire, from "Les Tresors de l'Indochine," 1922, gouache, 12⅜ x 7⅛ in. To be sold March 18 at Christie's East. Estimate: $20,000-25,000.

A detail of a set of three Tiffany leaded glass windows for the Waldo Newcomer (Albert) House, Baltimore, Maryland, circa 1904, all panels 79 in. high and 17, 31 and 17 in. wide respectively. To be sold March 16. Estimate: $100,000-150,000.

An important Tiffany "Hanging Head" dragonfly table lamp. To be sold March 16. Estimate: $200,000-250,000.

8

Laying Out Photo Spreads

The photos in *Auction News* must accurately represent original scenes, so the designer can't take artistic license by cropping. Photo layouts on inside pages demonstrate classic guidelines: Use an odd number of images and run one of them in a dominant size. The results are spreads such as those shown above.

Calendar of Future Sales

Park: 502 Park Avenue, 212/546-1

AMERICAN DECORATIVE ARTS	
Fine American Furniture, Silver, Folk Art & Decorative Arts	June 25, 2 p.m.
BOOKS	
The Stuart B. Schimmel Collection of the Book Arts	May 17, 10 a.m.
Printed Books & Manuscripts including Americana	May 17, 2 p.m. & May 18, 10 a.m.
CARS	
Important Motor Cars & Automobilia	May 20, 2 p.m.
CHINESE ART	
Fine Chinese Paintings & Calligraphy	May 29, 10 a.m.
Fine Chinese Ceramics & Works of Art	May 30, 10 a.m. & 2 p.m
COINS	
Ancient, Foreign & United States Coins & Important World Banknotes from the Archives of The American Banknote Company	June 5, 10 a.m., 2:00 p.m. & 6 p.m.
EUROPEAN FURNITURE	
Important French Furniture, Porcelain, Sculpture, Clocks & Tapestries	May 8, 10 a.m.
GENERAL SALES	
Nineteenth-Century English & Continental Furniture, Decorations & Porcelain	May 14, 10 a.m.
English & Continental Furniture, Decorations, Porcelain, Paintings & Oriental Works of Art	June 11, 10 a.m.
JEWELRY	
Important Jewels	June 11, 10 a.m. & 2 p.m
Antique & Fine Jewelry	June 13, 10 a.m. & 2 p.m
PAINTINGS, DRAWINGS & PRINTS	
Contemporary Art (Part I)	May 1, 7 p.m.
Contemporary Art (Part II)	May 2, 10 a.m.
Modern and Contemporary Paintings, Watercolors, Drawings & Sculpture	May 7, 10 a.m.
Impressionist & Modern Paintings & Sculpture (Part I)	May 8, 7 p.m.
Impressionist & Modern Paintings & Sculpture (Part II)	May 9, 2 p.m.

AUCTION NEWS FROM

CHRISTIE'S

502 Park Avenue, New York, New York 10022
Address Correction Requested

A Louis XV pôt-à-oille by Etienne-Jaques Marcq, Paris, 1955. To be sold April 18 in the Meyer de Schauensee Collection of French Silver. Estimate: $150,000-250,000.

Published 8 times a year by
Christie, Manson & Woods International, Inc.
502 Park Avenue, New York, NY 10022
Editor: R. Starr Collins
Design: Linda Stillman Inc.; Connie Circosta, designer
Annual Subscription Rates:
U.S. & Canada $15. Overseas $20.

Conway to oversee minority

Thomas E.H. (
has been named tl
of recruiting and
vices in the Colle;
ing at NCSU.

Conway, a nat
on, is working to
rate in counselir
CSU. He holds
ience degree in
bachelor of scie
gricultural educa
❑

Personalizing Mug Shots

Mug shots inside tinted boxes personalize the features and tie images to text. Using fine keylines and reverses gives the images maximum punch.

Name *North Carolina State University College of Engineering Newsletter*

Publisher *North Carolina State University, Raleigh, NC*

Purpose/audience *Service to faculty and alumni*

Production *PageMaker on Macintosh*

Printing *Black and metallic blue on white gloss-coated paper*

Format *8¹/₂-by-11 inches, eight pages*

Design *Martha K. Brinson and Mark R. Ransom*

Carbonell gets College of Engineering top award

Pettis memorial fund established

A fund in memory of Bobby D. Pettis has been established by the College of Engineering at North Carolina State University. Pettis, director of Student Services, died June 4 at the age of 45.

The Bobby D. Pettis Memorial Fund will be used to provide emergency short-term loans to undergraduate students in engineering and computer science. Pettis, considered by students to be both friend and counselor, was known to provide assistance to students from his own pocket when none was available from the college or university.

Pettis joined the College of Engi-

is met with a steady stream of
n thousands of one-on-one
vhich he was not just a counselor
ose friend.

und established for Stahel

ical engineering at NCSU
ory of Dr. Edward P. Stahel
gineering, Stahel died July

e used to purchase books for
was an excellent classical
widely recognized for his

n 1962 after receiving his
iversity. He also held a
ersity of Notre Dame and a
ton University. Contribu-
e to the Friends of the Library, Box 7111, NCSU,

Stahel

BOARD OF ADVISORS

Richard Applin
Marketing
Services Mgr.
Tennant Co.

Roland Dumas
Senior Baldrige
Examiner
Kaizen Institute

William Hummer
Customer
Service Manager
3M

Claire Kolmodin
VP, Client
Service Quality
IDS Financial
Services

Wayne Light
Manager,
Customer
Service
Strategies
Xerox

Laura Liswood
Senior Baldrige
Examiner
Liswood
Marketing Group

Patrick Townsend
Co-founder
Townsend &
Gebhardt

Ron Zemke
President
Performance
Research
Associates

Also Serving: *Ollie Parker*, Executive Vice President, Alexsis

Total Quality Newsletter — reporting on the "thousand little things" companies do to be more competitive — is published monthly to provide news, innovative ideas, practical skills, and tools for managers and executives working for overall quality improvement.

TQ®　　**TQ**®

Publisher, Philip G. Jones • **Editor**, Brian McDermott • **Managing Editor**, Dave Zielinski • **Associate Editors**, Christopher Busse and Randall Johnson • **Production Editor**, Julie Tilka • **Circulation Manager**, Nancy Swanson • **Customer Service**: Stella Dean and Lori Swanson

Designing Well With Mug Shots

By running mug shots of the advisory board immediately above the masthead, the editor adds both authority and personality to design space that is often routine. The mug shots all have similar cropping, contrast and backgrounds, unifying the spread. Note how the kerned initials of the name form a dingbat. For another example of good mug shots, see pages 118-119.

Name *Total Quality*

Publisher *Lakewood Publications, Minneapolis, MN*

Purpose/audience *Service to subscribers*

Production *PageMaker and FreeHand on Macintosh*

Printing *Black and red on white offset paper*

Format *8½-by-11 inches, eight pages*

Design *Mark Simonson, Brian McDermott and Julie Tilka*

Staying Power

DORA NOVICK (25)
"After 25 years, I still find this business fascinating. I have made many good friends in this, my second home."

JOAN PERRY CAIN (29)
"Think of the changes in television over the last 29 years. Wow! It's been exciting watching it grow and, indeed, watching Lintas grow. I'm happy to have been a part of it."

YVETTE SCHANTZ (15)
"Bills by the billions! Well, maybe more like millions. I must have seen at least that many over the years, but I'm glad they weren't mine."

DOUG GREENE (22)
"I've been stocking Lintas with supplies since its SSC&B days. Over the years, I've given you millions of pencils, billions of paper clips, and trillions of staples. Now that the letterhead has changed, I'll still be here to service you, but don't forget to bring your request form!"

Combining Type, Rules and Photos

The front page images work very well with the type and the heavy corner rules that run under the nameplate and on the left bottom corner. It all fits within a strict grid system but looks casually asymmetrical. That same graphic theme is used inside, where one dominant image balances three mug shots.

Name *Lintas Ink*

Publisher *Lintas:New York, New York, NY*

Purpose/audience *Service to employees*

Production *Ventura Publisher on IBM*

Printing *Black on white matte-coated paper*

Format *8¹/₂-by-11 inches, twelve pages*

Design *Rule Johnson-Morris*

hardware, are multiplying at an
blishers are now scrambling to
ks to the new hardware. Engi-
and making use of new soft-
ression (JPEG, MPEG), time-
QuickTime), and CD-quality
udiomedia).

ublisher to see the benefits of
s to existing products. A nor-
and animates when clicked on
high-fidelity sounds emanating
akers during a colorful slide
ctive. Most of these types of
bases are relatively simple, and
g to take advantage of that.
unced a new extension to the
led QuickTime, which will be
Time will provide the capabil-

industry," a notion that juxtaposes the unknown factors of
the fledgling market against the gut feelings that it could be
gigantic. Much of it is still a mystery. Clues to the market's
viability will have to be ferreted out by companies like Aldus.
As usual, those who are willing to risk early entry will be at
the forefront. Eventually—probably within the next two
years—the software industry will have a clear picture of what
is out there.

*Christopher Watson is an
engineer in San Diego.*

**The Vision Thing is your opportu-
nity to share your insights into
our industry, or your vision of
a new technology or market.
Submit articles and suggestions to Averill Curdy at
Aldus corporate.**

Bleeding Photos for a Fun Effect

Mug shots that bleed off one edge of the page help create a sense of fun. The premier issue was trimmed at the top to look like the roof of a house. The second issue settled into a 9-by-12-inch rectangular format. In addition to the software made by Campbell's employer, his production notes specify "an old 4-bit HP scanner, Lisa Mennet's Pentax K1000, and a Sanford Sharpie marking pen." Recycled paper, of course.

Name *Aldo*

Publisher *Aldus Corporation, Seattle, WA*

Purpose/audience *Service to employees*

Production *PageMaker and FreeHand on Macintosh IIcx*

Printing *Black and magenta on cream-tinted fiber paper*

Format *9-by-12 inches, eight pages*

Design *J. Scott Campbell*

The Vision

The strategic plan chart
By Jill Bamburg

business to enhance our succ
environment? What sort of s
work environment will we c

The discussions took pla
Seattle, San Diego, London,
Aldusians from virtually all le
company. The results of thes
in a 50-page draft document
executive staff prior to their
the plan should be complete
to the company a little later

Top-level observations of th

While I can't share the s
does make sense to pass on a
• The company's overall m
we will continue to "crea
people throughout the wo
information and ideas." W
zillion things we could do
generated a wealth of exc
will continue to be makin
attractive alternatives.
• As our customers expand
ers to communicate, we v
help them realize the full
tions." Yes, that undoub
means all kinds of "electro

". . . the future isn't what it used to be." — Paul Valery

worked at Ashton-Tate for a year, and then for
Rolm, a telecommunications company that was
ultimately bought by Siemens. Since Kathy had
no interest in moving to Germany—where Siemens has its headquarters—and Rolm's human
factors group was being phased out, she decided to
post her résumé at a conference she was attending
in Seattle. The position at Aldus was exactly
what she was looking for—to start a human factors
group at a small software company—and she
began working here in May of last year.

Kathy studied ballet
for many years and
used to race sail-
boats. She still
enjoys sailing,
in addition to
skiing and
camping.

for the people who develop the equipment or software. In software, we're
mostly concerned with the cognitive and
information processing capabilities of our
end users.

I define the things I work on as the
user-system interface. I go beyond its
narrow definition as just the look and feel
of a product, to define it as anything in
the product the user has to work with. It's
not only what the product looks like or
what the order of functions feels like, but
also what the functionality is and if it's
matched to the way people do their
tasks. I also consider all the other
elements of the product the
person deals with, like the
documentation and on-line help.

**Have we seen the results of any
of your work in the products that
have been released since you started
at Aldus?**

Not really, because the products
that have been released were started
before I got here. The work that I've
been doing in the last year will affect the
next generation of our products.

**How do you work with the development
teams?**

I see my role as a consultant to the
development teams. I can make recommendations, but they have the responsibility for the product. I do have influence,
but because I'm a part of the group it's

cost is
work aq,
also be Lotus,
You're in our
search t
What
work v

s have
sively ndus-
produ for us,
produ perous
"real ut I
action ons.
of a c he
this fo
I give
them

F
an org
attenti
figure
for hel
tation
on-lin
people
menus
point
were l
this pr
them?
they w

Outlining Product Shots for Interest

Outline halftones produce interesting product shots as well as images of people. These examples unite with their surrounding stories, taking their all-important captions along with them. Captions in bold type also form visual bases for the images. For more examples of captions, see page 110.

Name *Inside Extrusion Processing*

Publisher *Conair Gatto, Hauppauge, NY*

Purpose/audience *Service and marketing to customers*

Production *PageMaker and FreeHand on Macintosh IIcx*

Printing *Black and metallic silver on white matte-coated paper*

Format *8¹/₂-by-11 inches, twelve pages*

Design *The Morris-Lee Group—James Morris-Lee and Steven Smith*

Award *Newsletter Clearinghouse*

---

clutch engages, the blade spins to slice the material, returns to "park"

Accurate adjustments are easy to make on the plant floor—To adjust the new Conair Gatto clutch/brake for routine wear, operators simply remove 0.008-inch shims for a guaranteed parallel adjustment. Operators no longer have to carefully tighten opposing wedges to assure the plates remain exactly parallel.

position and then brakes to a stop. This whole process may repeat 10 times a second.

The best cuts come from quickly slicing material rather than chopping, which can distort the material and result in an uneven cut. We look at three criteria in selecting a knife for a particular cut:
• Attack angle
• Force required
• Cut time.

Attack angle describes the angle between a blade's cutting edge and its axis. A high attack angle means good slicing action; a zero attack angle means a chopping action.

Special knives improve cut quality—Some

Force required varies wi... size, density, hardness and d... tion of the product.

Higher force may require... knife, which, in turn, incre... requirements further to co... for wedging—the force req... work the thick blade down... the product.

In general, processors ch... thinnest knife that will do... without breaking or deflect...

Cut time describes how... actually takes for the knife... through the product. This... related to—but not necessa... inverse of—cutting rate.

For example, let's take a... cutting rate of 60 cuts per... a continuous cutter, the cut...

---

sively from one U.S. manufacturer. Other vacuum clutch/brake units had to be imported—and sent back overseas for repair.

But under a brand new agreement (see story on page 1), Conair Gatto now offers U.S.-manufactured models with the patented, U.S.-made Forêt vacuum clutch/brake. Processors whose application dictates the Forêt clutch brake—those with extremely high cut demands above 500 to 600 cuts per minute—can now also have Conair Gatto quality.

But many processors now find that a new generation of electromagnetic clutch/brakes make the advantages of the Forêt clutch/brake less obvious.

Better electromagnetic clutch/brake
...re are some less-attractive ...stics of vacuum clutch/ ...onsider as well:

...they run by vacuum, you'll ...mp, another piece of equip- ...rchase and maintain ...ump is noisy

...mum on-demand cut rates ...y much higher than the ...ily of cutters operated by ...gnetic clutch/brakes.

...nce the capabilities of elec- ...hical on-demand cutters, ...tto designed a new clutch/ ...m from scratch.

...than depend upon com- ...available, multi-purpose

Please see **Clutch/Brake**, *page 5*

---

tubing processors relied on breaker plates on 2.5-inch extruders to help block large contaminants. But in-

Add hydraulic control later—Processors can take advantage of polymer filtration today with this inexpensive manual screenchanger, then add hydraulic capability when and if they need it. All holes are pretapped, ready for field retrofit (right) without returning the unit to the factory.

creased regrind content—whether captive or bought on the open market—makes betting on a breaker plate an expensive gamble.

Large-volume processors may use continuous screenchangers which assure constant pressure and temperature. But they also cost upwards of $30,000.

Smaller processors have used manual- or hydraulic-activated screenchangers.

Retrofittable screenchangers
Now, smaller processors can get into filtration for less than $5,000

---

which remains in the melt flow at all times.

As pressure builds to the point at which the line should no longer run, the line is shut down and the operator uses a hand lever to insert a new screen block.

A wide range of screen media can be used, dependent upon desired filtration level. Sizes available are typically sized to the extruder and available in 2.5" and 3.5" sizes. The hydraulic unit and matching cylinder can be completely field retrofitted.

This series is compatible with most polymers, but is not suggested for rigid PVC. The units are in stock at the Conair Jetro division, and available through your Conair Gatto sales reps. ■

For more information, circle #6 on the reader service card.

Wrapping Text Around Outline Halftones

Tabloid size allows lots of photos and illustrations to merge with text. When the photos are outline halftones, they blend effortlessly into the story. The designer uses outline photos to keep the tone of the newsletter upbeat and personal for employees whose average age is twenty-seven.

Name *Acxiom News*

Publisher *Acxiom Corporation, Conway, AR*

Purpose/audience *Service to associates*

Production *PageMaker on Macintosh IIx*

Printing *Black and blue on white matte-coated paper*

Format *11-by-17 inches, eight pages*

Design *Julie Potter and Sandra Marbaise*

Award *Newsletter Clearinghouse*

ACXIOMNEWS

| Volume II | *A Bimonthly Publication for Acxiom Associates* | Issue V |

Acxiom's Goal—
100% Customer Satisfaction by 1995

November/ December 1990

One of Acxiom's corporate goals is to have 100% customer satisfaction by 1995. The following people are helping Acxiom reach this goal by going above and beyond the call of duty to service the customer.

Physician's Mutual has Complete Confidence in Acxiom
The dedicated customer service team of Linda Holt, Melissa Allgood, Karen Johnson, Robin Wait and Susan Maples always do whatever it takes to please the customer. According to Mike Peterson of Physician's Mutual, "Our Acxiom customer service team and everyone that we deal with at Acxiom are reliable and extremely easy to work with. They show genuine concern for our problems and do whatever is necessary to help us."
"We have complete confidence in both our customer service team and in the

The Physician's Mutual Customer Service Team

Superior Customer Service Is Our #1 Goal

took 24 hour coverage for an entire department.

The AT&T Customer Service Team Takes Pride in Their Work
"Acxiom has been an integral link in the success of the entire Universal Card 1990 acquisition process. The level of quality service is so consistent that at times it seems it is

"I find that Acxiom is just as the ad says—available 24 hours a day!"
-Uarco, Inc.

Customer Service, Continued on page 2

Acxiom Establishes a New Corporate Culture

ACXIOM IS OVERMANAGED AND UNDERLED

Child Development

Continued From Page 1

Potthast on doctor and hospital visits. Mrs. Potthast also received counseling at home from Child Development Counselor **Lynn Smart**.

The prognosis is excellent. Liske anticipates that Lucia will attend a community preschool without the program's assistance, and one day will be able to read regular-size print.

Four-year-old **Scott MacIntyre** was diagnosed as having retinitis pigmentosa approximately one year ago; this has left him with tunnel vision. In addition to a child development consultant's home visits, Scott and his younger brother **Todd** spend Thursday afternoons playing with other blind children at the Braille Institute Youth Center in Los Angeles, while his mother **Carole MacIntyre** meets with the Parent Support Group. Guided by a child

Tunnel vision caused by retinitis pigmentosa does not prevent **Scott McIntyre**, 4, above right, from playing with his brother **Todd** as his mother **Carole** looks on. Below, however, Scott seems displeased by Todd's curiosity, typical sibling behavior.

At left, **Paul Gonzalez** is again the center of attention, this time from his father **Frank** and brother **Frankie**, 4.

development counselor, parents discuss issues such as sibling relationships, discipline and separation.

Accompanied by a program preschool assistant, Scott attends a preschool three times a week. Plans by his parents, consultant and preschool assistant are underway for Scott to be mainstreamed into kindergarten.

Paul, Lucia and Scott are but three examples of the more than 155 individuals and their families who received aid from Braille Institute's Child Development Services in 1989.

"It's important to realize that a child's blindness has a profound effect not only on that child's development, but also on the family unit," Liske said. "Early intervention by our professionally trained personnel ensures that we can utilize every means we have to help visually impaired infants, toddlers, or preschoolers and their families."

4

Capture Interest With Action Shots

Action shots of people relating to their jobs or each other capture reader interest. Large type helps readers with poor vision. The second color (brown) creates a double keyline around the images that enhances the black halftones. In other issues, the designer uses a 20 percent screen of brown as a frame for halftones, creating the illusion of extended tonal range.

Name *Scene*

Publisher *Braille Institute, Los Angeles, CA*

Purpose/audience *Members of the institute*

Production *PageMaker on Macintosh IIcx*

Printing *Black and brown on natural offset paper*

Format *8¹/₂-by-11 inches, eight pages*

Design *Paul J. Porrelli*

Award *Press Club of Southern California*

Techniques That Emphasize Photos

An employee newsletter highlights people by running large mug shots. Techniques such as a drop shadow, printed keylines and a linking band of the second color help make photos stand out from the page. The drop shadow repeats above the standing headline to push copy downward into the page.

Name *Scorecard*

Publisher *Harry M. Stevens, Inc., Cranbury, NJ*

Purpose/audience *Service to employees*

Production *PageMaker and Typestyler on Macintosh IIcx*

Printing *Black and red on white offset paper*

Format *8 1/2-by-11 inches, eight pages*

Design *Anita V. O'Malley*

Award *Communications Concepts*

2

PRESIDENT'S DESK

It's a good feeling to glance through the SCORECARD and see scores of HMS employees that have put in countless years of service. Of our officials, we have Jerry Yates, who just received his 40 year pin. In the Maryland circuit, three employees are 40 years and over—that's half a lifetime of loyal service.

On another note, I would like to extend my best to the Meadowlands crew—who opened a totally renovated dining room and party area over the Christmas Holidays.

I'd also like to express my delight that both our Giants and '49ers made it to post season playoffs.

Wishing everyone a prosperous new year.   *Bill Koras*

SCORECARD

Published quarterly by and for employees of Harry M. Stevens, Inc.

Officials Awarded Pins

Jerry Yates—"The first impression youngsters in the ballpark get of work is from you."

As a kid of about 16, he recalls toting 50 gallon stockpots on the N.Y. subway from one HMS location to another. Jerry Yates, assistant manager, Shea Stadium, received his 40 year service pin this year and shares his memories with us.

Other 1991 award recipients:
10 YEARS
CANDLESTICK PARK
Greg K. Kramer
CORPORATE
Von Hilton Clarke
Dora Perri
Michele Turansick
Kathy Tammaro
EL COMANDANTE
Heinz Morgenthaler
FENWAY PARK
Cathleen Callahan
GIANTS STADIUM
Anthony Gerbino
HOUSTON ASTRODOME
Dan Guzman
Christa Kaiser
John Kehl
Shari Mauther
Rebecca Pena
Mary Smith
Gisela Woodward
MADISON SQUARE GARDEN
Tom Ehrlinger
Jose Smith
MEADOWLANDS RACETRACK
Steve Goodman

3

UP-CLOSE

120 Years of Serving the Action World

by John Cortezzo

This is a brief profile of three employees who each received their forty-year service pins for the Maryland thoroughbred racing circuit on November 4, 1990. HMS was built on the loyalty, hard work, and service of scores of employees such as these who have contributed to the success of our company for over a century.

Bill Gendemico   *Pennycoe "Kingfish" Parsons*   *Willie Rosen*

Bill Gendemico

Bill spent his 40 year tenure between all the tracks in Maryland and Charlestown, W.V. He went from waiter to captain to maitre d'. He traveled the entire route and did it well.

Bill was the happiest, I be-

Pennycoe "Kingfish" Parsons

To his family, he's Pennycoe Parsons, but to his friends, he is "Kingfish." Forty-four years ago he was working in the back stretch. At the time, Gus Hartshorn, manager of Pimlico, asked if he would work for HMS.

Willie Rosen

After 42 years as a bartender, he speaks of a love of racing which has kept him at the track longer than most.

"After the first ten years I had made so many friends and met government officials, the press,

Avis Benne

Continued from page 1

in this field. She practices what she preaches in the most literal sense. And now, 17 years later, she is still pain-free.

Avis Bennett, Ph.D.

Photo by Lynne E. Brown

A courageous story of will and determination almost too hard to believe. But just ask Avis Bennett, Ph.D., director of behavioral health at Canyon Ranch in the Berkshires, because she's lived it.

▼ ▼ ▼

To look at her now, an attractive, self-confident, stately woman, you couldn't guess where Avis has been. But to listen to her speak in her calming and reserved voice, you know you can benefit from her experience.

"I have a lot of energy because I practice what I preach," Avis said. "I meditate every day. I reach into that

4

Lenox is g

by Lynne E. Brown

What's more fun than a vacation at Canyon Ranch in the Berkshires? A vacation with all your friends or business associates at Canyon Ranch in the Berkshires!

Roxanne Housley, National Sales Director

Photo by Lynne E. Brown

"Many groups have already taken advantage of our facilities," reports National Sales Director Roxanne Housley. "From cultural arts to Hadassah to women's organizations to business

Upcoming

If you've been considering a return visit to either Canyon Ranch location, *don't!* Stop considering and start planning—and here are some great reasons why:

Discounts

Fall color season has arrived in the Berkshires. Past guests returning for a visit will receive a 15 percent discount off any package until October 27. OR, if you bring a first-time Canyon Ranch guest with you, each of you will receive 20 percent off your selected packages.

Winter Rates

Snowshoeing. Pole hiking. Cross-country skiing. These are a few of the active winter sports you can enjoy on and around the rolling hills

8

Planning Flexible Photo Layouts

Flexibility in photo layout originates with the grid and the format of images. The grid of *Canyon Ranch Round Up* allows images to use the scholar margin; the format includes lots of vertical images. Photos of people face into the page to link their images to the articles.

Name *Canyon Ranch Round Up*

Publisher *Canyon Ranch, Tucson, AZ*

Purpose/audience *Service to customers*

Production *Ventura Publisher on IBM*

Printing *Black and brown on white gloss-coated paper*

Format *8¹/₂-by-11 inches, eight pages*

Design *Lori Lieber and Lisa Goldsmith*

Cropping Photos for a Lively Effect

Although almost every newsletter has a vertical format, few editors take advantage of the shape by running vertical photos. The boys on the playground equipment look much livelier vertical than they would in a horizontal format. Mortising a second image at an angle and running text around it provides the professional finishing touch to the page.

Name *Ohel*

Publisher *Ohel Children's Home & Family Services, New York, NY*

Purpose/audience *Service to parents and friends*

Production *By hand*

Printing *Black and green on gloss-coated paper*

Format *8½-by-11 inches, six pages*

Design *Esther Lerner and Harvey Barnett*

Ohel

Photo Credit: Carol Goeltter

Outdoor recreation brings out the best in Ohel's boys

Even Disabled Kids Need to Get Away
Ohel's Summer Camp Program

A game of basketball is in progress down at the courts. Two boys are practicing their back-stroke in the outdoor pool. Later in the evening you'd find them roasting hotdogs around a campfire. What you may not notice is that all of these boys have different degrees of emotional and/or developmental disabilities. Yet they all formed a cohesive group, together with their counselors, to enjoy the summer at Ohel's special camp program, just like any other boys their age.

The boys living at the Ohel Residences during the year needed a secluded summer program where they could enjoy recreation, trips, outdoor sports, swimming and group activities. Their difficulty in adapting to new people and routines resulted in behavioral regression when returning from other summer programs. Due to their various disabilities it was necessary for the camp to be staffed by their year-round Ohel directors and counselors with whom they were familiar. A special Ohel camp with a therapeutic Torah environment was the perfect and necessary solution.

Ohel rented a camp with a communal dining and recreational room, swimming pool and spacious grounds. The boys excitedly settled in to begin two months packed with fun and adventure at their Ohel summer camp.

The wake-up signal sounded early in the morning, rousing the boys to prepare for calisthenics. Davening together in the synagogue was followed by a daily Jewish studies learning session. Sports, swimming, arts & crafts, rap sessions and even cooking classes were a part of every day's activities. Evening prayers, barbecues, camp fires and special night activities rounded out the day. There were trips to amusement parks, boat rides and a two-day color-war competition where the boys competed in sports, singing and creative artwork. At the end of the season trophies were presented to those who excelled.

Differences melted away and the boys merged to form one large happy family. A grand musical/dramatic production culminated the season. The boys, attired in white shirts and dark pants stood, side by side with arms up, as their voices resounded in song: "Consider yourself at home, Consider yourself part of the Ohel family!" The staff was proud to witness the camaraderie of these disabled boys.

We hope that soon Ohel will be able to establish permanent summer camp facilities to ensure continued summer camp experiences for its children every year, so that disabled boys can get away and enjoy two carefree months of fun and relaxation. ∎

Anna's Exodus
(Continued form page 1)

been estranged from her rich heritage for so many years. She also receives proper medical and psychological care. From all outward appearances, Anna is a typical teenager, shopping and talking on the phone with her friends.

But Anna's journey to freedom is not over. Her deep social and emotional scars are still healing. Continued therapy, education and much love and patience are still needed for her to meet all of the challenges she will face, until she can be truly free. ∎

CUNA Mutual Insurance Group Employee Publication

M U T U A L
Matters

Vol. 24, No. 2   February 1991

Talking works best
L/M Council builds strong ties
between union and management

Members of the Labor/Management Council are, from the top left, Barry Owens, Chuck Eikel, Steve Martin, Darlys Levinger, Kim Priemen, Bill Stevenson, Tom Olson, Don Davidson, Sue Carpenter-Skavnak and Kathy McCartney.

At monthly meetings of the Labor/Management Council, egos and job titles are left outside the room.

Inside, union and management employees take their seats and get down to business. This month's chairperson (on alternating assignment) calls the meeting to order and introduces the topics. Everyone has a chance to talk and say what he or she feels. For the next two hours various ideas and opinions flow around the table.

The Labor/Management Council, created as part of the current labor contract between Office and Professional Employees International Union and CUNA Mutual, has met four times since September 1990.

Their mission: communication. More specifically, it is to identify common goals of union and management, and, in the spirit of cooperation, discuss them in a manner that will lead to promoting CUNA Mutual's success and the well-being of all employees.

Union members are chief steward Darlys Levinger, stewards Sue Carpenter-Skavnak, Chuck Eikel, Kathy McCartney and John Priemen, the union's business manager. Three other stewards will take turns serving as members. Management members are Don Davidson, Steve Martin, Tom Olson, Barry Owens and Bill Stevenson.

"We began meeting in 1989 but discussions didn't move in the direction either side wanted them to go," says Darlys Levinger. "Then other concerns, such as work hours,

Please turn to page 8

Photos That Direct the Eye

Much forethought went into the photographs for this issue. The front page image above creates a strong diagonal pattern that works well against the opposing diagonal of the shadow-lettered nameplate. On pages six and seven the mug shots are sharply focused, all in the same contrast range, and all taken from the same angle. The off-center arrangement radiating up and out from the corner of the page anchors the outstanding group portrait on the right page.

Name *Mutual Matters*

Publisher *CUNA Mutual Insurance Group, Madison, WI*

Purpose/audience *Service to employees*

Production *By hand*

Printing *Black and silver-blue on white gloss-coated paper*

Format *8½-by-11 inches, eight pages*

Design *Jo-Dee Benson and Ralph Denu*

Awards *Communication Concepts, International Association of Business Communicators*

Employee Service

June Anniversaries

20 years: A. Jack Heartburg, North West; Vernon Lowell, MemberElect® Coverages; Mary Weichbrod, Collateral Insurance Center; Patrick Young, Finance and Administration, Southfield; Paul Butz, CUMIS PL Underwriting
25 years: Richard Bullington, Pomona; Price Legg, Field Operations; Frederic Nobles, South East

June Retirements

Jeanne Orvold, Real Estate; Norma Moyer, International Commons; Sylvia Heiser, CUMIS Claims; Evangeline Schneider, Quality Commitment; Betty Abramson, Pomona

July Anniversaries

20 years: David Lister, PLAN AMERICA;® Alberta Sullivan, Quality Commitment
30 years: Phillis Walmer, Employee Benefits Claims; Bertha Klemm, Quality Commitment

July Retirements

Barbara Johnsen, Medical; Robert Brokaw, North Central

A. Jack Heartburg
20 Years

Vernon Lowell
20 Years

Mary Weichbro[d]
20 Years

Paul Butz
20 Years

Richard Bullington
25 Years

Price Legg
25 Years

Norma Moyer
Retirement

Sylvia Heiser
Retirement

Evangeline Schnei[der]
Retirement

Betty Abramson
Retirement

David Lister
20 Years

Alberta Sullivan
20 Years

Phyllis Walmer
30 Years

Bertha Klemm
30 Years

Barbara Johnsen
Retirement

Robert Brokaw
Retirement

Take your

Summer vaca[tion] opportunity for With your cam[era] able to capture unique momen[ts]
And that uni[que] be a winner in annual *Mutual* Photo Contest.
Categories ar[e] "things;" and " may be color, b[ut] slides. Deadline
Entry form a[nd] will be publishe[d]

United Way keeps giving year 'round

DOWNTOWN MADISON — A man in a wheelchair bends over and rolls closer to hoarsely whisper something to the woman next to him.

Between them is a birthday cake with two candles burning bright. They reflect in the man's eyes as he speaks in a loud whisper. Anna moves closer because she can't hear as well as she used to.

"You know, Anna, I haven't had a birthday cake in 20, no, maybe 30 years," the man says in a scratchy, hoarse whisper. "This is the happiest day of my life."

A tear runs down the wrinkled face that has probably seen more than 80 birthdays. It matches the one on Anna's face. They blow out the candles together. Their companions politely applaud...

That was the scene one afternoon a few months ago at Madison's Adult Day Care Center, located at Bethel Lutheran Church. The Center is one of 79 agencies funded by Home Office employees' and retirees' generous contributions to Dane County United Way.

The Center allows people like the wheelchair bound gentleman and his ladyfriend Anna to get together in an easily accessible location for companionship, meals, activities and, especially, birthdays.

Thanks to your generous contributions these folks will continue to have a place to go. And, perhaps celebrate a few more birthdays than they otherwise would.

Thanks for giving! Ⓜ

United Way's success is up to you, says the 1990 campaign committee and executive supporters Irv Burling and Richard Heins. Members of the committee are, from left, Tom Heitpas, Jane Chesbro, Ron Jenkins, Lisa Otis, Scott Powell; center, Pam Andersen; bottom, Tom Kobinsky, Lois O'Rourke and Brenda Schuppe.

Photo by Jerry Jensen

Framing Words With Pictures

With a publication devoted largely to text (set 11/13 for readers fifty-five and older), a large image on the front and smaller images placed in a scholar margin frame information presented in words. Halftones in the margin can easily depart from rectangular shapes without needing runarounds.

Name *Solutions*

Publisher *Council of Better Business Bureaus, Inc., Arlington, VA*

Purpose/audience *Service to members*

Production *Ventura Publisher and Windows on IBM*

Printing *Black and a second color on white gloss-coated paper*

Format *8½-by-11 inches, sixteen pages*

Design *Erica Whitcombe*

An Open Door To ADR *by Steven J. Cole*

Editor's Introduction: Court-referred mediation and arbitration have become increasingly popular means of dramatically reducing court backlogs and avoiding long and costly trials. A recent survey by the National Center for State Courts identified over 700 court-annexed ADR programs nationwide, generally concentrating on civil and family disputes.

Ohio has been a leader in the establishment of such programs: state rules allow courts to refer cases to non-binding arbitration after pre-trial hearings are completed. And since 1986, several Ohio courts have held "settlement days" during which the regular work of the court is suspended, and judges and volunteer lawyers try to settle through mediation cases that have been on the courts' dockets for long periods of time. Courts in several other states now hold similar "settlement days."

their frustration. This is so because enforcement of these rights is, in fact, beyond the practical reach of most of us. The Ohio Supreme Court and the state leadership have played a prominent role in trying to eliminate this troublesome gap between reality and expectation.

Before I came to the Council of Better Business Bureaus, I had served as a private attorney representing poor clients, as a government regulator, and as a state consumer law enforcement official. I left each of these positions with a clearer understanding of the need for swift, inexpensive, and fair dispute resolution procedures.

While alternative dispute resolu-

Steven J. Cole,
Vice President and Senior Counsel

Committed to Precommitment *by Brian D. J. Peterkin*

Businesses in Seattle know that the Better Business Bureau of Greater Seattle, Inc., is serious about alternative dispute resolution. All businesses that become Bureau members are required to participate in BBB CARE®, a program that precommits the business to settle customer complaints through the Bureau's conciliation, mediation, or arbitration services.

"Ever since we started our dispute resolution programs in 1972 we felt that all members should be precommitted to dispute resolution," says Emilie Adams, the Bureau's president. "It re-establishes faith." Adams tells businesses that "it provides your customers with an alternative to court, which shows you are concerned about them." As it turns out, most people never use arbitration; "just knowing the business is precommitted to settling disputes often prompts both parties to settle before arbitration," Adams says.

Business-Activated ADR

The precommitment requirement is beneficial to businesses. When consumers call the Bureau with pre-purchase inquiries about businesses, they tend to have favorable views of businesses that are precommitted to settling disputes through the Better Business Bureau.

A unique aspect of Seattle's program is its use of a security account that is similar to an escrow account. To show they are serious about set-

tling a dispute, parties put whatever money may be in dispute into an account with the Bureau. "If the sticking point of a dispute is payment, the account removes that obstacle and allows the parties to concentrate on the dispute. Just knowing the other party's money is available will often lead to settlement," notes Bill Zook, the Bureau's director of professional services. Adams adds, "I couldn't run a program without it."

To show its own

BBB of Greater Seattle staff (from left):
Bill Zook, Emilie Adams, Lucy Armstrong,
Stacey Box, and Crish Lind.

Brian D. J. Peterkin is assistant editor of BBB Solutions.

An Expert Opinion *by Kate O'Byrne & Rod L. Davis*

Blown head gaskets. Warped cylinder heads. Burnt valves. What happened to this car, and how did it happen? When arbitrators deal with this sort of case, how can they be sure that they have all the information needed to make a fair decision?

BBB arbitrators do not have to be auto mechanics to render fair decisions in BBB AUTO LINE cases. And they don't have to be professional remodelers to decide home construction cases. But an arbitrator must understand the critical facts on which each party is basing his or her position, and the arbitrator must evaluate those facts to arrive at a fair decision. In cases involving technical issues, the arbitrator may decide that he or she needs the help of someone who is an expert in that specific technical field. The input of an expert can assist the arbitrator in reaching a decision that is fair and unbiased.

The BBB system gives parties the opportunity to present their cases in person. This process enables the customer and the business to explain their sides of the dispute, provide written and visual support for their positions, question the other party, and rebut statements with which they disagree. An inspection of the product or service or a test drive of automobiles can also give the arbitrator important factual information.

Parties are also allowed to bring in witnesses to corroborate their position, including witnesses who may

give "expert testimony" about technical issues. While the customer's and the business' witnesses may be knowledgeable and can provide insight into the issues in dispute, the arbitrator recognizes that the witnesses may have a vested interest in the outcome of the decision. Witnesses brought in by one of the parties may not be neutral, and the arbitrator must consider that as he or she evaluates the credibility of the information presented.

In some instances, verifying the accuracy of technical information can be accomplished through the exchange of questions and answers with the parties. The inspection and test drive also give the arbitrator an opportunity to evaluate technical evidence and its relevance to a specific case. But when the arbitrator feels a need for additional technical information from an independent source, he or she should ask the Bureau to call in an independent technical expert.

When Is a Technical Expert Needed?

The arbitrator is the sole judge of when to call in a technical expert. If the arbitrator feels that he or she needs the input of an expert in the field in order to render a fair decision, then the arbitrator should re-

Kate O'Byrne is research associate and Rod L. Davis is director of operations for the CBBB ADR Division.

Lennie Roberts

approved Measure A, closing several loopholes that the prior developers of Cascade Ranch had used to increase the density of their development. Yet developer Paul L. Gould, Inc. of Connecticut has used the old, pre-Measure A rules to determine a "base density" for the project, and has added several

Cascade
March

Committee for Green Foothills' challenge to the glitzy "executive spa" at Cascade Ranch finally got its "day in court," and we are very encouraged by the great interest in the case shown by Judge Harkjoon Paik of Monterey County Superior Court. CGF and co-plaintiff organizations have high hopes that Judge Paik will send this project back to the drawing boards.

from page 3, CASCADE

park acquisition of the rest of the Ranch, we continue to be troubled by TPL's role in lobbying for approval of this precedent-setting exception to the agricultural protections of the County's Coastal Plan.

Judge Paik asked all parties to attend a settlement conference in December before Judge McDonald in San Mateo County. CGF and our co-plaintiffs stood firm for a scaled-down campground and lodge, with on-site water, to serve coastal visitors. We were unwilling to accept any fitness center or conference facilities. Such "destination resort" facilities can be located anywhere, and do not belong in the agricultural area of the coast.

favor, finding that the Environmental Impact Statement was deficient in its analysis of noise. He has required Caltrans to prepare a study of the Bypass's impact on McNee Ranch State Park. Caltrans has refused to do the study, and has appealed Judge

CGF has taken this action because we felt there was an urgent need to demonstrate that if the county would not enforce the law, we would. Judge Bible's astonishing decision that there was no violation, and that our case was "frivolous," is on appeal. We have every confidence that this decision will be overturned.

MEASURE A - THE COASTAL PROTECTION INITIATIVE: Measure A was overwhelmingly approved by the voters in 1986. Landowner and development interests filed suit in 1987 to invalidate the election. For four years, they have allowed the case to languish in the courts. They are now activating the case, and it is expected to go to a hearing in San Mateo County Superior Court in late summer.

CGF provided key leadership in the campaign to pass Measure A. We have joined with other sponsors of Measure A to intervene in order to assure that the voters' mandate is vigorously and effectively defended.

Lennie Roberts is our San Mateo County Legislative Advocate.

from page 1, THREATS

Five amendments to the county's General Plan were proposed. The San Martin-Gilroy Greenbelt came under attack and seemed to be losing support, and a major new and precedent-setting resort plan was announced for Gilroy Hot Springs. The "Wild West" motif in Santa Clara hadn't stopped after all: it was merely in momentary remission.

In addition to this, at the end of the summer, two new apparent champions of development, John Vidovich and Victor Vasquez, took up their posts as county planning commissioners. The new appointees took the places, literally and figuratively, of "anything goes" Rex Lindsay and Jack "the Builder" Faris.

Here's a quick synopsis of what's happened since my last report to you.

Plan Amendments
Unfortunately the Planning Commission passed all five General Plan Amendments on a vote of 4 to 3. Not encouraging, as these amendments tend to make development easier.

Despite the responsible efforts of Commissioners Brown, Shotwell and Tanner, the majority of the seven member group seems compelled to grant whatever developers want. Vidovich spoke vehemently on development's behalf, and Vasquez spoke nary a word as he hit the "Yes" button on his console five consecutive times.

The Supervisors, an elected group after all, felt the need to act with more prudence. CGF was concerned with four issues (the fifth actually made development more difficult in a ranchland location). Three of the issues involved proposed density increases, one to change general requirements for ranchland parcel creation.

The supervisors, after being lobbied long and hard by CGF and other groups, denied the worst two of the three density proposals. A small victory, but a victory nevertheless.

As evidence of the influence Rex Lindsay still has over county planning, his proposal to change parcel creation in the ranchlands was passed 5-0. Mr. Lindsay went so far as to tell me personally that my "credibility" had been damaged for even having the gall to testify against his proposal.

Greenbelt
Residents of the proposed San Martin-Gilroy Greenbelt came out in force at the Supervisors' public hearings Dec. 4 to protest this latest threat to their membership in the millionaires' club.

The Greenbelt, if established, will pre-

Bruce Frymire is our Santa Clara County Legislative Advocate.

vent landowners in the area from developing their properties. It will *not* prevent them from farming, or from continuing their lives as they exist today, or from passing their property on to successive generations, but residents will not be able to subdivide their land.

Despite anguished testimony on the part of some residents (others supported the measure), the Supervisors stuck to their guns on this one and supported outgoing supe Susie Wilson's idea. A motion to "continue progress toward the greenbelt" was passed by a vote of 5-0.

New Foothill Threat
They are never going to leave our foothills alone. Fukuyama International announced plans in December to construct a $30 million resort complex in the east foothills at Gilroy Hot Springs (just above the Coyote Reservoir).

The plan comprises 21 $400,000 condominiums, a 76 room hotel with 22 separate cottages, restaurants, bars, shops, stores, a heli-pad and an "outdoor hill elevator." This is *not* a redesign of the historic, tiny resort on that spot, but a total revamp, creating a "recreational resort for a Japanese market."

The area now is quiet, undeveloped, prime mountain lion territory. A narrow road paralleling Coyote Creek winds up to the property. The site, an hour's drive from Los Altos, could be a hundred miles from civilization. That road, needless to say, will be widened if this plan goes through, and will carry up to 2000 more vehicles per day on weekends. *continued page 8, THREATS*

6

Dropping Text Into Pictures

When images are presented as large as on this front page, a story can begin in a box dropped into the halftone. On the inside, the negative space at the top of each page introduces the story using photos. Heavy horizontal rules at the head and foot of each page help blend words and images into one visual whole.

Name *Green Footnotes*

Publisher *Committee for Green Foothills, Palo Alto, CA*

Purpose/audience *Members and friends of the committee*

Production *PageMaker on Macintosh SE*

Printing *Dark green preprinted and black on light gray text paper*

Format *8½-by-11 inches, eight pages*

Design *Andrea Henrick and Barbara Brown*

Unifying Photos and Heads

These photos have an effective presentation centered over two or three columns and breaking the rule that creates the top portion of the box holding the text. Images hang directly down from headlines and subheads, with captions completing the eyeflow. The red second color is only used for headlines, initial caps and pull quotes. All of the graphic rules are in black.

Name *In Review*

Publisher *Seattle Community Colleges, Seattle, WA*

Purpose/audience *Service to students and community*

Production *PageMaker and FreeHand on Macintosh II*

Printing *Black and red on white offset paper*

Format *11-by-17 inches, four pages*

Design *Sharon Nakamura*

Award *Council for the Advancement and Support of Education*

---

*Burlington Northern Foundation
Faculty Achievement Awards*

Top teachers inspire gratitude

Seattle Community Colleges instructors (from left) Rochelle Dela Cruz, James Rondeau and Nancy Verheyden.

Three of the best teachers at the Seattle Community Colleges were honored in May with 1988-89 Burlington Northern Foundation Faculty Achievement Awards. The program, now in its fourth year, is based on nominations of full-time faculty members by students, former students, faculty, staff and the colleges' business partners.

This year, "the word that characterized the nominating letters for candidates is 'gratitude,' " said Jon Blake, chair of the awards committee at North Seattle Community College.

Recipients were presented awards of $1,500 at a May 9 recep-

to know what they bring with them is valuable and important. We would all lose so much, otherwise." One of her colleagues says this kind of understanding is appreciated by her students. "The number who return to visit or seek her out for counseling is telling. Several over the years have

Northwest History the same way — because the students aren't the same, and they make the class." The formula works: During winter quarter, Rondeau's "History of Washington" class was so popular with its senior citizen students that they petitioned the college to extend the session in spring.

■ Nancy Verheyden, Electro-Mechanical Drafting instructor at North Seattle Community College. Verheyden sets an "extraordinary example as a caring, involved faculty member who significantly impacts the lives of her students," according to a colleague. In the classroom, she has often helped

---

'Are we there yet?'

by Maralyn Thomas-Schier
**SCCC Instructor
Early Childhood and
Parent Education**

Summer often brings increased opportunities for travel with children.

However, vacations away from home do produce a stress of their own. They can be more fun for all if you plan ahead, include the children in preparations, sing a lot and tell stories. Here are some ideas that have helped other families enjoy their time together:

■ Having time for advance planning helps parents and children feel ready for a trip. Young children delight in having their own suitcase or backpack. Even the very young have ideas about what to take along. When children help with packing, they usually are more comfortable away from home. Of course, it is important to include a favorite toy or blanket for comfort.

Maralyn Thomas-Schier and friends at Seattle Central Community College. Bob Hereford photo.

pate in making a travel kit of generally non-messy materials they would enjoy using in their laps. For instance, the kit might include crayons, transparent tape, paper, washable felt tip pens, magic slates, sticker books and a roll of masking tape.

■ Include a viewfinder. You can often find new slide scenes along your route in tourist shops. You may also bring along slide photos from home, which are fun to look at and useful in countering feelings of homesickness.

eler, it is important to stop often and exercise a bit.

■ Snacks are a great help and can be purchased and prepared ahead to prevent some of the inevitable requests for junk food. It helps to tell children what you will purchase and what you will bring from home. (My favorite travel snack is 'O'-shaped dry cereals.)

■ Traveling together provides wonderful opportunities to talk with each other. Children love to hear about your childhood and trips you took when you were young.

Sometimes, the best vacation is in your own neighborhood. You can help neighborhood children create a circus; set up a pretend camp, school or store; stage a wedding; or put on an ice cream social. All these events are wonderful ways to get to know your neighbors and provide your children with opportunities to

'We all gain'

Students, families and school systems benefit from new partnership

schools have expressed interest," she said.

The programs help to motivate students — and help those who are already motivated. At Rainier Beach High School, for instance, College in the High School students have been studying English and political science. Coursework was developed by teams of faculty from the school district and the community colleges. This semester, college-level chemistry is being offered at Nathan Hale High School.

Franklin High Scho[...] Williams leads a sp[...] with students in his [...] Writing class.

ese [...]s offer [...] more [...] use of [...]hools' [...] and [...]rces'

Students who are taking a course for college credit are expected to maintain a specified grade level. They pay $50 per course (versus the $127 they would pay as community college students), and when they complete the course, they receive a transcript showing college credit.

Classes are a[...] dents who are takir[...] high school cred[...] plained.

Students who [...] training in high sch[...] of the Articulation cl[...] at advanced levels [...] at one of the Sea[...] Colleges; after one [...] work in that progra[...]

completed while in high school can be placed on their college transcript for a $10 records fee.

Fees generated by the students are used to pay stipends to community college faculty involved in the project, as well as to cover costs of registration, testing and tran[...]

'Ready to ride'

Interim chancellor leaves the West

and he applauds the diversity of the arts and the breathtaking scenery. Like most people who come to this region, Barringer had expected the rain — but not so much of it. And like most Northwest natives, he feels "when the sun is out, this is one of the most beautiful places on earth."

But by summer he'll be back in [...]

Seattle Community Colleges interim chancellor Dr. Bob Barringer (left) [...]lic Schools superin-[...]Kendrick, who [...]ment this spring [...]me classes and [...] the two systems [...]).

stepped into jobs at [...] Community College [...] Community College [...] Early on, Barringer [...]al, permanent posts [...] Albemarle in North [...] Catonsville Commu-[...]altimore; for six years [...] he was president of [...]mmunity College in [...]ges and rewards of

we've had in a decade." Barringer credits the coordinated effort of faculty, staff and students in getting the message across to lawmakers.

And he's confident of the outcome of the search that resulted in the choice of a Westerner, Dr. Thomas Gonzales, as the new Seattle Community Colleges chancellor. "I can say I'm pleased and proud of the results of the search process. Gonzales, I feel, is an outstanding educator, and will provide the colleges with strong leadership during the coming years."

One of Barringer's first accomplishments in Seattle was settlement of the union contract with the colleges' faculty, which happened "with as little acrimony as possible," and which "both sides worked very hard on."

Barringer would prefer to "let other people judge my

'Wher[...] back o[...] of the [...] I've live[...] the c[...] definite[...] appe[...]

What's cooking?

SCCC's culinary remodeling project nearly done

Whetting the appetites of the SCCC community is news that this fall, Seattle Central will reopen the kitchens and dining rooms of its Hospitality and Culinary Arts programs. The facilities were closed last year for a $5 million remodeling of the program's instructional areas.

The renovation will feature state-of-the art equipment and work areas for training students in hospitality technology. Students will learn a variety of skills, ranging from high-volume food preparation to contemporary cuisine and can specialize in baking, commercial food preparation or hotel and restaurant management.

Hands-on training will take place in the new main kitchen, which [...]

Hospitality/Culinary Arts Division chair Frank DeMartini (center) on the site of the $5 million SCCC remodeling project, with instructors (from left) John Lewis, Don Bullington, Ernie Kimberlin and John Balmores.

the national and international competitions in which Seattle Central students regularly participate.

The college community, as well as the students, benefit from retail facilities on the campus, including a [...]

skills. Classrooms also have a new look. The scullery, laundry and stockroom are all designed to serve as classrooms for teaching principles of sanitation and food storage.

Several changes in curriculum will accompany the remodeling. According to Frank DeMartini, chair of the Hospitality and Culinary Arts Division, the scope of the program will be broadened.

"We plan to develop our evening classload within the next year so we can provide evening dining facilities to the community," he said. A new management program will also be added to the cooking and baking programs.

The new facility will accommo[...]

INSIDE INFORMATION

The anatomy
of a dtp fish story

Here's the true story of how two dtp designers went fishing on the job — with a Mac instead of a worm — and created a catchy four-color brochure in only three days. It's a story with a moral for any designer who has to hook a quick design. (Turn to page for details.)

EDITORIAL GRAPHICS

Picture a table of contents

Congratulations! You got your audience to open your catalog, newsletter, booklet or informational brochure. With one obstacle hurdled, it's time to take on the contents page. What can you do to keep the pages turning? Add pictures.

Repeat the cover picture, tease with inside photos or use icons that suggest what the stories or products are about. Inside the publication, you can use icons in the margins, bleeding off the page for quick searching, enlarged to illustrate the page, or reduced to highlight an initial cap or a pull-quote. Take note of these examples, in which photos and illustrated icons lead readers on.

Left: Here's a contents page that, like the publication it previews, knows how to have fun. That's most appropriate for **The Rainbow Reporter,** *the quarterly of Binney & Smith Inc., the crayon makers. The page contains a cover reduction, kids' photos, and a detail from an inside-story — the full-page illustration is shown complete above.*

It's what's up front that counts in the contents page of **Intervue,** *the quarterly publication of Intergraph Corp., Huntsville, AL. Cover flags wave at half-size but full-color inside. The large navy logo and thick horizontal green rules on a white field look flag-like, so they work well with the flag theme.*

Left: Four-color, illustrated icons help to communicate the contents in the National Assn. of Printers and Lithographers' Publications & Services catalog. The icons provide the most color or in the otherwise black, gray and blue catalog. Above: Inside the catalog, here's how the enlarged icon begins a new category.

IN HOUSE GRAPHICS • 7

Illustrating Tables of Contents With Photos

In House Graphics often leads the way in innovative design. Here the editor shows how to use photos in a table of contents. On the opposite page, another editor applies the advice.

Name *In House Graphics*

Publisher *United Communications Group, Rockville, MD*

Purpose/audience *Service to subscribers*

Production *PageMaker on Macintosh*

Printing *Black and red on natural offset paper*

Format *8½-by-11 inches, eight pages*

Design *Ronnie Lipton*

Award *Newsletter Clearinghouse*

National Council on Compensation Insurance

Trends

Board Approves Move Toward Loss Costs

NCCI to shift focus to loss costs

New Communications Programs Tell NCCI Story to Employees, Board Members, Regulators and Legislators

A stepped-up communications effort, both within and outside of NCCI, is a major priority of new President William Hager.

Beginning with a weekly memo, detailing Hager's and NCCI's activities, which is faxed to all board members, the Council's communications program is expanding to encompass new publications intended for both internal and external audiences.

NCCI's newest internal communications vehicle is a monthly publication in which each NCCI department briefly reports its activities to the rest of the organization.

TRENDS, NCCI's employee magazine, will also begin to appear more frequently, with publication shifting from a quarterly to a bi-monthly basis.

In addition to communicating through these print media, Hager also plans to use video cassettes to personally address various issues of interest to all NCClers. These videotaped remarks will be for internal use only and will be played throughout the Council.

"Ideally, everyone at NCCI should have at least a feel for what other parts of the organization are doing," Hager said. "That enables all of us to have a better sense of how our role fits into the larger mission of NCCI, and how we might be called upon to help other departments in the future.

"We also want our many publics to have a better understanding of the full scope of our activities and concerns, and that is why we are introducing NCCI Update, a quarterly publication that will review these issues for our

To reach its internal and external audiences, NCCI uses a wide range of publications, some of which are displayed here.

members, regulators, legislators, etc."

"NCCI Update is closer in style and format to USA Today than to Scientific American," assistant vice president for Public Affairs Cheryl Budd explained. "We want to give readers a non-technical explanation of what we are doing, what we hope to do and where the problems are. Stories in NCCI Update will be kept short and, where possible, illustrated with graphs, charts, and drawings. The idea is to discuss 10 to 12 issues in each six-page edition."

"One of the important goals for NCCI," Hager observed, "is to help to set the agenda. By calling attention to the issues that concern us at NCCI, we hope to make others share our concerns and begin the process

of resolving the system's problems."

NCCI has entered into an agreement with North American Precis Syndicate, which will distribute "Noteworthy Trends," a series of six columns focusing on workers compensation and NCCI, to 3,800 suburban weeklies throughout the nation.

To reach a nationwide cable television audience of influential business and opinion leaders, NCCI has contracted with Nation's Business Today to produce five 90-second commentaries, each to be aired twice on the morning program "Perspective." The segments will feature NCCI senior executives. ■

6

Another Illustrated Table of Contents

The heavy rule bleeding off the top of the front page and its large drop sink lead all eyes to interesting photos illustrating the table of contents (TOC). The photographs complement the editorial slant of the inside articles by featuring reading material instead of the people. Note the excerpt from this image used in the TOC. Printing 150-line halftones on 100-pound glossy paper ensures high-quality reproduction of the halftones.

Name Trends

Publisher National Council on Compensation Insurance, Boca Raton, FL

Purpose/audience Service to members

Production PageMaker and Illustrator on Macintosh II

Printing Black and blue on premium white gloss-coated paper

Format 8½-by-11 inches, twenty-eight pages

Design Yvonne Oulton and Chris Bennett

Award Communications Concepts

Dual Previews Dazzle Members and Guests

On the warm and perfect summer evening of Friday, July 26, a total of 850 people attended combined preview openings for the Desertarium and "Wildlife: The Artist's View."

The enthusiastic crowd, consisting of donors, members, contractors, artists, exhibit designers and staff, seemed to go back and forth between the two exhibits as if wrestling with the age-old question of which is more important, "Life or Art?"

Special amenities for the evening included hors d'oeuvres from The Farmstead and refreshments donated by Clearwater Beverages and Pepsi Cola Bottling.

Both exhibits opened to the public the following day with a number of activities and events for all ages. ■

Right: Sherry Hossom (center) chats with Jim and Louise Castles.

Below: Curator Susan Harless shares a light moment with Grant and Mary Lou Woolley.

Center right: Volunteer Shirley Lennox stands by to usher members through new exhibit.

Right: Animal Care Specialist Mary Jo Douglas discusses exhibit with George and Stephanie Morton.

3

HIGH DESERT QUARTERLY September 1991

Mortising Photos for Space Efficiency

High Desert Quarterly achieves visual appeal while staying within budget by running four-color covers and two-color interiors. The paper remains identical throughout. Inside, photos mortised into one another use space efficiently and unify images. Keylines separate the images, telling readers to look for several photos.

Name *High Desert Quarterly*

Publisher *High Desert Museum, Bend, OR*

Purpose/audience *Service to members*

Production *WordPerfect on IBM*

Printing *Cover: four-color process; interior: black and rust on ivory matte-coated paper*

Format *8½-by-11 inches, twelve pages*

Design *Jack Cooper*

GUM SAN
LAND OF THE GOLDEN MOUNTAIN

Traveling Exhibit on Chinese in the West to Open September 21

"Almost no industry and no part of the economy on the Pacific Coast was left untouched by the resourceful Chinese laborers"

Robert G. Boyd
Curator of Western Heritage

"On the way to the mines," California goldfields. Courtesy California Historical Society

The history of the American West is a colorful fabric through which are woven the lives of a multitude of people. Over the course of the 19th and 20th centuries, the region, already populated by Native American Indians, became an ethnic melting pot, home to such diverse peoples as Scots fur traders, Hispanic vaqueros, Cornish miners, Irish tracklayers, and Chinese laborers. Few of the participants in the exploration and settlement of the western landscape faced the dramatic cultural change, not to mention the hardship and oppression, experienced by the Chinese.

"Gum San: Land of the Golden Mountain," an exhibition on the Chinese contributions to the development of the American West, will open in the Brooks Gallery, Earle A. Chiles Center on the Spirit of the West, on Saturday, September 21, 1991, and will run through Sunday, March 8, 1992.

The exhibit tells the story of the Chinese in the West from the California Gold Rush period to the early years of the 20th century, a history "...as full of hardship and oppression as it was of industry and opportunity," says Curator of Western Heritage Robert Boyd, principal organizer of the exhibit.

To many Chinese people, the American West was the "Gum San," or "land of the golden mountain." Their goal was to labor and save for a number of years, then return to their homeland where their modest savings could provide a measure of financial security and a better life for themselves and their families. Few attained this goal.

The Chinese worked their way across the Sierras and the deserts of Nevada in the construction camps of the nation's first transcontinental railroad; they labored in the goldfields from California to Montana; they hired on as chuck wagon cooks on High Desert ranches and cannery workers on the Pacific Coast, and performed a variety of domestic jobs within the settlements and cities. In short, they were active and essential participants in the great human adventure that resulted in the development and settlement of the West.

The purpose of "Gum San: Land of the Golden Mountain" is to interpret the often overlooked presence and importance of the Chinese in the region's history. Highlighted are over 40 Cibachrome prints of surviving Chinese sites in the West photographed by Barry Peril. They include interior views of temples, Chinese apothecaries, gambling houses, council chambers, as well as exterior views of aging canneries, ranch cookhouses, railroad construction sites, and the stacked stone "Chinese Walls" along the streams that ran through once-rich mining camps. Peril, who is best known for his landscape photography, has had numerous exhibits throughout the country, including one-man shows at the Museum of American Folk Art in New York City and The High Desert Museum.

Complimenting Peril's photographic record is a selection of historic black-and-white photographs that chronicle the daily life of the Chinese in the far flung corners of "Gum San." These photographs, together with over 50 artifacts, such as clothing, medicines, business documents, food containers, cooking utensils, gambling paraphernalia and personal objects of daily life, illustrate key themes of the Chinese experience in the American West.

The interpretive text for the exhibit and the accompanying catalogue were written by Dr. Jeffrey Barlow of Lewis and Clark College and Christine Richardson. Barlow and Richardson, authors of *China Doctor of John Day*, are recognized authorities on historic and contemporary issues concerning the Chinese in North America as well as in Asia. A poster and a full-color catalogue will be available at the Museum's store.

Guidance on "Gum San: Land of the Golden Mountain," two years in the making, has been provided by members of the Chinese communities in the region, in particular by George and Mary Leong of the Chinese Consolidated Benevolent Association, Portland, Oregon.

"Gum San: Land of the Golden Mountain," is the Museum's first major traveling exhibit. In 1992, it is scheduled to be shown at the Oregon Historical Society in April, the Umatilla County Historical Society in August, and the Southern Oregon Historical Society in December. Venues for 1993 include Coos Art Museum and Baker County Historical Society. ■

"Field hands," Sacramento Delta. Until Chinese labor diked the river and drained the tule swamps beginning in 1850, the Sacramento Delta, now one of the world's richest agricultural areas, was an uninhabitable marsh. By the late 1860s, thousands of Chinese agriculture workers labored in the area. Courtesy Henry E. Huntington Library and Art Gallery.

Historic Chinatowns of the West

Albany
Astoria
Auburn
Aurora
Austin
Baker City
Bellingham
Bodie
Boise
Carson City
Chico
China Camp
Coeur d'Alene
Elko
Eureka
Fort Colville
Granite
Idaho City
Idaho Falls
Jacksonville
John Day
Klamath Falls
Lewiston
Locke
Los Angeles
Lovelock
Marysville
Monterey
Port Gamble
Port Townsend
Portland
Sacramento
Salem
San Diego
Sandpoint
San Francisco
San Luis Obispo
Seattle
Silver City
Sumpter
Tacoma
Tuscarora
Unionville
Victoria
Virginia City
Walla Walla
Warrens
Weaverville
Winnemucca
Yuba City

This exhibit is sponsored by U S WEST, with special financial support from the Oregon Council for the Humanities, an affiliate of the National Endowment for the Humanities. Major support for the Museum's Changing Exhibits Program is provided by ARCO, the Ben B. Cheney Foundation, and Pacific Health & Life Insurance Company.

4   HIGH DESERT QUARTERLY   September 1991

5   HIGH DESERT QUARTERLY   September 1991

Creating an Effective Photo Spread

Effective photo spreads call for one image to dominate and other images to support. This spread blends the two images perfectly with the headline, pull quote and text into one story. The list at the right frames that side of the spread.

VISITING THE UNKNOWN

New York City
home care nurses
are equal to the
challenges they face

OUTSIDE A NEW YORK CITY APARTMENT BUILDING, gunshots echo through the streets as a visiting nurse toting a heavy backpack enters the building. Telling herself, once again, that "there are no safe neighborhoods these days" and saying a prayer that her car will be safe, she enters her patient's apartment. It is filthy. The patient hasn't eaten in days. Medication has been ignored.

By Kathy Aldworth and Fern Zela Nemeth

The nurse treats her patient, provides conversation, consolation. She might even take time to clean the dingy apartment, tackle the myriad insurance forms and bills or buy food and refill prescriptions for a debilitated patient who can't get out of bed.

Home care as an industry has doubled in size over the last 10 years. So, too, has the availability of "high-tech" health services for home-based care—better for the patient and tougher for the health professional. Tougher for the visiting nurse, too, is making home visits in the types of neighborhoods that the elderly can typically afford. And, thanks to a nursing shortage, there are fewer nurses to make those visits.

At the Visiting Nurse Service (VNS) Home Care of New York, which serves Manhattan, Queens, the Bronx and Brooklyn, staff nurses typically have case loads of anywhere from 28 to 50 patients, says Marge Callahan, chapter leader for the United Federation of Teachers/VNS Home Care Chapter, Federation of Nurses, local 2. Patients are released "sicker and quicker" from hospitals, which means seeing a patient sometimes two or three times a day. And, the agency provides around-the-clock service. That means evening and weekend visits—often in dangerous neighborhoods.

"One nurse recently told me she almost had her car taken from her," recounts Callahan, who is familiar with these incidents. "She was alone, going into a building, when two guys came up to her with a gun and told her to give them her car keys. She did. But she had an alarm system they couldn't operate. She ran into the patient's house and called the police."

Patricia Samuel, who works out of the VNS office in the Bronx, has lots of stories to tell: the time she discovered a man on top of the elevator she was riding or the sniping incident that occurred in the "projects," leaving one man dead and another paralyzed. The sniper is still at large, she notes.

There's also the time one of her colleagues was visiting a patient who needed a dressing changed; a drug raid was going on next door. The police broke into the patient's apartment so they could get to the fire escape. "The nurse had to stop in the middle of the dressing and put her hands up," comments Samuel.

It is for those reasons that Callahan says she encourages the nurses to use the escorts employed by the agency. These escorts have no special training, "they're just another body to be with you," says Callahan.

Visiting nurses know that if they didn't make these visits, many of their patients would suffer more than the lack of health care. The visiting nurse may be the sole contact with a certain patient, says VNS chapter member Ann Verderber. "Many problems don't hit a patient until they go home,"

Marge Callahan angles her patient information sheets to catch the only available light on the darkened staircase as she begins her daily rounds in the Bronx. At right, she contemplates the building in which her next visit will take place.

Patricia Samuel, whose home visits often take her into a housing project that has been called the "wild, wild west," checks in on Bronx patient Odell Johnson.

'One nurse recently told me she almost had her car taken from her,' says Callahan. 'She was alone, going into a building, when two guys came up to her with a gun and told her to give them her car keys. She did.'

Tips for a Strong Photo Spread

Photos often work better than words to convey feelings. Used in spreads such as these, they virtually become the story. Above, the pull quote doubles as a caption, leaving readers to contemplate the stark message of the images. Opposite, tight cropping and varied sizes of photos result in a dynamic layout.

Effective photo spreads meet the following guidelines.

- An odd number of images. Three or five images work best.
- One image is much larger than the others.
- Each image has its own caption.
- Keylines are not printed, ensuring that readers perceive photos as a group.

Child Development

Continued From Page 1

Potthast on doctor and hospital visits. Mrs. Potthast also received counseling at home from Child Development Counselor **Lynn Smart**.

The prognosis is excellent. Liske anticipates that Lucia will attend a community preschool without the program's assistance, and one day will be able to read regular-size print.

Four-year-old **Scott MacIntyre** was diagnosed as having retinitis pigmentosa approximately one year ago; this has left him with tunnel vision. In addition to a child development consultant's home visits, Scott and his younger brother **Todd** spend Thursday afternoons playing with other blind children at the Braille Institute Youth Center in Los Angeles, while his mother **Carole MacIntyre** meets with the Parent Support Group. Guided by a child

Tunnel vision caused by retinitis pigmentosa does not prevent **Scott McIntyre**, *4, above right, from playing with his brother* **Todd** *as his mother* **Carole** *looks on. Below, however, Scott seems displeased by Todd's curiosity, typical sibling behavior.*

At left, **Paul Gonzalez** *is again the center of attention, this time from his father* **Frank** *and brother* **Frankie**, *4.*

development counselor, parents discuss issues such as sibling relationships, discipline and separation.

Accompanied by a program preschool assistant, Scott attends a preschool three times a week. Plans by his parents, consultant and preschool assistant are underway for Scott to be mainstreamed into kindergarten.

Paul, Lucia and Scott are but three examples of the more than 155 individuals and their families who received aid from Braille Institute's Child Development Services in 1989.

"It's important to realize that a child's blindness has a profound effect not only on that child's development, but also on the family unit," Liske said. "Early intervention by our professionally trained personnel ensures that we can utilize every means we have to help visually impaired infants, toddlers, or preschoolers and their families."

4

One Family's Needs Reflect Complex Nature Of Services

Vicki Liske, Director
Child Development

What's in a name? A recent, desperate telephone call from the mother of an infant enrolled in our Child Development Services program shed a lot of light on this issue.

Rose Thompson called to say that her husband **James**, a Pfc. in the Army, had been informed of his imminent transfer from Long Beach to a remote area 300 miles away from Los Angeles.

In the hope that the Army would reconsider her husband's new assignment, she asked for a letter outlining the extensive services we provide to their six-month-old son **Tyrone**.

The Braille Institute department of which I am director recently changed its name from Preschool Services to Child Development Services.

As I began the letter for the Thompsons, I reflected on the new name and how it underscores the growth and vitality of our program and the focus of early intervention on the developmental needs of the family unit.

Mrs. Thompson had legitimate concerns because many of the services we provide are not readily available in the area her family would relocate to if her husband is reassigned. And, if the Army is to be influenced by Tyrone's needs, reporting that the infant was enrolled in a preschool program did not accurately describe the complex nature of the assistance we provide.

What began as Preschool Services was originally part of the multifaceted Student Services department. We have grown from one part-time person working with

a few families, to a separate department with a staff of 27 professionals who assisted more than 130 families in 1989.

Our clients range from infants at birth to kindergarten-age. The former name (Preschool Services) easily could be misunderstood as describing a program including nursery school children only. The new title incorporates both the actual ages served and the developmental focus.

The early years are a significant time for the child and parents. Referrals to us are often received when the baby is discharged from the hospital, thus enabling us to "begin at the beginning."

We offer comprehensive infant and preschool intervention, support for the families and coordination with other service providers.

Child development consultants visit the families in their homes to advise parents about activities that enhance development and to maintain up-to-date assessments of each child's developmental and functional status.

Consultants also assist families in obtaining ancillary services such as physical and occupational therapy, Social Security Insurance and state Regional Center for Developmentally Disabled follow-up.

Case management and coordination are essential to families who might otherwise feel overwhelmed by the systems and agencies with whom they need to negotiate.

Families of graduating children receive help during the transition from our early intervention program to school district kindergartens.

Parents are encouraged to participate actively and contribute to IEP (Individual Education Plan) meetings.

The consultants support parents during this time by demystifying the process, researching options and attending school meetings with them. Weekly Parent Support Groups are conducted by a child development counselor.

Because of the large geographic area covered by our program, two separate groups have been formed: one at the Braille Institute Youth Center in Los Angeles; the other at the Orange County Center in Anaheim. Parents discuss issues such as family stress, coping with parenting a special needs child and with discipline and separation.

The needs of families with young visually impaired children are complex. Child Development Services is there to provide assistance to them with the goal of enhancing the growth and development of both the child and the entire family.

Regarding the Thompsons, the Army is now in the process of looking for an appropriate position for Pfc. Thompson so that his family may remain in the Los Angeles area.

5

ATLANTA HISTORY CENTER
NEWSLETTER
News of the Atlanta Historical Society, Inc. • Vol. 22, No. 3 • May 1991

LIFE IN THE GREAT HOUSES
Symposium on Irish homes, gardens, arts

L-r, Woody Parsons, Marion Cole, Carmen Deedy, and more at the Atlanta Storytelling Festival.

Celebration of stories

John Ott resigns (p. 2)

Inside this issue:
- Log cabin donated .... p. 3
- Join our Members' Guild .... p. 4
- May calendar .... p. 5
- Best spring spot .... p. 8

Illustrating Calendars

Member involvement is so important to the Atlanta Historical Society that its calendar includes photos and runs as a full page. The photos, usually mug shots of speakers, establish an immediate connection with the events they advertise. Because the calendar gets so much space, the listing for each event includes a short description, almost like an article telling about the event before it happens.

Name *Atlanta History Center*

Publisher *Atlanta Historical Society, Atlanta, GA*

Purpose/audience *Service to members*

Production *By hand*

Printing *Black and a second color on white matte-coated paper*

Format *8 1/2-by-11 inches, eight pages*

Design *Elizabeth Tucker and Jo Phelps*

OCTOBER CALENDAR

Frances FitzGerald, Oct. 1

1 Livingston Lecture
Frances FitzGerald, Pulitzer Prize-winning author of *Cities On A Hill*, speaks on "The 20th Century: America in Revision." *Woodruff Auditorium, McElreath Hall, 8:00 p.m. Doors open at 7:00 p.m. Free for members—please bring your membership card. $5 nonmembers.*

7-11 Folklife Festival
Come enjoy 1840s fun–hearth cooking, spinning, blacksmithing, toymaking, storytelling, and more–at Tullie Smith Farm. Weekdays only from 9:00 a.m. to 2:00 p.m. School groups ($3 per student) and the public (included in regular admission price) are welcome. *Members free.*

14 Bus Tour
Join us for a bus tour of Atlanta's contemporary homes, "Buckhead and Modernism." 8:30 a.m.–2:00 p.m. $35 includes lunch at Azio's and a tour of five sites. Call Swan House, 238-0680, to reserve your place.*

14-18 Folklife Festival
1840s fun continues (see above).

20 Decorative Arts Lecture Series
Ronald Hurst, curator of furniture, Colonial Williamsburg Foundation, speaks on "Virginia Furniture in the

25-27 Member Trip
Visit the Georgia and Florida coasts with us. Tour St. Mary's, Ga.; Amelia Island and historic Fernandina, Fla.; and Jekyll Island. For more information or to sign up, call Dot Evans, 238-0652, by October 9.*

27 Book Signing
William R. Mitchell, Jr., and Van Jones Martin autograph copies of *Classic Atlanta: Landmarks of the Atlanta Spirit* (see p. 5). Book available for sale. RSVP to 261-1837 by October 21. *McElreath Hall, 2:00-5:00 p.m. Free.*

Current Exhibits
Atlanta Resurgens, permanent exhibit
Atlanta and the War, 1861-1865, permanent exhibit, Mr. and Mrs. Clyde Lanier King Gallery
On the Set of GONE WITH THE WIND: Photographs by Fred A. Parrish, McElreath Hall
The Atlanta Historical Society Plans for the Future, Atrium
Philip T. Shutze Collection of Decorative Arts, Swan House

Atlanta History Center Downtown at 140 Peachtree Street
Monday-Saturday, 10:00 a.m.-6:00 p.m.
Exhibit, Atlanta's Hotel Heritage: Proms, Politics, and Prime Rib

Hedrick Smith, Oct. 23

7

APRIL CALENDAR

4 Stump Franklin
Bring your questions, trivial or profound, and try to Stump Franklin, official historian for the city of Atlanta and the Atlanta Historical Society (see p. 3). Reception follows. *Woodruff Auditorium, McElreath Hall, 8:00 p.m. Free.*

8 Livingston Lecture
John Kenneth Galbraith, Ph.D., internationally known author, statesman, and professor emeritus of economics at Harvard University, speaks on "The Twentieth Century: Dollars and Sense." *Woodruff Auditorium, McElreath Hall, 8:00 p.m. Doors open at 7:00 p.m. Free for members–please bring your membership card. $5 nonmembers.*

John Kenneth Galbraith, April 8

13-14 Tasteful Tables and Teapots
Come view creative tablesettings using 18th-, 19th-, and 20th-century antique and contemporary ceramics (see p. 3). This exhibit is sponsored by the Ceramic Circle of Atlanta and features unique pieces from its members' private collections and from the Society's Philip Trammell Shutze Collection of Decorative Arts. *Members Room, McElreath Hall, Saturday, 9:00 a.m.-5:30 p.m., Sunday, noon-5:30 p.m. $5.*

20 Sheep to Shawl
During this day-long event, our sheep are sheared and the fleece is handwoven into a shawl (see p. 1). *Tullie Smith Farm, 9:30 a.m.-5:30 p.m. Free for members.*

Book Signing
Carmen Deedy, local author, professional storyteller, and founder of the Atlanta Storytelling Festival, reads and autographs copies of her new book, *Agatha's Featherbed: Not Just Another Wild Goose Story*. Book available for sale; members enjoy a 10 percent discount in the Museum Shop. *McElreath Hall, 1:00-3:00 p.m. Free.*

AGATHA'S FEATHER BED — Not Just Another Wild Goose Story

Carmen Deedy autographs book April 20.

Volunteer and Member Trip to Nashville and Memphis
25-29 Call 238-0652 for information or to make your reservation.

27 Genealogy

Current Exhibits
Atlanta Resurgens, permanent exhibit
Atlanta and the War, 1861-1865, permanent exhibit, Mr. and Mrs. Clyde Lanier King Gallery
The Atlanta Historical Society: A Family Album, Atrium
The Atlanta Historical Society Plans for the Future, Atrium
A Vision of What Atlanta Can Be:

*Preregistration or tickets required. For more information on any program or event, call 261-1837.

JULY/AUGUST CALENDAR

JULY

4 Fourth of July
Celebrate our nation's birthday–bring a picnic lunch and spend the day exploring Atlanta's history. Noon-5:30 p.m. Free for members.

Boyd Lewis, July 10

10 Points on Peachtree
Boyd Lewis, WABE Radio classical disc jockey, on "Voices from Peachtree's Past." Lewis shares his memories of living in "The Dump," the apartment building at Tenth and Peachtree where Margaret Mitchell wrote *Gone with the Wind*. He will also recount his experiences as a stringer for National Public Radio covering many Peachtree Street happenings. Points on Peachtree is presented in conjunction with The Real Peachtree: Past and Present exhibit at the Atlanta History Center Downtown and is made possible through the generosity of A. Montag and Associates and EDAW, Inc. *Georgia-Pacific Center Auditorium, 133 Peachtree Street, noon. Free.*

The Civil War Revisited: Atlanta
20-21 Encampment 1991
Union and Confederate soldiers set up camp at the Atlanta History Center (see p. 1). Atlanta Historical Society members receive reduced rates: $5 adults, $3.50 seniors and students 18+, $2 children 6-17, and free under 6. Weekend pass good for both days is $8, $6, $4, and free, respectively. *Atlanta History Center, 10:00 a.m.-5:00 p.m.*

23 Guided tours of Atlanta and the War
Beginning today take advantage of regularly scheduled guided tours of the exhibit, Atlanta and the War, 1861-1865. The one-hour tour is offered every Tuesday and Saturday at 2:00 p.m. It's free for members and reservations are not required. *Meet at the reception desk, McElreath Hall.*

AUGUST

5 Exhibit opens
The exhibit, Atlanta's Hotel Heritage: Proms, Politics, and Prime Rib, opens at the Atlanta History Center Downtown, 140 Peachtree Street (see p. 4). Free.

Current Exhibits
Atlanta Resurgens, permanent exhibit
Atlanta and the War, 1861-1865, permanent exhibit, Mr. and Mrs. Clyde Lanier King Gallery
The Atlanta Historical Society: A Family Album, Atrium
"The Face of America": Selections from the Linda Schaefer Collection, McElreath Hall, through September 2
Philip T. Shutze Collection of Decorative Arts, Swan House*, through August 5

Atlanta History Center Downtown at 140 Peachtree Street
Monday-Saturday, 10:00 a.m.-6:00 p.m.
Exhibit, The Real Peachtree: Past and Present, through August 1
Exhibit, Atlanta's Hotel Heritage: Proms, Politics, and Prime Rib, opens August 5

Upcoming Events
Autumn offers many special events for our members, so please make a note of these important dates: Open house for new volunteers, September 8; exhibit opening, On the Set of GONE WITH THE WIND: Photographs by Fred A. Parrish, September 17, McElreath Hall; former U. S. president Jimmy Carter, September 17, Livingston Lecture series; annual symposium, Refining the Garden: The Trowels and Pleasures of Gardening, September 28-29; and Frances Fitzgerald, October 1, Livingston Lecture series. Watch your September newsletter for details.

*Preregistration or tickets required. For more information on any program or event, call 261-1837.

Faces on parade. *Don't miss our fascinating exhibit, "The Face of America": Selections from the Linda Schaefer Collection, at McElreath Hall through September 2. Here, a woman pauses on New York City's Fifth Avenue to watch a Dick Gephardt rally. Schaefer's photos are of politics, people, and the 1988 presidential campaign.*

7

Another Photographic Calendar

A calendar can use photos to introduce speakers or, as shown at right, to entice readers to attend events. In *Canyon Ranch Round Up* the vertical image frames the upper right corner of the page, enclosing the headline to make the calendar one unified image.

Name *Canyon Ranch Round Up*

Publisher *Canyon Ranch, Tucson, AZ*

Purpose/audience *Service to customers*

Production *Ventura Publisher on IBM*

Printing *Black and brown on white gloss-coated paper*

Format *8½-by-11 inches, eight pages*

Design *Lori Lieber and Lisa Goldsmith*

Expand your horizons in the great outdoors

Feeling a bit claustrophobic? Are you ready to abandon hectic meetings and stress-filled days and opt instead for a relaxing break amidst mountains and fresh air? If so, head for Canyon Ranch in either Lenox or Tucson for Outdoor Sports Activities and Hiking Weeks.

Make new friends as you spend exhilarating days working your body and resting your mind. You'll see why guests return year after year to hike their favorite trails and discover new ones.

For more information or reservations, call 1-800-742-9000.

LENOX

Outdoor programs include full use of Ranch facilities, meals (including one welcome group dinner) and a daily massage. Lenox outdoor sports participants receive a 15 percent discount on their rates (*cannot be used with any other discounts or promotions*).

December 4 – 9: BERKSHIRE WINTER INTERLUDE. Pole and regular hiking in the hills around Canyon Ranch for the advanced-beginner to intermediate hiker. Approximately 4 to 7 miles daily.

1991

February 12 – 17: VALENTINE'S WEEK: LEARN TO SKI SPECIAL. Geared for beginning cross-country skiers, this program includes lessons and a special Valentine's Day meal.

March 5 – 10: WINTER SPORTS PACKAGE. Combine

hiking and cross-country skiing (weather permitting) in this 5-day treat in the Berkshires.

June 5 – 9: INTRODUCTION TO OUTDOOR SPORTS. Hike wilderness trails, ride via mountain bikes through the woodlands, and canoe in nearby lakes (able swimmers only) during this athletic extravaganza. A workshop and sunset hike with supper are included. Beginner level.

June 12 – 16: OUTDOOR SPORTS CHALLENGE. Similar in content to the Introduction to Outdoor Sports, only geared more for the intermediate athlete.

July 10 – 14: BICYCLE TOURING 101. Rides for the novice of 8 to 20 miles daily include stops to enjoy local culture and nature. Workshop included.

TUCSON

The Tucson program includes use of all Canyon Ranch facilities, meals, six massages and an herbal wrap.

January 12 – 19: MILEAGE MONSTER. For advanced hikers who enjoy longer, more challenging hikes. Expect an average of 10 to 16 miles daily with rugged terrain and striking scenery.

May 11 – 18: SONORAN SPRING. Hikes of 5 to 8 miles daily in both upper and lower elevations. Interpretation of spring flora unique to the Sonoran ecosystem by our staff naturalists. A great intermediate week.

September 21 – 28: PEAK EXPERIENCE. Advanced hikes of from 8 to 12 miles every day to a different peak or high ridge. Primarily high elevations above 7,000 feet depending on temperature. No technical climbing involved. An exceptional hiking experience.

Hiking Weeks in Tucson are always popular (above).

Photo by Mark Black.

Learn to cross-country ski at Canyon Ranch in the Berkshires (left).

In September 1990, the hiking and biking departments combined at Canyon Ranch in Tucson. Look for joint hiking and biking programs in the coming year. In the meantime, enjoy a broad selection of hikes and bicycle rides through Sabino Canyon and elsewhere.

9

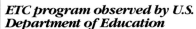

The Value of Photo Captions

Readers look at photos first and captions next. Then they read headlines and text. For that reason, no writing deserves more careful attention than captions. Designers and editors work together closely to pack lots of information into captions. These captions not only identify the image but amplify its meaning to incorporate it into the story. Or is the story incorporated into the photo?

Name Commons News

Publisher Chicago Commons Association, Chicago, IL

Purpose/audience Service to members

Production QuarkXPress on Macintosh

Printing Black and green on white laid text paper

Format 8¹/₂-by-11 inches, six pages (six-panel foldout)

Design The Newsletter Group, Inc.

From her home desk area designed by her husband to meet her working needs, Kathy Werdahl, Transportation Planning Technician 2, is one of seven employees taking part in the Washington State Energy Office's Puget Sound Telecommuting Demonstration Project. While telecommuting, Kathy is able to work out of her home three days a week and avoid the morning and evening commute.

The College installed 200 workstations and servers in fall 1990. Over the next two years, 550 more workstations will arrive. Dr. William Willis, director of Computer Operations, helps with the first arrivals.

Cynthia Mackey, left, of ISD and Linda Lindley of CUNA & Affiliates were recently named the Credit Union Center's first "Community Service Volunteers of the Year." Judges recognized Mackey for her work at Briarpatch, a United Way family counseling agency. Lindley is a leader of the Waunakee Parent Support Network, an organization providing a forum for adults to work together to share parenting skills. The award was established this year to recognize employees who have made a significant volunteer contribution to their community.

The Bird Road Center (above) is being renovated while the East Hialeah Medical Center (right) is undergoing a complete make-over.
El Centro Médico de Bird Road (arriba) está siendo renovado mientras el Centro Médico del Este de Hialeah está siendo remodelado completamente.

Designing Effective Captions

Research reveals that readers read captions before reading stories and often before reading headlines. Make each caption count by setting it in clear type and putting it under the image to which it refers.

Publishers Represented in This Book

United States

AR Acxiom Corporation, Conway, AR

AZ Best Western International, Inc., Phoenix, AZ

AZ Canyon Ranch, Tucson, AZ

AZ Samaritan Health Services, Phoenix, AZ

CA Braille Institute, Los Angeles, CA

CA Committee for Green Foothills, Palo Alto, CA

CA Graff Advertising, Inc., Palo Alto, CA

CA Griffin Printing, Glendale, CA

CA Hemming Morse Co., San Francisco, CA

CA Institute of the Americas, La Jolla, CA

CA Ruddle and Associates, Milpitas, CA

CA Wine Institute, San Francisco, CA

CO Tattered Cover Bookstore, Denver, CO

CT Coalition of three magazines and a cable TV channel, Darien, CT

CT Pitney Bowes Co., Stamford, CT

DC Federation of Nurses and Health Care Professionals/AFT, AFL-CIO, Washington, D.C.

DC Kaiser Permanente Mid Atlantic States, Washington, D.C.

DC International Food Information Council, Washington, D.C.

FL CAC Ramsay, Coral Gables, FL

FL Greater Miami Convention and Visitors Bureau, Miami, FL

FL Kleinfeld & Zabludowski, Attorneys, Miami, FL

FL National Council on Compensation Insurance, Boca Raton, FL

GA Atlanta Historical Society, Atlanta, GA

GA Haverty Furniture Companies, Inc., Atlanta, GA

GA Kennestone Healthcare Systems, Marietta, GA

IL Chicago Commons Association, Chicago, IL

IL Financial Institutions Marketing Association, Chicago, IL

IL Heidrick and Struggles, Inc., Chicago, IL

IL Loyola University Chicago, Chicago, IL

IL Triangle/Expercolor, Skokie, IL

MA Chase Access Services, Lexington, MA

MA Medical Center of Central Massachusetts, Worcester, MA

MA Millipore Corporation, Bedford, MA

MD United Communications Group, Rockville, MD

MI Kalamazoo Public Museum, Kalamazoo, MI

MN Free Spirit Publishing, Inc., Minneapolis, MN

MN Lakewood Publications, Minneapolis, MN

MN Mayo Foundation, Rochester, MN

MN The John Roberts Company, Minneapolis, MN

MO Leadership St. Louis, St. Louis, MO

NC CIBA-GEIGY Dyestuffs & Chemicals, Greensboro, NC

NC Engineering Foundation, Inc., Raleigh, NC

NJ Harry M. Stevens, Inc., Cranbury, NJ

NY American Demographics, Inc., Ithaca, NY

NY Bank Street School for Children, New York, NY

NY Christie, Manson and Woods International, Inc., New York, NY

NY Gannett Foundation Media Center, New York, NY

NY Conair Gatto, Hauppauge, NY

NY Gruntal & Co., Inc., New York, NY

NY Ithaca College, Ithaca, NY

NY Lintas:New York, New York, NY

NY Ohel Children's Home and Family Services, New York, NY

OH Shaker Heights City School District, Shaker Heights, OH

OR Eugene/Springfield Metro Partnership, Inc., Eugene, OR

OR High Desert Museum, Bend, OR

OR L.grafix, Portland, OR

OR Mt. Bachelor Ski Area, Bend, OR

OR Port of Portland, Portland, OR

OR SAIF Corporation, Salem, OR

PA Bestinfo, Inc., Media, PA

SC Imagine, Inc., Clemson, SC

TX Continental Airlines, Houston, TX

TX National Wildflower Research Center, Austin, TX

TX Texas Elementary Principals & Supervisors Association, Austin, TX

UT WordPerfect Corporation, Orem, UT

VA Certified Professional Insurance Agents Society, Alexandria, VA

VA Council of Better Business Bureaus, Inc., Arlington, VA

VA Editorial Experts Inc., Alexandria, VA

VA McGuire, Woods, Battle & Booth, Richmond, VA

VA National Fisheries Institute, Arlington, VA

VA Town of Leesburg, Leesburg, VA

WA Aldus Corporation, Seattle, WA

WA Seattle Community Colleges, Seattle, WA

WA Spokane Teachers Credit Union, Spokane, WA

WA Washington State Department of Transportation, Olympia, WA

WA Weyerhaeuser Credit Union, Longview, WA

WI CUNA Mutual Insurance, Madison, WI

Canada

BC The Commonwealth of Learning, Vancouver, BC

ON Canadian Centre for Active Living in the Workplace, Gloucester, ON

ON Sterling Communications, Inc., Toronto, ON

Index

Improve your skills, learn a new technique, with these additional books from North Light

Graphics/Business of Art

Artist's Friendly Legal Guide, by Floyd Conner, Peter Karlan, Jean Perwin & David M. Spatt $18.95 (paper)

Artist's Market: Where & How to Sell Your Graphic Art, (Annual Directory) $22.95

Basic Desktop Design & Layout, by Collier & Cotton $27.95

Basic Graphic Design & Paste-Up, by Jack Warren $14.95 (paper)

Business & Legal Forms for Graphic Designers, by Tad Crawford $15.95 (paper)

Clip Art Series: Holidays, Animals, Food & Drink, People Doing Sports, Men, Women, $6.95/each (paper)

COLORWORKS: The Designer's Ultimate Guide to Working with Color, by Dale Russell (5 in series) $9.95 each.

Creative Self-Promotion on a Limited Budget, by Sally Prince Davis $19.95 (paper)

The Creative Stroke, by Richard Emery $39.95

Design Rendering Techniques, by Dick Powell $29.95

Desktop Publisher's Easy Type Guide, by Don Dewsnap $19.95 (paper)

The Designer's Commonsense Business Book, by Barbara Ganim $22.95 (paper)

The Designer's Guide to Creating Corporate ID Systems, by Rose DeNeve $27.95

The Designer's Guide to Making Money with Your Desktop Computer, by Jack Neff $19.95 (paper)

Designing with Color, by Roy Osborne $26.95

Dynamic Airbrush, by David Miller & James Effler $29.95

59 More Studio Secrets, by Susan Davis $12.95

47 Printing Headaches (and How to Avoid Them), by Linda S. Sanders $24.95 (paper)

Getting It Printed, by Beach, Shepro & Russon $29.50 (paper)

Getting Started as a Freelance Illustrator or Designer, by Michael Fleischman $16.95 (paper)

Getting the Max from Your Graphics Computer, by Lisa Walker & Steve Blount $27.95 (paper)

Graphically Speaking, by Mark Beach $29.50 (paper)

The Graphic Artist's Guide to Marketing & Self Promotion, by Sally Prince Davis $19.95 (paper)

The Graphic Designer's Basic Guide to the Macintosh, by Meyerowitz and Sanchez $19.95 (paper)

Graphic Idea Notebook, by Jan V. White $19.95 (paper)

Great Type & Lettering Designs, by David Brier $34.95

Handbook of Pricing & Ethical Guidelines, 7th edition, by The Graphic Artist's Guild $22.95 (paper)

How'd They Design & Print That?, $26.95

How to Check and Correct Color Proofs, by David Bann $27.95

How to Find and Work with an Illustrator, by Martin Colyer $8.95

How to Get Great Type Out of Your Computer, by James Felici $22.95 (paper)

How to Make Money with Your Airbrush, by Joseph Sanchez $18.95 (paper)

How to Make Your Design Business Profitable, by Joyce Stewart $21.95 (paper)

How to Understand & Use Design & Layout, by Alan Swann $21.95 (paper)

How to Understand & Use Grids, by Alan Swann $12.95

Make It Legal, by Lee Wilson $18.95 (paper)

Making a Good Layout, by Lori Siebert & Lisa Ballard $24.95

Making Your Computer a Design & Business Partner, by Walker and Blount $10.95 (paper)

Papers for Printing, by Mark Beach & Ken Russon $39.50 (paper)

Presentation Techniques for the Graphic Artist, by Jenny Mulherin $9.95

Type & Color: A Handbook of Creative Combinations, by Cook and Fleury $39.95

Type: Design, Color, Character & Use, by Michael Beaumont $19.95 (paper)

Type in Place, by Richard Emery $34.95

Type Recipes, by Gregory Wolfe $19.95 (paper)

Typewise, written & designed by Kit Hinrichs with Delphine Hirasuna $39.95

To order directly from the publisher, include $3.00 postage and handling for one book, $1.00 for each additional book. Allow 30 days for delivery.

North Light Books
1507 Dana Avenue, Cincinnati, Ohio 45207
Credit card orders call TOLL-FREE
1-800-289-0963

Stock is limited on some titles; prices subject to change without notice.